Crime in TV, the News, and Film

Crime in TV, the News, and Film

Misconceptions, Mischaracterizations, and Misinformation

Beth E. Adubato
Nicole M. Sachs
Donald F. Fizzinoglia
John M. Swiderski

LEXINGTON BOOKS
Lanham • Boulder • New York • London

Published by Lexington Books
An imprint of The Rowman & Littlefield Publishing Group, Inc.
4501 Forbes Boulevard, Suite 200, Lanham, Maryland 20706
www.rowman.com

86-90 Paul Street, London EC2A 4NE, United Kingdom

Copyright © 2022 by The Rowman & Littlefield Publishing Group, Inc.

All rights reserved. No part of this book may be reproduced in any form or by any electronic or mechanical means, including information storage and retrieval systems, without written permission from the publisher, except by a reviewer who may quote passages in a review.

British Library Cataloguing in Publication Information Available

Library of Congress Cataloging-in-Publication Data

Names: Adubato, Beth E., author. | Sachs, Nicole M., author. | Fizzinoglia, Donald F., author. | Swiderski, John M., author.
Title: Crime in TV, the news, and film : misconceptions, mischaracterizations, and misinformation / Beth E. Adubato, Nicole M. Sachs, Donald F. Fizzinoglia, John M. Swiderski.
Description: Lanham : Lexington Books, [2022] | Includes bibliographical references and index. | Summary: "With a combination of field experience and criminological research, this book gives insight to the news and drama programming that shapes the way viewers perceive crime and the formation of policy"—Provided by publisher.
Identifiers: LCCN 2022003964 (print) | LCCN 2022003965 (ebook) | ISBN 9781793628688 (cloth) | ISBN 9781793628701 (pbk) | ISBN 9781793628695 (epub)
Subjects: LCSH: Crime in mass media. | Crime and the press—United States. | Television broadcasting of news—Political aspects—United States. | Television series—United States. | Journalism—Political aspects—United States—History—21st century. | Mass media and race relations—United States. | Journalism—Objectivity—United States. | United States—Race relations—Press coverage.
Classification: LCC P96.C74 A33 2022 (print) | LCC P96.C74 (ebook) | DDC 364.2/54—dcundefined
LC record available at https://lccn.loc.gov/2022003964
LC ebook record available at https://lccn.loc.gov/2022003965

Contents

Preface	vii
Acknowledgments	xi
Introduction: The Following	1
Chapter 1: What's So New About News?	9
Chapter 2: Murder in the First Degree	21
Chapter 3: Murder in the First Block	39
Chapter 4: "True" Crime Shows	57
Chapter 5: News You Can't Use	73
Chapter 6: It's All in the Genes	87
Chapter 7: The Unbearable Weight of Being Black	101
Chapter 8: Damsels in Distress	115
Chapter 9: Missing Pretty White Girls	129
Chapter 10: It's Hard Being a Girl . . . Even Harder Being a Girl of Color	143
Chapter 11: Good Cops, Bad Cops, Dirty Cops, and Mad Cops: Five Hollywood Films	157
Chapter 12: From the TV Screen to the Ballot Box	169
Conclusion	177
Bibliography	191

Index	207
About the Authors	217

Preface

The planning and much of the research for this book began before our world turned upside down with the onset of a global pandemic. No one could have imagined how reliant on media we would become. When the reality of 2020 became clear and staying at home was no longer a choice but a necessity, Americans turned in droves to television drama, streaming content, and nonstop "breaking news." By mid-April of 2020, after at least six weeks of growing uncertainty about the Coronavirus, the most watched TV show in America was ABC's "World News Tonight."[1] The cable news networks saw a rise in viewership never before seen—CNN's numbers were up 168 percent, Fox News was up 45 percent, and MSNBC's numbers increased by 24 percent.[2] Is the answer that everyone was home with schools, jobs, gyms, and restaurants shutdown? Is it that people were terrified about the growing concern over a spreading virus? Whatever combination spurred on this sudden dependence on news, it was clear that Americans were watching.

Was America returning to the time when Walter Cronkite, Dan Rather, Tom Brokaw, and Peter Jennings were regular nightly visitors in our living rooms? When Walter Cronkite anchored the news, it was common for 25 to 30 million viewers to tune in, when he considered to be "the most trusted man in America." In the sixteen years of teaching on a university level, this author has yet to come across a student who either watches the nightly news or even understands the concept of the national nightly news. And they do not know the name Walter Cronkite. Clearly, this increase in 2020 was a cultural anomaly for our time.

After the news was over, with a considerable percentage of the population in quarantine and having nowhere to go, channels were changed. The actual method of consuming media does not resemble those Cronkite days. Cable and streaming services supplement network broadcasts and are most popular among younger people. These streaming services are often observed on non-traditional equipment; in other words, not on "regular" TVs. As the effects of the pandemic ebbed and waned—in other words, states opening and states shutting down—clear patterns of entertainment content became apparent and the focus was on crime. While entertainment and infotainment have always been reliant on crime stories, the proliferation of crime-related shows and documentaries proved mutually enjoyable to both the producers' bottom lines and to satisfy the hunger of a shocked and worried people for such distraction.

Streaming platforms such as Netflix, Hulu, and Amazon Prime offered an array of crime-focused shows—some of them new, some old, some in the form of documentaries. According to Nielsen Ratings, *Tiger King: Murder, Mayhem, and Madness* garnered 34 million viewers within the first ten days of its release. The story of a notorious zookeeper who was arrested for murder-for-hire seem to fit the mood of a nation stuck at home during the initial phase of the COVID-19 lockdown. With approximately thirty-four other crime shows on Netflix from which to choose, *Tiger King* seems to have benefited from social media mentions that propelled interest in the series. Hulu, a rival streaming platform, offered more than fifty shows with an element of crime. Amazon, the dominant online retail store, has its own platform, "Amazon Prime," which streams crime show programming; much of it is older or repetitive, but does include three original crime series.[3] These streaming platforms are in addition to the major television networks that have been broadcasting crime shows since their very existence; in other words, everyone is getting in on the action.

A pandemic out of control, a nation sheltering in place, the daily death toll climbing—it was against this background that less than three months after quarantine orders kept millions of Americans glued to TVs, computers, and phones, the videotaped death of George Floyd on May 25, 2020, captured the attention of the world. This was not fictionalized crime, this was a death involving a Black man and the Minneapolis Police Department, captured on video by iPhones, surveillance footage, and body cameras—new forms of media that are encroaching upon the long-observed media landscape. The ensuing protests following the death of George Floyd transfixed a nation. The combination of protests around the world over police brutality with daily hospitalization numbers from the Coronavirus filled our airwaves, but did not produce the same reactions from all of those who watched. The resulting chasm in our country comes complete with charges of "fake news" being leveled at both sides of what is now a political issue.

This is not a book about politics, but events of this recent year increased political rancor to a crescendo perhaps not witnessed since the 1960s. Once again, law and order proclamations directly clashed with demands for civil rights as the specter of police brutality loomed over protests in the streets. It is with this in mind that we added a small survey to assess whether the relationship between police and the media had been strained enough to impact public perception.

We call this book *Crime in TV, the News, and Film: Misconceptions, Mischaracterizations, and Misinformation*. We come from a mixture of backgrounds—a documentary maker and film professor, a police officer who teaches criminal justice classes, a young criminologist with a specialization in interpersonal crime who is also a criminal justice professor, and a former television anchor/reporter who is now a criminal justice professor, as well. What we know is that alleged perpetrators have had a certain "look" for decades and likewise, victims are also stereotyped by gender and race. We know that murder is the most popular subject for news and entertainment and that the use of DNA excites audiences but does not play the role in crime-solving that audiences at home would believe. Media and crime dance a complicated tango, but we hope that we provide some insight into their footwork.

NOTES

1. Jones, Tom. "America Is Watching the Evening News Again. TV News Numbers Are Up. Way Up." https://www.poynter.org/newsletters/2020/america-is-watching-the-evening-news-again-tv-news-numbers-are-up-way-up/.

2. Ibid.

3. Hersko, Tyler. "'Tiger King' Had 34 Million Viewers Within 10 Days of Launch, Fox to Air Special." *IndieWire*. April 8, 2020 https://www.indiewire.com/2020/04/tiger-king-netflix-viewership-fox-special-1202223808/.

Acknowledgments

Two decades ago, while working as a television journalist, I decided to return to school to pursue a master's in criminal justice. I felt it was a useful degree for my profession. I never imagined that I would end up with a PhD in the subject and as a criminological researcher. I first created a class called Media, Crime, and Public Policy while a grad student at Rutgers University (at that point, I had an MA in Criminal Justice and a master's in public affairs in politics). This class was a "special topics" class that I created which basically combined all of my career and academic knowledge base. It was at this point that I realized just how important the topic of media and crime is and how much crime coverage affects our everyday lives.

So, in this spirit, I want to give credit to all of my co-authors on this project. I want to thank John Swiderski, who brings his field perspective to the subject and Donald Fizzinoglia, who writes from the communications perspective (and brought his artistic talent to the cover!). They added flavor that complemented our criminological research.

In truth, I would not be able to accomplish half of what I do if it were not for Nicole Sachs. Nicole was a grad student in a class I taught at Rutgers School of Criminal Justice almost ten years ago and she was superior. At the end of the semester, Nicole said, "Whatever you do, I want to do it with you," and she is. Nicole is simply amazing—brilliant and competent and never-tiring. I cannot possibly express my gratitude with mere mortal words. I look forward to the other ten projects we have brewing.

I would like to thank Kari Larsen, Chair of the Criminal Justice Department at Saint Peter's University, where I am an associate professor. Kari is completely supportive of my research agenda and I am grateful for that. I would also like to thank WeiDong Zhu, Dean of the College of Arts and Science, for his backing. The provost, Fred Bonato and the president, Eugene Cornacchia encourage faculty research in a school where we have an emphasis on teaching. They are patient and understand our need to balance these aspects of academia.

Speaking of Saint Peter's University, I must thank special contributor, Leanna Hernandez, who was my advisee on her senior honors project. It was her project that provided much of the research for the chapter on portrayal of Latina women. The survey on "defunding the police" was part of a senior seminar project by Saint Peter's student Daniel Lodato. A huge thank-you goes out to the students at Saint Peter's and the undergraduate students at Rutgers School of Criminal Justice in Newark (where I am a part-time lecturer)—they served as data collectors for ALL of the research in this book.

Thank you to Becca Beurer at Lexington Books for her guidance and her patience!

Finally, I want to thank our families—Don and I have three daughters between us (Allegra, Eve, and Julia, alphabetically) and they have been hearing about this book for a long time. They will be overjoyed at its publication. We will, however, write another one soon.

Beth E. Adubato, PhD

It has been rewarding, demanding and downright exhilarating to work so closely (and at the same time from the distance dictated by a pandemic) with a team of scholar-citizens who are dedicated to criminal justice and who aren't afraid to make changes at 11:51 p.m. on a manuscript due at midnight!

Special thanks are reserved for the first authors, whose scholarship, work ethic, and patience have been tested throughout.

Donald F. Fizzinoglia, MA

Working with Beth and Don has been an absolute pleasure. From mailing data back and forth in the middle of a pandemic, to texts long after midnight, all while teaching more courses than we all anticipated, we astonishingly submitted our drafts on time, crafted cohesive and compelling chapters, and had a few laughs in between. We are long overdue for a glass (or two) of wine, and we cannot thank them enough for taking us along for the ride on this fun and exciting project that even our parents can understand and read!

Thank you to our family and friends who constantly support us in whatever we pursue individually and as a team. To our parents, Kathy and Mike Sachs, and Ann and Joe Swiderski, you have loved us through all walks of life; even as we get older, we never stop trying to make you all proud. To Nicole's late grandparents, Shirley Sachs and Vincent Guido, who never fail to provide strength from above in the most challenging of times. To Nicole's grandmother, Violet Guido, who provided, and continues to provide, unsolicited and unintentional comic relief as we checked in with her during writing breaks. To Nicole's brother, Cody Sachs, and his fiancée, Christina Marchi,

John's sister, Michelle Milos, and her husband, Keith Milos, our niece, Mikayla Milos and nephew, Kaiden Milos, and our aunts, uncles, cousins, and friends, we thank you for always cheering us on, for listening to us talk about our work, and for recommending some of the very TV shows in this book for us to binge.

At the start of the pandemic, we lost our beloved pit bull, Polo. We want to dedicate this book to him. Writing this book helped to distract us from this profound loss. While putting the finishing touches on our chapters, we decided it would be an excellent idea to adopt a rescue puppy. Rocky, you bring endless joy to our lives, and we are so thrilled to have you join the family.

Our personal and professional lives would be far less interesting, and our hearts far less full, if not for all of you.

Nicole M. Sachs and John M. Swiderski

Introduction
The Following

A handsome prison guard walks briskly down a hallway and using a security fob, enters into a locker room, where he gathers his belongings. As another officer tells him to, "Have a good one, Pete," the guard doesn't turn his head, but gives a wave. While the guard appears to drive his car out of the parking lot and we hear, "Good night, Pete!" the two replacement officers enter an office where five men have been brutally slaughtered. The guard in his jeep drives away, distancing himself from the penitentiary, as Patsy Cline continues to sing "Sweet Dreams" from the jeep.

We then see another locator in the "bottom third"—this time it says Brooklyn, New York. Well-known actor Kevin Bacon wakes up when his phone rings. He groggily pushes the covers aside and we see him gulp down an entire bottle of water and toss it into a wastebasket, already filled with empty liquor bottles.

The Kevin Bacon character offhandedly turns on the TV but turns around abruptly when he hears a news anchor say, "when he was a professor of literature. So far, five guards are confirmed dead . . . " Bacon switches the channel and the chyron reads, SERIAL KILLER AT LARGE. This news anchor reports, "Carroll was convicted of the murder of 14 young women, who attended the university where he was a professor of literature." Bacon finally picks up his phone. The FBI wants him (we learn his name is Ryan). They want him back because he caught Carroll and "no one knows him like you do." And we're hooked!

Given the plethora of crime dramas on television, it is clear that TV viewers are fascinated with crime. This opening scene from the television pilot of *The Following* checks off many boxes that viewers desire: murder with plenty of gore, a handsome and obviously brilliant criminal (we see him escape from a penitentiary and we hear that he is a university professor—twice), a well-known actor in the role of a troubled, former FBI agent (close-up on the liquor bottles), and we hear that "fourteen young women" (they would have been called "co-eds" in less enlightened days) were murdered and we know that they were the villain's students. We learn this all in under three minutes.

This book is not a psychological treatise, but rather a summary of what we know to be true about crime versus what Americans and non-Americans who witness our various forms of media perceive to be true about crime. Just a quick search of imdb.com,[1] known as the standard international movie and television database, shows over 33,000 shows or movies with murder in the title or the subject. While not all of these movies and television shows portray police procedurals or even crime in the United States, it reveals much about the prurient nature of human beings that we are obsessed with murder—the most terrible crime we can commit, because of its very essence, its finality.

Obsession with crime and the "dark side" of humanity is nothing new. Greek tragedies gave us patricide, infanticide, and gruesome suicide. Elizabethan audiences who were not members of royalty or the upper classes, the groundlings, would stand for hours to watch plays that featured murders most foul. In 1927, Alfred Hitchcock released *The Lodger: A Story of the London Fog*—only his third movie and clearly about a character much like Jack the Ripper. Documentarian Joe Bellinger has produced two projects on serial killer Ted Bundy—for Netflix alone—and countless other movies and documentaries have been made about this one man who killed perhaps 100 women.[2] Students who decide to major in criminal justice often mention their interest in the subject because of a desire to learn more about the mind of a killer.

With an abundance of shows already airing, new shows premier each year. Studies have shown that dramas such as *CSI* and *Law & Order* may have had a negative effect on how juries view actual trials. Additionally, studies show that the inaccurate portrayals of the demographics of victims, perpetrators, and the types of crime most often depicted can seriously skew public perception of the criminal justice system.

According to criminologist Ray Surette, "The portrait of criminals found in today's media has almost no correspondence with the official statistics of persons arrested for crimes." Other research indicates the following mischaracterizations of the criminal justice system:

- When described, victims tend to be portrayed as female, very young or old, or a celebrity.
- News coverage also routinely depicts criminal violence against females differently from that against males and underplays the victimization of minorities.
- The ideal crime victim from a news perspective is a child or pregnant woman.

- In the entertainment media, victims normally play one of two extremes—either helpless fodder or wronged heroic avengers.
- Overall, the victimization rates of persons in the media correlate more with fear of crime than with the public's actual victimization risk.[3]

Because public opinion often informs public policy, this focus on fear of crime allows for a serious shift against rehabilitation, against social programs, and for more punitive sentencing. A popular show, for example *Cops*, highlights criminal activity with absolutely no reference to the underlying social ills that contribute to criminality.

FEAR OF CRIME

Jack the Ripper, Ted Bundy, and countless "scary men of color"—what do they have in common? They evoke fear. Criminologists, sociologists, and media scholars have been researching the connection between media and fear of crime for decades. Beginning in the 1970s, criminologists in New Jersey conducted an experiment designed to reduce crime in some targeted neighborhoods. The Safe and Clean Neighborhoods Program was established in twenty-eight New Jersey cities. Police officers were taken from their comfortable patrol cars and given foot patrol. Rules were enforced to keep "frightening people" away from those people who were on their way to and from work or school.

Five years after the program went into effect, the Police Foundation found that the foot patrols did not reduce crime. The interesting finding was that fear of crime was reduced. Even with no reduction in crime, having a stronger presence of police officers in their midst enabled the residents of these areas to feel safer. So, while violent crime is the actual source of fear of crime, fear of crime itself heightens the level of insecurity.[4] In a twist on FDR's "nothing to fear but fear itself," statement, we see that fear of crime is often increased or decreased in some cases by the imagination. Media sources have an awareness of this concept. Even with the best intentions of keeping the reader and the viewer informed, there is an underlying knowledge that fear sells.

There is an ever-expanding body of research on fear of crime. In this book, we stand on the shoulders of these researchers but also bring to bear the most recent developments concerning media and crime—in a fast-changing media world. As noted in the preface of this book, the calendar year 2020 alone brought circumstances that forced a major proportion of the world's population to remain indoors with media as the lifeline to the outside world. With uncertainty over a rampantly spreading deadly virus ratcheting up the stakes of leaving our homes, media loomed larger than ever before as the purveyor of the path to certainty. While the world was glued to their screens, we saw violent crime played out in real time. Yet fear of crime still takes different forms and differing degrees for non-indifferent audiences.

Studying the connection between television and fear throughout the 1970s, George Gerbner and his associates theorized that television may "cultivate a mean view of the world."[5] Decades later, in his book, *The Culture of Control*, David Garland wrote of media images that highlight an "alienated, angry self-destructive 'underclass'" which may contribute to fear of crime that is closely related to "fear of strangers . . . especially black males."[6] Other research points to the TV/fear relationship depending on specific content and the specific cultural makeup of the audience; in other words, depending on your point of view, you will glean a different "take-away" on crime. In a survey of over 500 participants in Indiana, Maria Grade and Dan Drew found that respondents overestimated the probability of becoming a crime victim.[7] Just ask young people in a university criminal justice class if their grandparents fear crime and you will find solid anecdotal support for this idea. Cultivation theory, which speaks to this issue, will be defined more fully in chapter 2. Let's step back to how and when media presentations became so frightening.

IT STARTED WITH SOUND . . . AND THE FURY?

So how did we get here? What follows is an extremely brief history of media. As alluded to earlier, in antiquity we had theater, folktales, and myth. The tales included in Greek and Roman mythology were not for the faint of heart. Citizens of these eras were not reading these plays and stories in a paperback, because they were most likely not reading at all. Aeschylus and Sophocles wrote dramas that could rival some of today's violent presentations. They attended plays in open-air theaters. The theaters provided the entertainment, but these playwrights knew what power they had to disseminate information.

As early as 400 B.C.E., the Greek poet Euripides stated, "The tongue is mightier than the blade."[8] The mighty tongues of those days were town criers. Town criers gave weather and markets reports on the streets of Rome. Town criers in Germany provided the "news," even if the news only asked villagers not to urinate in the river when water was being drawn to make beer.[9] These early news reporters were present across Europe, using their voices to provide a liaison of sorts between the government and local denizens.

Included in this genre are minstrels. Although stereotyped by white Americans as a way to denigrate Black American culture, the minstrel has been a "sound media figure" through much of known history and certainly did not originate in the United States. Turkey, Iran, and Egypt, for example, have long histories or minstrels in coffee shops. It was through these minstrels that men (as women were not allowed) learned of news and history and political dramas in their culture.[10] For fans of Monty Python, the knight who serves as a minstrel in *Monty Python and the Holy Grail* sums up the events in song as a sort of "live reporter on the scene." His clever observations are often annoying to the knights going through the travails, but in this Arthurian England set comedy, the minstrel adds to the fun.

A PRESS BEFORE THE FREE PRESS

Julius Caesar commissioned a daily newspaper of sorts—the *Acta Diurna* (the acts of the day)—which was written on a white tablet and displayed. Obviously, there was a limited the number of people who would be able to obtain this information. It was an invention in the mid-1400s out of Mainz, Germany that revolutionized communication. When Johannes Gutenberg invented the printing press, the era of mass communication was begun. Gutenberg has been named by A&E Network as number one on their list of important people of the millennium[11]—not a bad ranking!

Newspapers sprang up across Europe, but governments had varying degrees of control over the press. It took over fifty years between the publication of John Milton's essay "Areopagitica" (1644), a diatribe against English censorship laws enacted in 1534 under Henry VIII, and the abolishment of these laws in 1695. Even so, the government was still able to take action on grounds of seditious libel against those who criticized government policies.[12] The British government was able to restrict almost anything that related to government through the use of the Official Secrets Act.[13]

Because of these restrictions, pamphlets were a mainstay of the colonial political activists who rebelled against English rule in young America. Thomas Paine, one of the leaders in this movement, printed his anonymous pamphlets in a hiding place. There is a reason that freedom of the press falls under the First Amendment; the framers of the Constitution were keenly aware of the necessity to protect the right to criticize the government.

Historically, freedom of the press has been attached to the general concept of censorship. We see examples of countries without the right to publish news, information, and opinions because there is extensive censorship. The Council on Foreign Relations says that the Chinese government has long kept tight reins on both traditional and new media to avoid potential subversion of its authority.[14] The government uses libel lawsuits, arrests, and other means to force Chinese journalists and media organizations to censor themselves. Thirty-eight journalists were imprisoned in China in 2017. In Russia, the official news organization, TASS, is controlled by the government. We often see reports in our own country about Russian activity that Russian citizens themselves will not see.

> "Wherever people are well informed, they can be trusted with their own government."
>
> —Thomas Jefferson[15]

ANCHORS AS MEN YOU CAN TRUST

Speaking of trust, some of us have grandparents who recall the "good old days" when the network nightly news was anchored by Edward R. Murrow and Walter Cronkite and even Peter Jennings. These were men you could trust. They were men. They were white.

In 1976, the first woman to co-anchor the national nightly news was Barbara Walters. She was paired with Harry Reasoner on ABC Evening News and remained in that position until 1978.[16] On September 6, 2006, Katie Couric[17] made history as the first female solo anchor of the nightly news, the CBS Evening News with Katie Couric. As of this writing, the three major nightly network news programs are anchored by:

ABC—David Muir
CBS—Norah O'Donnell
NBC—Lester Holt

These anchors are respectively—a white male, a white female, and an African American male. Times do change.

In reality, if you compare the headlines and the reporters and the producers and the editors, you will see little differences among the broadcasts of these nightly newscasts. You will see vast differences between cable news networks Fox News and MSNBC, but CNN may seem somewhat similar to MSNBC. Undergraduate students seldom "get their news" from sources such as network news. Younger people may rely on social media for information flow. Local news provides viewers in their region or community with news that touches on world news and national news but focuses on local issues. In chapters 3 and 5, we will explain the differences among newscasts and just exactly how what you watch affects what you will learn.

For the most part in this book, we will be dealing with the "norm," we will be learning about law enforcement's portrayal over the years on television and film and in the news. As we discussed in the preface, however, the year 2020 saw Americans—and most global citizens—at home, with no place to go. That may have temporarily or permanently changed the media landscape . . . time will tell. We do know that social media have become a great influence in how we receive news, infotainment, and entertainment and in how we encounter the criminal justice system through these media.

CONCLUSION

A good portion of this research divides crime related programming into news and drama, which we also do in this book. Further, we delve into another medium often associated with crime drama—film. This is a lot to explore, but in today's media landscape, news, television drama, and film may all be viewed on the same device in the comfort of one's own home. Actress/comedian Amy Poehler remarked on a broadcast of the Golden Globe Awards, "TV is the one that I watch five hours straight, but a movie is the one I don't turn on because it's two hours. I don't want to be in front of my TV for two hours, I want to be in front of the TV one hour five times."[18] People born before 1970 may find this inconceivable, but those born after 2000 cannot conceive of it being any other way. With lines blurred between fictional television programming and news, between television and film, between opinion shows and informational shows, is it any wonder that it is difficult to comprehend what is real about crime?

NOTES

1. https://www.imdb.com/search/title/?genres=crime&explore=title_type,genres&title_type=tvSeries.
2. https://www.businessinsider.com/inside-2-ted-bundy-netflix-movies-by-joe-berlinger-extremely-wicked-2019-5.
3. Surette, Ray. *Media, Crime and Criminal Justice: Images, Realities, and Policies.* Belmont, CA, Cengage Learning, 2011.
4. Kelling, George. Class lecture, Rutgers University, November 2000.
5. Gerbner, George and Larry Gross. "Living with Television: The Violence Profile." *Journal of Communication*, vol. 2, 1976, pp. 171–80.
6. Garland, David. The Culture of Control. Chicago, The University of Chicago Press, 2000.
7. Grabe, Maria Elizabeth and Dan G. Drew. "Crime Cultivation: Comparisons across Media Genres and Channels." *Journal of Broadcasting and Electronic Media*, vol. 51, 1, 2007.
8. Harr, J. Scott, Kären M. Hess, Christine H. Orthmann, and Jonathon Kingsbury. *Constitutional Law and the Criminal Justice System.* Boston, Cengage Learning, 2018.

9. Brown, Chris. "Twin Town Crier Help Keeps the Beer Flowing." *Windsor and Maidenhead Town Crier*. 19 April 2013.

10. Çobanoğlu, Özkul. "Cultural interrelationships between Turkish minstrel tradition and Egyptian folk culture in the socio-cultural context of coffeehouses in Alexandria and Cairo." *International Journal of Modern Anthropology*, vol. 2, 2009.

11. History.com. "The Printing Press." https://www.history.com/topics/inventions/mankind-the-story-of-all-of-us-videos-the-printing-press-video.

12. Op cit., Harr, p. 161.

13. Ibid.

14. Xu, Beina and Eleanor Albert. "Media Censorship in China—Backgrounder." Council on Foreign Relations. 17 February 2017, https://www.cfr.org/backgrounder/media-censorship-china.

15. Op cit., Harr, p. 162.

16. History.com. "This Day in History, September 6, 2005." This Day in History, September 5, 2006, https://www.history.com/this-day-in-history/katie-couric-makes-network-anchor-debut#:~:text=Barbara%20Walters%20was%20the%20first,University%20of%20Virginia%20in%201979.

17. Ibid.

18. Blake, Meredith, staff writer. "Tina Fey, Amy Poehler Lampoon HFPA, Life in Lockdown in Golden Globes Monologue." *Los Angeles Times*, February 28, 2021, https://www.latimes.com/entertainment-arts/tv/story/2021-02-28/golden-globes-2021-tina-fey-amy-poehler-monologue#:~:text=%E2%80%9CTV%20is%20the%20one%20that,five%20times%2C%E2%80%9D%20said%20Poehler.

Chapter 1

What's So New About News?

"Printers are educated in the belief that when men differ in opinion, both sides ought equally to have the advantage of being heard by the public, and that when Truth and Error have fair play, the former is always an overmatch for the latter."

—Benjamin Franklin[1]

Who first introduced you to the "news"? Was it your parents? Your grandparents? When you were a child and you were forced to sit and watch the news, did you understand what was going on? Do you remember when you heard your first "big" news story? Perhaps you remember 9/11? In 2012, the East Coast of the U.S. experienced Superstorm Sandy, but those who were dealing with its aftermath were not watching it on the news, because most people lost electricity. It was one of the events in more recent history during which people really had to turn to the radio for news. Many people (who were able to buy gasoline!) would sit in their cars and listen to the radio. Listening to transistor radios was a way of life for many generations but is virtually unheard of today.

Our modes of media obviously change. In the introduction, we took you on the proverbial whirlwind tour through the history of media from town criers to TASS, but now we will break down the history of media in the United States. As mentioned, the framers of the Constitution were particularly concerned over potential governmental interference in a free press. So, we have mention of it right there in the First Amendment:

> Congress shall make no law respecting an establishment of religion, or prohibiting the free exercise thereof; or abridging the freedom of speech, or of the press; or the right of the people peaceably to assembly, and to petition the Government for a redress of grievance.[2]

The Constitution serves as the law of the land, but that of course originally meant the federal law. This concept became binding on state governments via incorporation of the Fourteenth Amendment in *Near v. Minnesota* (1931), in which the Court ruled that no newspaper could be banned because of its contents, regardless how scandalous they might be.[3]

So, those who produce the "news" have protections and rights and the government cannot stop stories that show its actions in a poor light, but how can the consumer of news be sure that the news source is reliable? Has this "free press" always operated with integrity? Are "true stories" always true? Does news lie outside of popular culture or is it part and parcel of popular culture? What even is popular culture? Whoa . . . that's heady stuff. Let's explore it.

POOR RICHARD, PURITANISM, POPULAR CULTURE, AND OTHER NON-ALLITERATIVE BEGINNINGS OF AMERICAN MEDIA

It's All About the Benjamins . . .
. . . Seven zeros, over in Rio Dijanero
Ain't nobody's hero, but I wanna be heard[4]

—Sean "P. Diddy" Combs

The former Harvard literature professor and Puritan historian Perry Miller claims that Benjamin Franklin has become the most "massively symbolic" figure in American history.[5] Franklin was the only signer of all three documents that "freed" young America from British rule—the Declaration of Independence, the Treaty of Paris, and the Constitution. He is widely known as the person in history who flew a kite attached to a key, illuminating the ability of electricity to travel and leading to the invention of the lightning rod. John Adams, our second president, feared that with all of the lore around George Washington and Benjamin Franklin in early American society, that future generations could elevate these two men as though they single-handedly formed the country.[6]

Most recently, as witnessed by these lyrics from Sean "P. Diddy" Combs, it's all about the Benjamins—meaning, the presence of Benjamin Franklin's image on the hundred-dollar bill. Franklin was a journalist, a scientist, a statesman, and the first United States Postmaster General—just to name a few of his accomplishments. It is fitting, then, that we posit the introduction of Franklin's publication, "Poor Richard's Almanack" as the beginning of an American popular culture.

Franklin borrowed the name Richard Saunders from the author of a popular, London-based almanac. Saunders was an astrologer and almanac maker in the 17th century. Publication of the almanac began in 1732 and continued through 1758 and it was one of the main sources of Franklin's acquired wealth. As many as 10,000 copies sold every year and considering the proportion of those sales to the population, this was an overwhelming bestseller. The almanac included poems, weather predictions, and pithy sayings. Every year, Franklin needed to include new and exciting information that would entice readers to buy the latest edition. He found that "predictions" would increase sales.[7] Eventually, the work was hailed worldwide—for example, Napoleon had it translated into Italian.

While John Adams's fears were not realized, we can see how a nation's story develops over time and the role it has in establishing a symbolic "national" agenda.[8] Professor Carla Mulford contends that, "Franklin's figure offers a representative case of the multiple ways in which Americans have searched for a national culture."[9]

Professor Mulford says that narratives about Franklin were widespread throughout the "life of the country," but particularly during the decades crucial to the construction of American nationalism. She points out that the most contentious times—when the country was sectionalized and heading toward civil war—present the most auspicious times for memorializing who we are as a country.[10]

What does this all mean? It means that while Old World countries already had established popular cultures, our new country had to find its own. Franklin was fighting for freedom of the press while controlling the press, profiting from the press, and helping to create who we are as Americans while fighting for autonomy. It seems like another American conundrum. Does this not inherently contradict the specific intention of a "free press," if the key figure in the founding of a young country's free press is simultaneously crafting what it means to be a patriot? This is a question to be pondered and we will do so right up to the end of the last chapter of this book.

PENNY PRESS

While 10,000 almanacs sold per year was an incredibly high number for the time, approximately 70 years after the end of Poor Richard's Almanac came the proliferation of the daily newspaper. Benjamin Day's *New York Sun* was among the first such papers, known as a "penny press" paper. The *New York Sun* featured a daily police-court news column in 1833 and after doing so, experienced a notable circulation boost.[11] Several other daily papers popped up after the successes of the *Sun*. Criminologist Ray Surette points out that human-interest crime stories "quickly became a staple of these inexpensive, popular newspapers." He goes on to posit that these "early papers portrayed crime as the result of class inequities and often discussed justice as a process manipulated by the rich and prominent."[12]

Barbara Friedman contends that there is a relationship between the growth of the middle and working classes and the increased desire for more scandalous stories and gossip.[13] John Nerone proposes that the definitive innovation of the penny press was the introduction of a newspaper that sold daily for one cent, therefore, making them accessible to new readerships.[14] In comparison, the newspapers for the so-called upper classes sold for about six cents apiece and were part of subscriptions. Additionally, these "upper-class" papers were far more political.[15] A more affordable news source—with a simple vocabulary and less politics, directed at less educated and socio-economically lower readers—could bring about a sea-change in 19th-century media literacy (we will discuss media literacy as a concept in chapter 5).

Another change brought about by these penny press publications was the way it was sold. Following the tradition of London newsboys, when "liveboys" were the distributors, they concentrated far more on street sales and less on subscriptions, thereby bringing the papers to the people, so to speak.[16] Street sales dictated sensational content and better, more easily read type.

The push for larger circulations is claimed to have been the catalyst for seeking out more readers, leading to an increase in sensationalism. Earlier papers had been considered the "special property of elites,"[17] but some researchers and historians say that these dailies made significant changes in content that revolutionized the industry. Three main claims dominate the literature:

- The penny press initiated a policy of political neutrality.
- It emphasized news over opinion, pioneering in sensationalism and human-interest stories.
- It simplified writing styles.

There was a detractor from enthusiasm toward this revolution—one of the most influential publishers of the 19th century, Horace Greeley. Greeley, who was the founder of the *New York Tribune* and the *New Yorker*, waged a long and litigious battle against the idea of the penny press.[18]

Greeley withstood lawsuits, fights with the postmaster, and threats of personal violence to challenge what he called "grave threats" to freedom of the press. He believed that the commercial nature of this enterprise limited the ability of the press to stand as a watchdog and agent of social reform. While Greeley later seemed to forsake these values when he made a secret deal with then-President Abraham Lincoln to give favorable coverage for the Union's cause in return for the "inside scoop," his concerns are important to note.[19] It is also critical to see that this balance between "commercial" and "free" is one that has been waged throughout our nation's history and is still being fought today.

POLICE AND COURT "NEWS"

As previously mentioned, the addition of a police-court column in 1833 precipitated a major increase of sales of the *New York Sun*. Students of criminal justice may be aware of other police and court developments around that time—the formation of official police departments in major American cities. Although we cannot conduct a study that asks the editors and publishers of these daily newspapers where they got their information, it does make considerable sense that with the organization of police departments, reliable crime information was more readily available. Here is a brief history of police departments and how they were forming at the same time as the advent of these daily papers.

English colonists coming to America in the 17th and 18th centuries brought with them the system of policing that existed in England at the time.[20] In towns such as Boston, Charleston, and Philadelphia, justices of the peace, constables, and sheriffs were appointed and "watches" created.[21] Law enforcement was mostly reactive at that time because the responsibility of enforcement of the law lie with citizen volunteers.

The colonists had fought a seven-year war ending in 1782 and an almost three-year war ending in 1815. By the 1820s, society could begin to recover from war and begin addressing local issues. Without a common enemy to fight, citizens had both more time to engage in social interactions and fewer figures of authority in their midst (e.g., British soldiers). The growing society produced more complex human problems and the responsibility of law enforcement shifted from these volunteers to paid specialists.

Between 1830 and the 1850s, a growing number of cities decided that the constable-nightwatch system was inadequate.[22] This paved the way for the formation of paid daytime police forces. These daytime forces ultimately joined with the nightwatch to create integrated day/night, modern-type police departments. In 1833, an ordinance was passed in Philadelphia creating a paid force consisting of 24-person daytime crews and a 120-person nightwatch. Boston followed suit in 1838 and New York in 1844.

(Just a note to illustrate how disorganized the initial organization really was—Philadelphia disbanded its police force two years after establishing it and did not reinstate it until 1854!)

FROM PENNIES TO DIMES AND YELLOW, NOT MELLOW

Police forces were formed in both Chicago and Milwaukee in 1855. Just the mere mention of these Midwestern cities reminds us that population shifts were occurring in the United States. No longer were the eastern seaboard cities the only viable population centers. As populations increased, so did human interaction and what follows is often unlawful behavior, a.k.a. *crime*. The pioneering spirit of Americans pushed its borders and initially there was little effective government in place. The vacuum created by this lack of government was often filled by vigilante groups in the American West.

VIGILANTE GROUP

A group of private citizens taking the law into their own hands by tracking down criminals and punishing them. These groups typically consisted of a few hundred people organized by the "town elite." They would track down criminals or disorderly people in the settlement and administer "justice." Occasionally the captured outlaws were given a chance to present a defense. Determination of guilt often resulted in the execution of the "defendant," usually by hanging. Vigilante groups were generally well organized along military lines and had written manifestos or constitutions to which the members would subscribe.[23]

In the East, increased immigration and population shifts contributed to growing urban centers. The ensuing stress caused by social dislocation frequently erupted into riots, a phenomenon considered the most important precipitating factor in the creation of professional police forces.[24] Throughout the nation crime became the central social concern. According to criminologist Ray Surette, in the latter half of the 1800s, the dominant image of the criminal in popular culture shifted from a romantic, heroic portrait to conservative, negative images. The newspapers, dime novels, and magazines of that time created many themes of crime and justice that dominate movies and television today.[25]

Schroth et al. explain that as literacy rates in the United States increased during the th century, a market developed for reading material that was entertaining and inexpensive. Published in 1941, *The Murders in the Rue Morgue* by Edgar Allen Poe has been called the first detective story. Well-known crime and detective authors such as Arthur Conan Doyle and Edgar Wallace explored this genre and dime novels became a hit as soon as they emerged.[26]

Unlike the stories in the penny press newspapers, however, dime novels took the central theme of crime as originating in individual personality or moral weakness rather than being due to broader social forces. Surette posits that by downplaying wider social and structural explanations of crime, these novels helped reinforce the existing social order, the status quo.[27]

Dime novels have had a lasting influence as portraits of crime and justice produced during this time are similar to those found today—promoting the notion that heroic individuals are pursuing and capturing criminals and encourage the belief that criminals can be readily recognized and crime ultimately curtailed through aggressive law enforcement efforts.[28] Although often simplistic and/or violent, the themes developed have a durable appeal that continue to entice and enthrall readers.[29] These same things are regularly witnessed in crime shows on television and film, both of which will be discussed at length in upcoming chapters.

As the 19th century rushed toward its close, newspapers came to be mass produced by corporations with large advertising revenues, staffs, and circulations. Crime coverage, in fact, increased at this time because of a trend called *yellow journalism*. This new journalism emphasized the details of individual crimes and police officers replaced court personnel and witnesses as the primary source of crime information.[30]

The term yellow journalism came into vogue when William Randolph Hearst and Joseph Pulitzer endeavored to compete for viewership for their newspapers in New York City in the late 1890s.[31] The term was a pejorative as labeled by the "upper-class" journals to indicate a level of illegitimacy, since Hearst and Pulitzer relied on sensationalism, populism, and socialism to address the interests of new, working class, urban, and immigrant readers.[32]

Here is a further explanation of this term by sociologist Richard Kaplan:

The "yellow" label refers to how journalists handled news content. Pulitzer, and in his footsteps the competitive acolyte Hearst, emphasized reporting on crime and scandal and launched populist crusades against governmental corruption and corporate power. Sensational journalism in the World and the Journal violated the tastes and social understandings of the American upper and middle classes. In response, competitors from the genteel press condemned the focus on crime, scandal, and reform, saying that Hearst and Pulitzer were pandering to the tastes of the masses. The New York Press coined the term "yellow journalism" in 1897 to denote the sensationalist coloring of the news. In fact, in Western Europe "yellow" had long been a depreciating expression for cheap, popular, sensationalist fiction. In New York City, however, yellow had a more specific reference in one of the World's and Journal's most prominent features: comic strips and, in particular, Richard Outcault's brightly colored Yellow Kid, a gap-toothed ragamuffin from the city slums. Conflicts over the correct conduct of journalism and proper public discourse produced a movement aimed at chastising the two New York publishing magnates. Elite papers joined with upper-class magazines, reforming social scientists, and political leaders in criticizing the yellow press and calling for the banning of sensational sheets from libraries and clubs.

Outcault's Mickey Dugan was depicted as, a "bald, buck-toothed, Irish slum urchin, who was identified with the over-sized—presumably a hand-me-down—nightshirt in yellow."[33] His head was portrayed as shaved because it was commonly thought that these poor kids regularly had head lice. "The Yellow Kid was not an individual but a type," Outcault said in an interview. "When I used to go about the slums on newspaper assignments I would encounter him often, wandering out of doorways or sitting down on dirty doorsteps. I always loved the Kid. He had a sweet character and a sunny disposition."[34]

What would students of today call "yellow journalism"? It is a question you may want to ponder after completion of this book. In the end, Kaplan points out that Pulitzer himself ended the race "to the gutter" with William Hearst in that he pursued a "veneer of respectability" in the early 1900s by founding the Columbia University School of Journalism and the Pulitzer prizes. Kaplan adds that "although centered on American history," yellow journalism was a precursor to sensationalism elsewhere in the media.

ON THE TWENTIETH CENTURY

The 20th Century Limited, known by train buffs as the greatest train in the world for 65 years, rolled out on its track in 1902.[35] The 20th century may seem . . . oh . . . *so last century* . . . but the developments during those hundred years were—just like Superman—faster than a speeding bullet.

Around the same time this train made its 20-hour run from New York to Chicago, developments in technology were chugging along. The world of media was about to change forever—from print . . . to radio . . . to film and television.

One year after the 20th Century Limited took its maiden voyage, the first narrative film *The Great Train Robbery* was filmed in West Orange, New Jersey, by Thomas Edison. Those who have watched this film may be shocked that in 1903, there was portrayed a considerable number of killings and a somewhat cavalier manner in which those bodies were disposed. By its title, we can tell that the film itself is about a crime, so it may not be surprising that there is violence. It may surprise some to know, however, that crime was also prominent as a secondary plot in love stories, Westerns, comedies, and dramas.[36]

Throughout the 20th century, all forms of media evolved—probably beyond the imaginations of the likes of William Hearst, Joseph Pulitzer, Edgar Allen Poe, and of course, the Benjamins, both Franklin and Day. (Notice how women are conspicuously absent from this group! That is a subject for another book.) What was so different about the twentieth century that the world drastically changed in such a short time? Mass communication and technology are the answers to this question.

The 20th Century Limited took its last trip in 1967. The train was half-full and there was little fanfare. Perhaps 67 years into this century, there were so many technological advances that people were unfazed (two years later, we saw Americans walk on the moon). College students today would probably find media from 1967 to be limited—no Internet, no cell phones, and only three major news networks. If we look at what preceded the 20th century, we can clearly see how those previous centuries moved rather slowly in comparison—at least in terms of media. While we talk about the dime novels and newspapers of the late 19th century in terms of mass communication, any ingenuity from that time rather pales in comparison to what developed after the turn to the 1900s.

THE TWENTY-FIRST CENTURY AND AN EVER-CHANGING MEDIA LANDSCAPE

The ensuing chapters in this book will pick up the story at the beginning of the 1900s in the United States. While it is difficult to imagine how much quicker mass communication can become, we must realize that computer technology only represents a blip in history—timewise—but dominates our society now.

So, what is so new about news? The obvious answer is technology and heretofore unimaginable mass communication. What is not new? Media as a source of information for the receiver and an income source for the producers. Does that create a conflict or is media controlled by government even "less free" than media with a bottom line? And have trends really changed all that much? Do we still struggle with a free press and a national identity? Do we still have larger-than-life characters and disagreements about public policy that seems unsolvable? And finally . . . is it really all about the Benjamins?

CHAPTER SUMMARY

So, what is news? Is it the late-breaking, up-to-date information we see flashing across our television screens or streaming on our laptops or is it the annual report of climate change and weather patterns? In this chapter, we traced American media from its origins, which were greatly influenced by Benjamin Franklin. Franklin wore many hats in early America and two of those chapeaus involved establishing both a free press and a national identity. We discussed the possibility that there could be an inherent conflict in that both goals would often be at cross-purposes.

The Penny Press brought news to more Americans—easier and cheaper to obtain and written in more accessible language to the less educated—it was both more egalitarian and more sensational. While we often think that sensationalism is a recent phenomenon, it clearly had its foothold in American media by the 1830s. After two long wars with the British, the denizens of this young country could redirect their focus to local issues and one of those issues was crime. Police and court news became prevalent around the same time that police departments were forming in the larger American cities. Additionally, prisons were being built and our court system was expanding.

In the post–Civil War America, we had the difficult period of Reconstruction, followed by the Industrial Revolution and countless changes to everyday lives and the migration of workers from more rural areas to urban areas. Journalism followed all these changes and the political cartoon was an oft-used tool to both instruct and inspire.

Throughout the 20th century, rapid advances in technology brought us access to news at an even quicker pace than the printing press. Radios, newsreels at movie houses, and ultimately televisions brought media to the people. Twenty-four-hour cable news dawned in the latter part of the 1900s and now news directors and producers had to fill 24-hours' worth of news every day. While cable television completely altered the media landscape, it seems slow and stodgy when compared to today's instant ability for everyone to record events as they happen, on a personal device. Who can envision what will be the next iteration of media?

NOTES

1. Franklin, Benjamin. Apology for Printers. Retrieved from: https://www.pbs.org/benfranklin/pop_apology.html.

2. Harr, J. Scott, Kären M. Hess, Christine H. Orthmann, and Jonathon Kingsbury. *Constitutional Law and the Criminal Justice System*. Boston, Cengage Learning, 2018.

3. Ibid.

4. Puff Daddy & The Family. "It's All About the Benjamins." EMI Music, 1997.

5. Murphey, Murray G. "Perry Miller and American Studies." *American Studies*, vol. 42, no. 2, 2001.

6. Mulford, Carla. "Figuring Benjamin Franklin in American Cultural Memory." *The New England Quarterly*, vol. 72, no. 3 (Sep., 1999), pp. 415–443 https://www.jstor.org/stable/366890.

7. Rich, Paul. "Poor Richard in 2011." *Policy Studies Journal* retrieved from: https://onlinelibrary-wiley-com.proxy.libraries.rutgers.edu/doi/pdfdirect/10.1111/j.1541-0072.2010.00387.x.

8. Op. cit., Mulford.

9. Ibid.

10. Ibid.

11. Gordon and Heath in Surette, Ray. *Media, Crime and Criminal Justice: Images, Realities, and Policies*. Belmont, CA, Cengage Learning, 2011

12. Surette, Ray. *Media, Crime and Criminal Justice: Images, Realities, and Policies*. Belmont, CA, Cengage Learning, 2011.

13. Friedman, Barbara. "The Penny Press: The Origins of the Modern News Media, 1833–1861." *Journalism History* vol. 31, no. 1 (2005): 56–56. Research Library Core, ProQuest. Web. 27 Oct., 2009.

14. Nerone, John C. The mythology of the penny press. Critical Studies in Mass Communication, 4:4, 376–404, DOI: 10.1080/15295038709360146.

15. Fellow, R. Anthony, *America Media History*. California State University, Fullerton, Ed. Rebeckah Matthews and Megan Garvey. 2005.

16. Op. cit., Nerone.

17. Ibid.

18. Stewart, Daxton R. "Chip." "Freedom's Vanguard: Horace Greeley on Threats to Press Freedom in the Early Years of the Penny Press," *American Journalism*, vol. 29, no. 1, 60–83, DOI: 10.1080/08821127.2012.10677814, 2012.

19. Ibid.

20. Novak, Kenneth and Gary Cordner, Bradley Smith, and Roy Roberg. *Police & Society*. New York, Oxford University Press, 2017.

21. Adler, Freda and Gerhard Mueller and William Laufer. *Criminal Justice: An Introduction*. New York, McGraw Hill, 2000.

22. Op. cit., Novak.

23. Op cit., Adler.

24. Ibid.

25. Op. cit., Surette.

26. Schroth, *Dime Novels, Pulps, and Thrillers in The Social History of Crime and Punishment in America: An Encyclopedia*, ed. Wilbur R Miller, SAGE Publications, 2012

27. Op. cit., Surette.

28. Ibid.

29. Op. cit. Schroth.

30. Op. cit., Surette

31. Kaplan, Richard. Yellow Journalism. *International Encyclopedia of Communication*, edited by Wolfgang Donsbach, Volume XI, 2000.

32. Ibid.

33. Canemaker, John. "The Kid from Hogan's Alley." *The New York Times*, December 17, 1995. Retrieved from: https://www.nytimes.com/1995/12/17/books/the-kid-from-hogan-s-alley.html.

34. Ibid.

35. Browne, Malcolm W. "The 20th Century Makes Final Run; Economics Force Central to End Luxury Service." *The New York Times*, December 3, 1967. Retrieved from: https://timesmachine.nytimes.com/timesmachine/1967/12/03/84990019.html?pageNumber=31.

36. Op. cit., Surette.

Chapter 2

Murder in the First Degree

The gray, overcast city of Seattle is pictured from overhead. People are walking around outside, umbrellas opened, as they navigate to work through the rain. A bird's eye view of an office, with colorful cubicles of green plants, multicolored files, and diverse employees typing away on keyboards, is featured. Eventually, the camera focuses in on a red-headed White woman, in her late 20s, with curly hair, fair skin, and a pink cardigan. She is instant messaging an unknown seller about an orange-colored classic car. The seller asks her to meet, and she agrees.

The scene changes to the woman standing outside in the rain, waiting for the classic car to pull up and the seller to exit, so she can take it for a test drive. The seller switches to the passenger seat, and the woman begins to drive through Seattle traffic. We do not see the full profile of the seller, but from a peek we are offered of his mouth we can tell he is a White man. He asks the woman if she wants to see underneath the hood of the car, so the woman pulls over to inspect it. After inspection, the seller takes the wheel, the woman under the impression that he is driving her back to her office. However, he purposely misses the turn-off. The woman becomes wide-eyed with panic as the seller ignores her frequent requests to stop the car. She turns to the lock on the door, seeing there is none; the woman is trapped. The seller punches her in the face.

Over three-thousand miles away we meet behavior analysts—individuals who work to solve some of the most infamous murder cases. As one lectures new recruits, he is interrupted, only to be told about a strangler in Seattle who has taken the lives of four victims, and who seems to have abducted a fifth. We are told the strangler keeps the women alive for seven days before ending their lives. His message to police, found on the woman's computer, says he cannot control himself. Does he want to be found? Four days have passed, and the team is left with three days to save the red-headed office worker with a love of classic cars.

The analysts quickly board a private FBI plane, taking them from Washington, D.C. to Seattle. They are reviewing the deaths of the strangler, building a profile of the suspect based on the evidence from past crime scenes. While they work, the red-headed woman is seen in an oversized dog's crate, lock on the door. She is blindfolded with duct tape, gagged with fabric, and chained. She is wailing as the strangler opens the crate, yelling at her for trying to remove her bindings and clipping her fingernail.

As time progresses, we are introduced to additional evidence and the full profile of the suspect by the analysts: White male, late 20s, a typical "guy next store," with a criminal record, psychopathic and organized, sexually inadequate, an anger rapist who experienced the death of a family member as a child that led to paranoia. Killing gives this suspect power, as does inserting himself into the investigation. In fact, the analysts believe this is a suspect the Seattle police have already interviewed. Soon after delivering the profile, the agents make an arrest. But the suspect doesn't match the profile. Or does he?

The agents interview the suspect and analyze his statements to determine that he is working with someone. A second suspect is now being sought; he is thought to be the dominant in the pair. The agents believe the pair met in prison, and investigate the old cell mate of the first suspect. But, as they visit the prison, they learn the cell mate died. Still, their trip to prison turned into a success, as they spoke to a corrections officer with a keychain reminiscent of the orange-colored classic car. This second suspect is also a White male, late 20s to early 30s, who protects the weak. Knowing the identity of the second suspect, the team leaves the prison without making an arrest and returns to the evidence, and to the first suspect, hoping to gain a confession.

Does the red-headed woman end up dead? We learn her fate as half of the agents successfully tapped into the first suspect's computer and see the victim, alive, on a webcam. They suspect she is being held in some boat, as the light over her cage is moving. Meanwhile, the other half of agents are pursuing the second suspect, hoping they catch him and can save the victim. But quickly, the sense of urgency rises, as suspect number two reaches the victim in a shipping yard. Agents are close behind. Before the suspect can complete the kill, the agents shoot him dead. The case is solved.

If you have ever watched fictional crime dramas on TV, then you may recognize the above plot from the pilot episode, "Extreme Aggressor," of *Criminal Minds*.[1] While not the first of its kind, *Criminal Minds* lasted fourteen seasons before the series ended in 2020. This chapter takes a look at murder and its depiction in television crime dramas. We present a content analysis examining whether murder on TV accurately represents murder in the real world. In doing so, we first define murder and its types, and later discuss the popularity of dramas featuring murder.

TV crime dramas have been on air since the 1950s. Dragnet is recognized as one of the first police dramas, moving from radio to television in 1951.[2] Much has evolved in the realm of crime-fighting since then, but one thing has not changed—the publics' fascination with murder. Murder is typically classified as either first-degree, second-degree, or manslaughter.

TYPES OF MURDER

Before we describe the different types of murder, we first want to differentiate between murder and homicide. Homicide is defined broadly as the killing of another person. Murder is the illegal or unjustified killing of another person. So, all murders are homicides, but not all homicides are murders. In this text we will use the terms homicide and murder interchangeably, keeping in mind that most acts we refer to are those of first-degree murder.

First-degree murder best characterizes what many crime dramas depict. First-degree murder refers to the taking of a person's life with premeditation, deliberation, and malice. In other words, a perpetrator consciously intends to take the life of another person, knowing that killing is wrong. Indeed, the inclusion of malice suggests an evil thought or indifference to another's life. First-degree murder may also include felony murder, which refers to murder committed during some other felony. An example of felony murder is killing someone while robbing a gas station.

Second-degree murder, on the other hand, involves no premeditation or deliberation. So, while a person intends to kill another at the time of the murder, up until that moment there was no plan to kill. Say, for example, you and a family member have been arguing over an heirloom piece of your grandmother's you both want. One day, you decide to go to your family member's home to talk about who the heirloom should go to. As you talk, the discussion gets more and more heated. You walk to the kitchen to cool off, but while there you grab a knife from your family member's kitchen. As you return to the conversation, you stab your family member, killing him or her. While you did not go over your family member's home with the intent to kill that person, in the moment you grabbed the knife you meant to kill, or at the very least cause serious bodily harm that you knew could lead to death. This act would be classified as second-degree murder.

Manslaughter occurs when a person does not intend to kill another, but winds up doing so as a result of being neglectful, reckless, or so emotionally distraught that his or her judgment is clouded. Voluntary manslaughter involves intentional killing, but without malice. Some refer to voluntary manslaughter as "heat of passion." Perhaps the best example of this is the wife who walks in on her husband with another woman, so high on emotions that she grabs a gun and shoots him dead. While the intent to kill was present the moment the woman picked up the gun, so overcome with emotion was she that she did not appreciate the wrongfulness of her actions. Involuntary manslaughter occurs when someone's reckless behavior causes death. For example, you know that texting while driving is wrong and distracts you from paying attention to the road. You do so anyway and, while typing out a text, you strike a pedestrian, killing him or her. You consciously chose to take a risk by texting, knowing you could cause harm to another, even if you did not intend to kill when you looked down at your phone to send that fateful message.

TYPES OF MULTIPLE MURDER

Murder can involve a single victim, or multiple victims. When multiple victims are involved we apply the term multiple murder. In the case of multiple murder, we distinguish between serial murder, mass murder, and spree murder. The Federal Bureau of Investigation (FBI) defines serial murder as, "the unlawful killing of two or more victims by the same offender(s), in separate events."[3] These separate events may occur over a period of days, months, or years.[4] And, this definition suggests that there is a "cooling off" period between the murders. While none seem to agree on the length of a "cooling off" period, Edelstein suggests the more important aspect is that there is a clear distinction between each of a serial killer's murders.[5] Famous serial murderers include Ted Bundy, Jeffrey Dahmer, the BTK Killer, and John Wayne Gacy.

In contrast, mass murder is defined as the killing of four or more victims, "during the same incident, with no distinctive time period between the murders."[6] School shootings, like those at Virginia Tech, Sandy Hook, and Parkland, fall into this type of multiple murder. Similarly, the 2016 shooting at Pulse nightclub in Orlando and the 2017 shooting at the Route 91 Harvest music festival in Las Vegas can also be classified as mass murder. And Richard Speck, who killed eight nursing students in their college home in one night, is classified as a mass murderer.[7]

Finally, spree murder is defined as, "the killing of three or more victims in different locations but within the context of one event."[8] Spree murder does not include the "cooling off" period of serial murder. Instead, a killer moves from one location to another, killing along the way, without losing sight of his or her murders. For example, a man kills his boss at work, then drives to the gas station, killing an attendant, then continues to his home, killing his wife, and then immediately drives his child's school, killing a teacher, with no break in between these events. Other examples of spree murder are the DC/

Beltway Snipers, who killed ten people over the course of three weeks in the Baltimore area, and William Cruse of Florida, who killed several people in different locations without a break in between.[9]

MURDER IN THE FIRST DEGREE, ON TV

Research suggests that murder is the crime portrayed most often in crime dramas.[10] This applies to present-day crime dramas as well as crime dramas from decades ago.[11] So it seems fitting that we begin our discussion and present our findings on murder first, before moving on to other crimes in later chapters.

Over the course of four years, we collected data on television crime dramas. Specifically, we were interested in content including the crime(s) depicted, and perpetrator(s) and victim(s) demographics. In Adubato's Research Methods courses, students were trained on data collection and recording observations. They were then tasked with watching four to five episodes of a crime drama of their choosing. Table 2.1 displays the data collection table used by students.

Students completed a separate data collection table for each crime drama episode viewed. They were instructed to draw a check or tally mark in the open space next to each type of crime and characteristic of each offender and victim as they saw the crime(s), perpetrator(s), and victim(s) in the episode. If there were multiple perpetrators and victims per episode, students attempted to separate the characteristics of each individual offender or victim in the space provided. If there were multiple crimes, whether the same of different, students simply tallied the crimes they viewed.

A total of 449 hours of crime dramas were viewed (with all episodes lasting one hour). Crime dramas included episodes from shows on cable and subscription services (e.g., Netflix and Hulu) and included both newer releases (e.g., *The Blacklist* and *The Sinner*) and long-running programs (e.g., *Law & Order* and *Criminal Minds*). Table 1 includes a list of all shows viewed. Of the 449 hours, we collected non-aggregated data for 169 hours, meaning that we have data on the individual crimes committed, individual perpetrator information, and individual victim information. We have aggregated data for 280 hours of crime dramas. We discuss our results below and throughout this text, and compare the crime drama data to past research and official statistics. It is important to note that in regard to perpetrator and victims' race and age, the student researchers may have recorded their perceptions if the age and race were not directly stated in the episode. We will discuss the implications of this in chapter 7.

- *Blue Bloods*

Table 2.1. Data Collection Table

Type Of Crime					
Drug Smuggling					
Drug Distribution					
Drug Use					
Bribery					
Extortion					
Sexual Assault					
Homicide					
Kidnapping					
Animal Cruelty					
Terrorism					
Robbery					
Child Pornography					
Aggravated Assault					
Arson					
Burglary					
Serial Bomber					
Hijacking A Plane					
Forgery					
Theft					
Trafficking					
Credit Card Fraud					
Total:					
Age Of Victim	18 and under	19–30	31–45	46–65	Over 65
Gender Of Victim	Female	Male			
Race Of Victim	Black	Hispanic	Other	White	
Age Of Perpetrator	18 and under	19–30	31–45	46–65	Over 65
Gender Of Perpetrator	Female	Male			
Race Of Victim	Black	Hispanic	Other	White	

Source: Table created by author.

- *Breaking Bad*
- *Brooklyn 99*
- *Castle*
- *Chicago PD*
- *Criminal Minds*
- *CSI: Miami*
- *CSI: NY*
- *Dexter*
- *Gotham*
- *Hawaii Five-O*
- *Homeland*
- *How to Get Away With Murder*
- *Law & Order: Criminal Intent*

- *Law & Order: Special Victims Unit*
- *Mindhunter*
- *Money Heist*
- *Murder in the Thirst*
- *NCIS*
- *Orange is the New Black*
- *Ozark*
- *Power*
- *Quantico*
- *Psych*
- *Queen of the South*
- *Snowfall*
- *The Blacklist*
- *The First 48*
- *The Punisher*
- *The Sinner*
- *The Wire*

Of the 169 episodes (hours) of which we have non-aggregated data, at least one homicide was included in 110 (65 percent) episodes. And, of those 110 episodes, 55 (50 percent) included homicide as the only crime featured (the remaining episodes including multiple crimes). In the 280 episodes (hours) of aggregated data, a total of 922 individual crimes were recorded, 292 (31.7 percent) of which were homicides.

WHO ARE THE PERPS?

Of the 110 episodes (hours) of crime dramas involving a homicide, 73 (66.3 percent) included a sole perpetrator, 31 (28.2 percent) included more than one perpetrator, and in 6 episodes the gender of the perpetrator was not identified (5.4 percent). Of the sole perpetrators (73), 66 (90.4 percent; 60 percent of total episodes) sole perpetrators were male, and 7 (9.6 percent; 6.3 percent of total episodes) were female. There were 10 (9.1 percent) pairs of one male and one female perpetrator, and 15 (13.6 percent) instances of multiple male perpetrators. In only one (.9 percent) episode was there multiple female perpetrators, and another five (4.5 percent) episodes had multiple offenders, which consisted of both males and females. And, in the 104 episodes where a perpetrator's gender was identified, at least one male was a perpetrator in 96 (92.3 percent).

In regard to race, in 79 (71.8 percent) of the episodes only White perpetrators were depicted. This applies to both sole and multiple perpetrators. Conversely, Black perpetrators only were featured in 11 (10 percent) episodes, Hispanic perpetrators only in 6 (5.4 percent) episodes, and Asian perpetrators only in one (.9 percent) episode. Another one (.9 percent) episode featured a multiracial perpetrator, three (2.7 percent) episodes featured perpetrators of "other" race/ethnicity, and eight (7.3 percent) episodes depicted multiple perpetrators of different racial/ethnic backgrounds.

We have data on age of perpetrator for 108 hours. Some episodes included more than one perpetrator of the same or different age. With that, we identified the age of 138 perpetrators. The majority of perpetrators (38.4 percent) fell into the 31–45 age category. There was nearly an equal amount of perpetrators in the 19–30 (27.5 percent) and 46–65 (23.2 percent) age categories. Thirteen (9.4 percent) perpetrators were 18 years or younger, and only two (1.4 percent) were identified as 65 years or older.

Taken together, the above analysis suggests that the "typical" homicide perpetrator in a crime drama is a sole White male between ages 31–45. Perpetrators who fit this exact profile were present in 27 (26 percent) episodes (based on 104 episodes in which perpetrator gender was recorded). This profile remains consistent with homicide perpetrators in crime dramas in the 1970s and 1980s, demonstrating that our portrayal of killers on TV has not changed much, if at all, over time.[12]

WHO ARE THE VICTIMS?

Of the 110 hours of crime drama episodes involving a homicide, 58 (52.7 percent) included a sole victim, while 52 (47.3 percent) included more than one victim. Of the sole victims, 30 (51.7 percent) were male, and 28 (48.3 percent) were female. In episodes where more than one victim was identified, 16 (30.8 percent) involved multiple males only, 4 (7.7 percent) involved multiple females only, and 32 (61.5 percent) involved both male and female victims.

Whites only were featured as victims in 68 (61.8 percent) episodes, compared to Blacks only in 14 (12.7 percent) episodes, Hispanics only in nine (8.2 percent) episodes, multiracial victims only in three (2.7 percent) episodes, and a victim of "other" race/ethnicity in one (.9 percent) episode. Further, multiple victims of differing race/ethnicities were included in 15 (13.6 percent) episodes.

In 108 hours of episodes we identified 137 victims' ages. The majority of victims (33.6 percent) fell into the 19–30 age category, with victims aged 31–45 (31.4 percent) nearing the same number. Similarly, there was close to an equal amount of victims aged 18 and under (14.6 percent) and 46–65 (16 percent). Only six (4.4 percent) victims aged 65 and older were identified.

Taken together, the above analysis suggests that the "typical" victim in a TV crime drama is likely to be a single victim who is White. There were close to an equal number of male and female victims, with males slightly surpassing females. And age range was again close in number, suggesting a typical victim may be anywhere between ages 19 and 45. As such, the "typical" victim profile is not as simple to build given the near exact numbers surrounding gender and age.

COMPARING TV CRIME DATA TO OFFICIAL STATISTICS

In criminal justice, crime statistics come from three primary sources: the FBI's Uniform Crime Report (UCR; publication titled *Crime in the United States*), the Bureau of Justice Statistics's National Crime Victimization Survey (NCVS; publication titled *Criminal Victimization*), and self-report surveys. The UCR relies on information provided by police departments. In other words, the UCR only captures crime reported to the police. The NCVS obtains data by first randomly selecting households in the United States and then surveying all members of a household ages 12 and older. The NCVS captures (some of) the dark figure of crime, or crime not reported to police. Self-report surveys are often completed by adolescents and young adults in high school and college, asked to report their own deviant or criminal behavior.

Official homicide statistics are published by the FBI in its Uniform Crime Report (note that the NCVS does not publish homicide data, as it relies on survey completion by living household members). As of the writing of this text, the most recent data available were from 2019. Overall, murder accounted for 1.4 percent of all violent crime.[13] Aggravated assaults are the most common form of violent crime, accounting for over two-thirds of violent crimes in 2019.[14] This suggests that homicides are overrepresented in television crime dramas.

OFFICIAL STATISTICS: MURDER PERPETRATORS

Of the 16,245 homicide reported to and recorded by police departments in 2019, gender of perpetrator was known in 11,743 (72.3 percent) incidents. Males overwhelmingly made up those committing murder; 10,335 (88 percent) of perpetrators identified as male. Race of perpetrator was known in

11,493 (70.7 percent) events. Over six thousand (55.9 percent) perpetrators identified as Black, 4,728 (41.1 percent) of perpetrators identified as White, and 340 (2.9 percent) of perpetrators were another race. As for ethnicity, the FBI records this separately in two categories: Hispanic or Latino and Not Hispanic or Latino. The ethnicity of 7,633 perpetrators was recorded, and 6,102 (79.9 percent) offenders were not Hispanic or Latino.[15]

The FBI records age in different increments. For example, it reports the number of perpetrators ages 13 to 16, 17 to 19, 20 to 24, 25 to 29, 30 to 34, and so on (in five year increments after age 19). Age was recorded for 11,265 perpetrators. Over 1,000 perpetrators were recorded in the 17 to 19 (12.8 percent), 30 to 34 (12.3 percent), and 35 to 39 (9.5 percent) age categories. Over 2,000 perpetrators were recorded in the 20 to 24 (20.8 percent) and 25 to 29 (18.3 percent) age categories, with the 20 to 24 age category having the greatest number of offenders.[16] Given this data, it appears the "typical" perpetrator per official data is a Black male between the ages of 20 and 24. While these data are for 2019 only, homicide trends over the past couple of decades suggest that the profile of a murderer has not changed.

Returning to the data, we counted the number of episodes where the perpetrator in the episode matched the most common perpetrator identified through official data sources. Because our age categories differ from the FBI's we considered perpetrators in our dataset ages 19–30 as fitting the age of the "typical" homicide offender. Of the 104 episodes where gender, age, and race/ethnicity of perpetrators were recorded, only 4 (3.8 percent) episodes featured a Black male in the 19–30 age category. As a reminder, the "typical" offender in crime dramas is a White male between ages 31 and 45. In sum, television crime dramas do not accurately represent perpetrators of murder in the real world (in the United States), as they overrepresent White male perpetrators and underrepresent Black male perpetrators. We will return to this in chapter 7 when we discuss the effect of crime dramas on perceptions of Blacks and other People of Color.

OFFICIAL STATISTICS: MURDER VICTIMS

In 2019 there were a recorded 13,927 victims of homicide, 10,908 (78.3 percent) of which were male. A remaining 2,991 (21.5 percent) of victims were female, and 28 (.2 percent) victims' gender was unknown. In regard to race, 7,484 (53.7 percent) victims were Black, 5,787 (41.5 percent) were White, 422 (3 percent) were of another race, and 234 (1.7 percent) victims' races were unknown. As with perpetrators, the FBI reports ethnicity separately, with 8,881 (63.8 percent) victims not Hispanic or Latino and 2,193 (15.7 percent) Hispanic or Latino (ethnicity was unknown for 1,808 [13 percent] victims).[17] Information on age was recorded in the same way for victims as detailed above for perpetrators. Over 1,000 perpetrators were recorded in the 17 to 19 (8.1 percent), 30 to 34 (12.6 percent), 35 to 39 (9.8 percent), and 40 to 44 (7.9 percent) age categories. Over 2,000 perpetrators were recorded in the 20 to 24 (15.4 percent) and 25 to 29 (15.4 percent) age categories, with the 25 to 29 age category having the greatest number of offenders.[18] Given this data, the "typical" victim per official data is a Black male between the ages of 25 to 29. Of the 104 episodes where gender, age, and race/ethnicity of perpetrators were recorded, only three (2.9 percent) episodes featured a Black male in the 19–30 age category. As a reminder, the "typical" victim in crime dramas is a White person between ages 19 and 45. Like with perpetrators, television crime dramas to not accurately represent victims of murder in the real world (in the United States), again overrepresenting White victims and underrepresenting Black male victims.

OTHER OFFICIAL MURDER PATTERNS

Most homicides are intraracial, meaning the race/ethnicity of the perpetrator(s) and the victim(s) is the same.[19] With that, we again returned to our data set and identified the number of episodes featuring intraracial homicide. Of the 109 episodes where race of perpetrator(s) and victim(s) were recorded, 70 (64.2 percent) were intraracial. Specifically, 60 of the episodes featured White perpetrators and victims, seven featured Black perpetrators and victims, and three featured Hispanic perpetrators and victims. The remaining 39 episodes involved multiple perpetrators and/or victims of different racial and ethnic backgrounds.

The majority of murders in the official data involve male offenders and male victims.[20] And female victims are more likely to be killed by male offenders. Female-on-female murder is the least common sex-on-sex relationship in the official data.[21] These same patterns were found in the television crime drama data, whereby male-on-male violence was most common, followed by male-on-female, female-on-male, and female-on-female murder.

A single victim and single offender is the most common murder situation in both official and television crime drama data. In the official data, 7,047 (50.6 percent) murder incidents involved a single victim and perpetrator in 2019; in the television crime drama data, 42 (40.4 percent) of 104 episodes featured one murder victim and one offender.[22] This is where the similarities between official data and crime drama data end as it relates to situation. In our crime drama data, multiple victims and a single offender was the second most frequent represented murder situation, with 32 (30.8 percent) episodes featuring this scenario. In the official data, however, a single victim and multiple offenders was second in frequency (when offender[s] information was known) with 1,782 (12.8 percent) cases. In our crime drama data, the third most common situation was multiple victims and offenders, with 17 (16.3 percent) episodes portraying this. The multiple victims and offenders scenario is least common in official data (when offender[s] was known).[23] Finally, in our crime drama data the least common situation was that of a single victim and multiple offenders, which was found in 13 (12.5 percent) of the episodes. All considering, while television crime dramas get the perpetrator and victim profiles wrong (when comparing to official data sources), they (mostly) get the patterns of murder right.

IT'S NOT ALWAYS AS IT SEEMS: CULTIVATION THEORY

The above results demonstrate that television crime dramas tell a different story than official statistics about perpetrators and victims of murder. But crime dramas are fictional, so there is no harm done, right? Evidence suggests otherwise. As it applies to television crime dramas, cultivation theory argues that people who watch more hours of crime dramas (compared to those viewing less or no hours of such shows) are more likely to perceive crime through the lenses of these shows.[24] In other words, television shows shape, or cultivate, people's social realities.[25] And they do so for people exposed to shows over a long (versus short) period of time.[26] For example, a person who has only watched two or three episodes of *Criminal Minds* is not likely to alter his or her perceptions of crime compared to another person who has watched every episode in the series' 14 seasons.

Cultivation theory was proposed by George Gerbner. He and his colleagues conducted several studies demonstrating that those who watched more violent television shows perceived: (1) violent crime as more prevalent in society compared to its low rates in the real world, (2) more law enforcement officers employed than in actuality, (3) people in general to be less trustworthy (i.e., the mean world syndrome), (4) their chances of being victimized heightened compared to their actual risk.[27] Indeed, Gerbner states that more than half of television characters experience violence each week.[28] This can lead us, the viewers, to also have a heightened fear of crime.[29] In reality, less than 1 percent of people are victims of violent crime annually in the U.S.[30]

Shrum offered a social psychological explanation that supports cultivation theory, arguing that people who watch television often use television, and the content of episodes, as a cognitive shortcut when evaluating the world around them.[31] For example, let us say a person has been asked how much crime occurs in his neighborhood. Because this person views many hours of crime dramas per week, he reports that crime is rampant in his neighborhood. Why does he do this? Rather than think about how much crime he has seen in his neighborhood, or think about a recent report of his neighborhood's crime rate, the person uses this cognitive shortcut, or heuristic, to report level of crime as high. This person sees crime so often on television shows that such images of the episodes are strong in his mind and are recalled first when being asked the question about neighborhood crime.

Since Gerbner and his colleagues published their works in the mid-to-late 1970s, other researchers have explored cultivation theory and the impact of watching television crime dramas on people's construction of crime. For example, Sarapin and Sparks found that people who regularly watched fictional crime-related television shows were more likely to overestimate the number of murders in the U.S. compared to those who watched crime-related shows less often.[32] This finding was especially true for female viewers of crime shows, who overestimated nearly all crime.[33] Jamieson and Romer looked at violent content in television shows and Americans' fear of crime from 1972 and 2010. The authors found that violence in television shows was directly related to fear of crime.[34] Holbert and colleagues found that television crime drama was related to support for capital punishment, or the death penalty.[35]

Other researchers did not find support that television crime dramas predicted viewers' perceptions of crime and viewers' protective behaviors (e.g., owning a gun); however, they did find that reality and/or news programs related to crime or police did predict outcomes like gun ownership, greater perceptions that the criminal justice system is effective, greater confidence in police, and fear of crime.[36] We will return to crime on reality (nonfiction) shows in chapter 4.

It is also worth mentioning that Hughes returned to Gerbner and colleagues' studies and reanalyzed the data, including additional variables that may influence people's construction of reality. In his reanalysis, Hughes concluded that Gerbner and colleagues' findings were not supported after including additional variables, like race, hours worked, and church attendance.[37] Hughes suggests that Gerbner's cultivation theory is either wrong, correct but in need of better data, or too simple, because other factors interact with television to shape our worldviews.[38]

Television alone is not responsible for our perceptions of crime. Indeed, Hughes demonstrated that the variables previously mentioned and sex, income, size of place, age, and others affect our perceptions of crime.[39] For example, those with a college education tend to be less influenced by television dramas.[40] Direct experience can also play a role in how people perceive crime.[41] For example, if one was previously victimized, he or she may overestimate how much crime occurs, and may report a greater fear of crime compared to a person who has never been a victim of crime.

Before moving on we will leave you with this question: If cultivation theory is correct, and crime dramas are depicting White males as those most likely to commit murder, then why do many Americans still associate murder suspects, and criminals in general, as Black men? We will return to this question, and provide some possible answers, in chapter 7.

SUCCESS OF CRIME DRAMAS

Despite the apparent differences between murder in the first degree on TV and actual homicide data, crime dramas remain one of viewers' top show preferences and are typically met with success. For example, the original *Law and Order* ran for 20 seasons. One of the series' spin-offs, *Law & Order: Special Victims Unit* (*SVU*), was renewed for three seasons in 2020, which will take the spin-off into its 24th season. SVU is currently the longest-running primetime drama and live-action show in television history.[42] Similarly, *Law & Order: Criminal Intent* ran for 10 seasons, and *Law & Order: Organized Crime* was recently announced as of the writing of this text, with a fall 2021 anticipated premier date.[43]

Outside of the *Law & Order* universe, other television crime dramas have received spin-offs due to the original show's raging success. Indeed, *NCIS*, a drama surrounding crime committed by or against naval officers, has run for 17 seasons and includes two spin-offs, *NCIS: Los Angeles* and *NCIS: New Orleans*. *CSI: Crime Scene Investigation* ran for 15 seasons and resulted in the productions of *CSI: Miami*, *CSI: New York*, and *CSI: Cyber*.[44]

New crime dramas continue to be met with success and renewals by their broadcasting companies. *Prodigal Son*, for example, follows Malcolm Bright, son of (fictitious) serial killer the Surgeon, as he assists local detectives in solving homicide cases. *Prodigal Son* debuted in 2019 and was renewed for its second season in 2020 (airing in 2021). Its first season averaged 3.4 million viewers per episode.[45] Generally speaking, crime dramas comprise about one-fifth of scripted shows on television today, and outnumber all other show types in the drama category.[46] Given this, we can be certain that crime dramas, especially those surrounding murder, will remain in primetimes television spots for years to come.

WHO GETS MURDER RIGHT?

We know that many shows get murder "wrong" as it relates to official statistics, but is there any crime drama that does it right, or at least comes close? *The Wire* is one television show that has been recognized as portraying the victims and offenders of murder (and crime more generally) more accurately than other crime dramas airing during similar years.[47] Interestingly, *The Wire* was broadcasted by Home Box Office (HBO), a premium channel for which television subscribers typically pay an extra monthly fee. Britto and colleagues note that *Law & Order: SVU*, "does a good job not demonizing minorities in their portrayal as offenders and this is different than many previous media studies in recent years" (but see our discussion about more of Britto and colleagues' findings in chapter 7).[48] However, as you will see in chapter 8, SVU misrepresents official statistics in other ways.

CHAPTER SUMMARY

This chapter began with describing the pilot episode of *Criminal Minds*, which ran for 15 seasons and ended in 2020.[56] Crime dramas remain popular with the public, and often receive the coveted 8 p.m., 9 p.m., and 10 p.m. time slots on major networks (like ABC, CBS, FOX, and NBC). The most common crime depicted in crime dramas is murder, specifically murder in the first degree. As such, this chapter examined the differences between the portrayal and "typical" profiles of perpetrators and victims of murder on crime dramas and in official statistics. What we found is a general misrepresentation of the most common victim and offender profiles in crime dramas.

Crime dramas most often portray killers as sole, middle-aged White men. Similarly, the majority of victims in crime dramas are White men. If cultivation theory is correct, then our perceptions of real-world offenders and victims should be affected so that we believe the most common perpetrators and victims of murder are White men. However, official statistics tell us that the most common perpetrators and victims of murder are Black men in their early to mid-20s. Thus, there is a clear disconnect between murder on TV and in the real-world.

NOTES

1. "Extreme Aggressor." *Criminal Minds*, created by Jeff Davis, season 1, episode 1, The Mark Gordon Company, 2005.

2. "Crime Dramas." Public Broadcasting Service, 2014, https://www.pbs.org/wnet/pioneers-of television/pioneering-programs/crime-dramas/#:~:text=%E2 percent80 percent9CDragnet%E2 percent80 percent9D,leap%20to%20television%20in %201951. Accessed 27 Feb. 2021.

3. "Serial Murder." Edited by Robert J. Morton and Mark A. Hilts, FBI, 21 May 2010, www.fbi.gov/stats-services/publications/serial-murder.

4. Fox, James Alan, and Jack Levin. "Multiple Homicide: Patterns of Serial and Mass Murder." *Crime and Justice*, vol. 23, 1998, pp. 407–455.

5. Edelstein, Arnon. "Cooling-off Periods among Serial Killers." *Journal of Psychology & Behavior Research*, vol. 2, no. 1, 2020, pp. 1–15.

6. Morton and Hilts, "Serial Murder," p. 8.

7. Fox, James Alan, et al. *Extreme Killing: Understanding Serial and Mass Murder*, fourth ed., Sage, 2018.

8. Keeney, Belea T., and Kathleen M. Heide. "Serial Murder: A More Accurate and Inclusive Definition." *International Journal of Offender Therapy and Comparative Criminology*, vol. 39, no. 4, 1995, pp. 299–306.

9. "Beltway sniper attacks," *Encyclopedia of Race and Crime*, ninth ed, 2009; Keeney and Heide, "Serial Murder: A More Accurate and Inclusive Definition," p. 301.

10. Donovan, Kathleen M., and Charles F. Klahm IV. "The Role of Entertainment Media in Perceptions of Police Use of Force." *Criminal Justice and Behavior*, vol. 42, no. 12, December 2015, pp. 1261–1281.

11. Donovan and Klahm, "The Role of Entertainment Media," pp. 1261–1281; Rhonda Estep and Patrick T. Macdonald, "How Prime Time Crime Evolved on TV, 1976–1981," *Journalism Quarterly*, vol. 60, no. 2, 1983, pp. 293–300.

12. Estep and Macdonald, "How Prime Time Crime Evolved on TV," p. 293.

13. "Violent Crime." Federal Bureau of Investigation (FBI), Fall 2020, https://ucr.fbi.gov/crime-in-the-u.s/2019/crime-in-the-u.s.-2019/topic-pages/violent-crime.

14. Ibid.

15. "Expanded Homicide Data Table 3." Federal Bureau of Investigation (FBI), Fall 2020, https://ucr.fbi.gov/crime-in-the-u.s/2019/crime-in-the-u.s.-2019/tables/expanded-homicide-data-table-3.xls.

16. Ibid.

17. "Expanded Homicide Data Table 1." Federal Bureau of Investigation (FBI), Fall 2020, https://ucr.fbi.gov/crime-in-the-u.s/2019/crime-in-the-u.s.-2019/tables/expanded-homicide-data-table-1.xls.

18. "Expanded Homicide Data Table 2." Federal Bureau of Investigation (FBI), Fall 2020, https://ucr.fbi.gov/crime-in-the-u.s/2019/crime-in-the-u.s.-2019/tables/expanded-homicide-data-table-2.xls.

19. "Expanded Homicide Data Table 6." Federal Bureau of Investigation (FBI), Fall 2020, https://ucr.fbi.gov/crime-in-the-u.s/2019/crime-in-the-u.s.-2019/tables/expanded-homicide-data-table-6.xls.

20. Ibid.

21. Ibid.

22. "Expanded Homicide Data Table 4." Federal Bureau of Investigation (FBI), Fall 2020, https://ucr.fbi.gov/crime-in-the-u.s/2019/crime-in-the-u.s.-2019/tables/expanded-homicide-data-table-4.xls.

23. Ibid.

24. Gerbner, George, and Larry Gross. "Living with Television: The Violence Profile." *Journal of Communication*, Spring 1976, pp. 172–199.

25. Gerbner, George. "Cultivation Analysis: An Overview." *Mass Communication & Society*, vol. 1, no. 3/4, 1998, pp. 175–194.

26. Ibid, p. 181.

27. George Gerbner et al., "TV Violence Profile No. 8: The Highlights," *Journal of Communication*, vol. 27, no. 2, June 1977, pp. 171–180; Gerbner et al., "Cultural Indicators: Violence Profile No. 9," *Journal of Communication*, vol. 28, no. 3, Summer 1978, pp. 176–207; Gerbner and Gross, "Living with Television: The Violence Profile," pp. 191–194.

28. Gerbner, "Cultivation Analysis: An Overview," p. 184.

29. Gerbner and Gross, "Living with Television: The Violence Profile," p. 194.

30. Gerbner, "Cultivation Analysis: An Overview," p. 184.

31. Shrum, L. J. "The Role of Source Confusion in Cultivation Effects May Depend on Processing Strategy: A Comment on Mares (1996)." *Human Communication Research*, vol. 24, no. 2, December 1997, pp. 349–358.

32. Sarapin, Susan H., and Glenn G. Sparks. "Eyewitnesses to TV Versions of Reality: Th Relationship between Exposure to TV Crime Dramas and Perceptions of the Criminal Justice System." *How Television Shapes our Worldview: Media Representations of Social Trends and Change* (2009): 145–170.

33. Ibid, p. 159.

34. Jamieson, Patrick E., and Daniel Romer. "Violence in Popular U.S. Prime Time TV Dramas and the Cultivation of Fear: A Time Series Analysis." *Media and Communication*, vol. 2, no. 2, 2014, pp. 31–41.

35. Holbert et al. "Fear, Authority, and Justice: Crime-Related TV Viewing and Endorsements of Capital Punishment and Gun Ownership." *J&MC Quarterly*, vol. 81, no. 2, Summer 2004, pp. 343–363.

36. Maria Elizabeth Grabe and Dan G. Drew, "Crime Cultivation: Comparisons Across Media Genres and Channels," *Journal of Broadcasting & Electronic Media*, vol. 51, no. 1, March 2007, pp. 147–171; Holbert et al., "Fear, Authority, and Justice: Crime-Related TV Viewing and Endorsements of Capital Punishment and Gun Ownership," p. 343; Sarah Eschholz et al., "Race and Attitudes towards the Police: Assessing the Effects of Watching 'Reality' Police Programs," *Journal of Criminal Justice*, vol. 30, 2002, pp. 327–341.

37. Hughes, Michael. "The Fruits of Cultivation Analysis: A Reexamination of Some Effects of Television Watching." *The Public Opinion Quarterly*, vol. 44, no. 3, Autumn 1980, pp. 287–302.

38. Ibid, p. 300.

39. Ibid, p. 293.

40. Ibid.

41. Gerbner, "Cultivation Analysis: An Overview," p. 182.

42. Stacey Lambe, "'Law & Order: SVU': How Season 22 is Handling COVID-19, Stabler's Return and More (Exclusive)," *Entertainment Tonight*, 12 Nov. 2020, https://www.etonline.com/law-order-svu-season-22-coronavirus-elliot-stabler-preview-155899; Gabbi Shaw, "The longest-running TV dramas of all time," Insider, 2 Mar. 2020, https://www.insider.com/longest-tv-dramas-2018-10.

43. Ibid.

44. Ibid.

45. Mitovich, Matt Webb. "TV Ratings: Prodigal Son Slips with Tuesday Move, This Is Us Tops Night." *TV Line*, 13 Jan. 2021, https://tvline.com/2021/01/13/tv-ratings-prodigal-son-season-2-premiere/.

46. Porter, Rick. "TV Long View: How Much Network TV Depends on Cop Shows." *The Hollywood Reporter*, 20 June 2020, https://www.hollywoodreporter.com/live-feed/heres-how-network-tv-depends-cop-shows-1299504. Accessed 27 Feb. 2021.

47. Sabin, Roger, and Jane Gibb. "Who Loves Ya, David Simon? Notes towards Placing The Wire's Depiction of African Americans in the Context of American TC Crime Drama." *Darkmatter*, 2009, pp. 1–14.

48. Britto, Sarah, et al. "Does 'Special' Mean Young, White, and Female? Deconstructing the Meaning of 'Special' in Law & Order: Special Victims Unit." *Journal of Criminal Justice and Popular Culture*, vol. 14, no. 1, 2007, pp. 39–56. Shaw, Gabbi. "Longest-Running TV Dramas of All Time."

Chapter 3

Murder in the First Block

On June 17, 1994, Game 5 of the NBA Finals between the New York Knicks and the Houston Rockets was interrupted for breaking news. For reasons that slowly came out over the 90-minute broadcast of this police/car chase, former NFL star and well-known celebrity O.J. Simpson was being driven in a white Ford Bronco and the LAPD drove behind him. Americans watched in amazement and were completely entranced in this unfolding drama. As the unusually dragged-out car chase continued on, viewers learned that Los Angeles Police were going to charge the Hall-of-Famer, Simpson, with the murder of his ex-wife, Nicole Brown Simpson and the murder of a waiter, Ronald Goldman. At least a dozen police cars trailed behind the white Bronco that was driving the speed limit and LAPD helicopters flew along-side. Commenters from KCAL, a news station in Los Angeles, reported that O.J. Simpson, who was the passenger in the front seat, held a gun to his head at various times. The conjecture was that this was the reason police allowed this slow chase to continue for such a long time period. The police chase itself lasted more than two hours, until Simpson finally surrendered at his own home.

According to CNN, Domino's Pizza reported record sales of pizza delivery during the chase.[1]

The O. J. Simpson story had a profound effect on media coverage. Ninety-five million Americans watched "The Chase" unfold and everyone had to know what led to the arrest and what would transpire subsequently. For 15 and a half months, the O. J. Simpson story dominated the headlines and the first block of newscasts. Court TV, which was just a small cable news station previously, carried the Simpson trial—known as the Trial of the Century—and this catapulted the station to a much higher stature than it previously enjoyed. Overall, CNN devoted 900 hours to the O. J. Simpson story.[2] The networks devoted 84 minutes of their nightly newscasts in one week alone!

FIRST BLOCK

So, what is it meant by first block? A "news block" is simply the content divided around the commercial breaks. Obviously, to draw viewers in, the first block should provide as much excitement and allure as possible. As we will discuss later in this chapter, the O. J. Simpson story had it all—gory murders and a celebrity arrested for these murders. A story like this could easily occupy that top block indefinitely . . . and it did.

You may not have put form to thought on this subject, but you probably understand on a basic level that most of the violent crime and scary news happens at the beginning of a newscast. If you thought about it harder, you would probably agree that the news seems to get "softer" as the half-hour goes on, wrapping up after weather and sports with a cute story—maybe puppies or kids or sometimes the "dumb criminal" story. What is the dumb criminal story? That is the hilarious story of the bank robber who wrote the "give me all your money" note on an envelope that has his name and address written on it. This is actually a popular genre of what is called a "kicker." The kicker is the story at the end that makes you feel okay about the world after the newscast has frightened you. The news station does not want you to never turn on the news again; as a matter of fact, the entire news team wants you to tune in regularly.

So how does a news station cajole the viewer into watching regularly? Interestingly, local news stations across the United States employ the exact same formula. Over the years, some stations have experimented with non-traditional newscasts, but they often return to the well-known format. As mentioned in the first chapter, the expression goes, "If it bleeds, it leads." This is often literally about blood, referring to either violence, strife, natural disasters, or terrible accidents. Obviously, these events are unwanted by any rational human beings, but when they occur, they make headlines. In the case of television, the expression is "top story."

Top story does not always have literal blood either, the carnage could come in the form of great monetary loss or celebrity scandal. The unfortunate expression for a story like this is—it's sexy. Calling sex crime or murder or overturned tractors on a highway "sexy" is particularly onerous, but it is a truth of media. This absolute need for a sexy top story drives a reporter's day. More than once in a 20-year news career has this author been part of the ghoulish attitude that accompanies this drive. Driving by a car wreck, a reporter and a videographer may slow down to check out the scene, but without a multi-car pileup or fatality, it is not worth stopping.

TOP STORY

One particularly pointed event illustrates this overwhelming need for a sexy top story—and if it is an exclusive in the TV market, all the better! At a network affiliate in Birmingham, Alabama, a story came across the news wires that there was a counterfeit $20 bill passed in a lunchroom in a grade school in New York. It was not New York City, but rather a small town six hours west. It seemed like a nothing story to this reporter, but the news director felt otherwise. The news audience only sees the resulting story and associates the reporter wholly with that reporter, but news is either made from the top down or approved by the top. When a news director tells a reporter to cover a story, she or he usually has no choice.

On the way out the door to "create" this story, the news director yelled out, "And it's top story!" The team of videographer and reporter set off to find a story about counterfeit money in Birmingham, without any actual event to cover. The first interview was an FBI agent in Birmingham, who spoke on camera about the problems of counterfeit money in general. When asked if there was any heightening of concern over counterfeit money at the time, he clearly said no. Next, we went to a bank branch and had the manager explain how to tell the different between counterfeit and real money. This gave us some footage to add to the story. Finally, we asked three POS (people on the street) if they were worried about counterfeit money. The POS who agree to be on camera often really want to be on camera. They made various comments. The videographer took some exterior shots and we went back to the station to write and edit the story.

Making a sexy story out of a non-story happens to a reporter much more often than reporters like. Even though the idea of "fake news" stories has permeated our collective conscience, the truth is that the vast majority of news reporters—local and national—are people of integrity who present fair and balanced stories with a very short amount of time to do so.

Having said that, the story was written in the hypothetical; in other words, without writing a fake story I wrote about what counterfeit money looks like and what damage it could do to the city of Birmingham and its denizens. The story was approved and edited and given to the 5:00 news producer.

Just to give a bit more insight to what goes on in a newsroom, televisions and monitors cover a couple of walls. Everywhere you look, you will see broadcasts from your station's competitors, you will see CNN, Fox News, and maybe MSNBC. (In the sports department, you will see ESPN and other local games.) Additionally, you will see "feeds" coming down from the "mother ship." Translation: Whatever news affiliate your station is receives footage from all over the world, all day long. If you are a CBS affiliate, you will receive video from the headquarters in New York, throughout the day. This footage is available to use in all your broadcasts. But I digress . . .

As the Oprah Winfrey Show was playing (our lead-in to our 5:00 newscast), I heard the voice-over of a professional announcer who recorded our announcements from his home studio. The voice-over said, "Coming up at 5:00 . . . Birmingham, your money is not safe!" And there was more. I was livid. I never intimated any such thing in my story.

When the 5:00 news began, I watched and listened while the story was teased and then introduced and wrapped up—around my "package"—in a way that truly would scare our viewers into thinking they could be losing money or even worse be caught distributing fake money and could be in legal trouble. There was nothing I could do. The phone rang in my office and it was the FBI agent I had interviewed. He was even more livid than I. The worst part is that I could not convince him that it wasn't my doing. He told me he would never give me a story again and that I was a dishonest person and he hung up.

Why the push for this top story? Our ratings were bad. We were number four in a four-station market. There is intense pressure on these news organizations and on the news directors in particular. It does not excuse the sexy-top-story-at-all-cost, but it explains it.

From the Field . . . Beth Adubato

THE ART OF THE TEASE

What exactly is a news tease? It is the verbal and often visual equivalent of a news "headline." Remember the town crier? The town crier is purported to have yelled, "Hear ye! Hear ye!" and would proceed to yell out the juiciest part of a story. Watch an old movie and you may hear a "newsie" yell, "Hot off the presses!" and proceed to give a glimpse of what titillating story is available for just the purchase of a newspaper. The television tease comes from this tradition. The television tease calls you to tune in exactly at the top of the hour; the "deep tease" will keep you watching throughout the news program. The tease is not a once-in-a-while event, it is part of every newscast—often part of every news block.

- "Coming up, a devastating winter storm could be headed our way!"
- "Are your children safe in school? Join us at 5:00!"
- "A grizzly murder reveals bodies dumped in a ravine . . . we'll have the shocking story tonight at 6:00."

The "deep tease" refers to something coming up later in the broadcast. If you can have a sexy story at the beginning of the broadcast and one later on to keep viewers from switching the channel, that is a solid broadcast. This is the goal of every news organization—attract and keep viewers. Nothing does that better than fear; therefore, fear sells and that takes up back to murder in the first block.

THE CRIMINAL JUSTICE WEDDING CAKE

The opening voice-over of the long-running TV series *Law & Order* announces:

> *In the criminal justice system, the people are represented by two separate but equally important groups: the police, who investigate crime; and the district attorneys who prosecute the offenders. These are their stories.*[3]

Then, there is some kind of convincing sound effect and we are in the story. It is an extremely effective opening for a show that ran for 20 seasons, was nominated for 203 awards, and produced two successful spin-offs—*Law & Order: Criminal Intent* and *Law & Order: SVU*. Although we are dealing with news media in this chapter, it is worth noting the phrase that begins the famous narration, "In the criminal justice system . . . " It is assumed by viewers of all media that there is a criminal justice system. We hear the words all the time; we, therefore, believe that there is a system in effect. Further, it indicates that within this system, criminal justice cases will be treated the same way.

To dispel this notion, criminologists offer the "Wedding Cake Model." Originally developed by Lawrence Friedman and Robert B. Percival in *The Roots of Justice in Alameda County, California, between 1870 and 1910*, the model has been updated by criminologists Michael and his father, Don Gottfredson.[4] With additional support based on contemporary evidence, the Gottfredsons posed this theory in their work, *Decision Making in Criminal Justice*.[5]

The wedding cake model emphasizes two points: (1) there are significant differences between types of cases, based primarily on the seriousness of the offense, the offender's prior record, and the relationship between the victim and the offender, and (2) there are fairly consistent patterns of disposition within each category.

Chapter 3

TOP LAYER

The top layer consists of a crime that dominates the news. This crime will be either a celebrated case including a famous person or a particularly gruesome crime. Sadly, there are many recent examples of a crime that fits onto the top layer of this cake.

- College admissions scandal—More than 50 wealthy parents paid thousands of dollars to an alleged mastermind named Rick Singer to rig their children's SAT scores or have coaches claim they are athletes or many other ways of getting children of privilege admitted to prestigious universities. These young people took the spots of students who would have rightfully earned acceptance on their own merits. This scandal would never have made it to the top of the wedding cake, if it were not for two famous Hollywood actresses being charged, Felicity Huffman and Lori Loughlin. Huffman immediately plead guilty for paying to have her daughter's SAT scores changed. She served two weeks. Loughlin, charged with more serious crimes, faced 45 years in prison. She served two months.[6]
- Jeffrey Epstein—Epstein started his career as a teacher, but switched to a banking career and ended up extremely wealthy. His wealth put him in an elite social circle and he cavorted with the rich and powerful. A financier worth more than $550 million, Epstein was accused of abusing a 14-year-old girl by her parents in Palm Beach, Florida in 2005. In 2008, he was convicted by a Florida state court. He served 13 months in custody, but with extensive work release. On July 6, 2019, Epstein was arrested on federal charges for the trafficking of minors in New York and Florida. Epstein died on August 10, 2019 in his New York City jail cell, where he was found hanging. The medical examiner ruled his death a suicide.[7]
- Harvey Weinstein—Weinstein, an award-winning and powerful movie mogul, was sentenced to 23 years in prison in March of 2020, for forcible sex crimes. He had been charged with two felony sex crimes in New York. He faces charges on six additional counts of sexual assault in Los Angeles. Twenty-one women who have accused Weinstein of sexual misconduct have formed a group called the Silence Breakers, which includes well-known actresses Ashley Judd and Rosanna Arquette.[8]
- Breonna Taylor—In March of 2020, 26-year-old Taylor was shot and killed in her own apartment by Louisville Metropolitan (LMPD) police officers in Louisville, Kentucky. Shortly after midnight on March 13, plainclothes officers forced entry to her apartment while executing

what was initially a no-knock warrant. When the officers breached the door, Kenneth Walker (Ms. Taylor's boyfriend), believing the police to be intruders, fired one shot from his legal firearm. In response to this shot, three police officers shot 32 rounds into the dark apartment. Five of these rounds struck Ms. Taylor, with one causing her death. The killing of Breonna Taylor set off a year of protests in the city and across the country.[9]
- George Floyd—The 46-year-old Texan native was detained by police in Minneapolis, where he had gone to seek employment. The *New York Times*, using bystander footage along with police body camera and security tapes, put together a video timeline that shows the 17 minutes from initial contact between Floyd and the police and his loss of consciousness. Mr. Floyd spent almost eight minutes and 46 seconds with Minneapolis Police Officer Derek Chauvin's knee on the back of his neck, with his face down on the pavement. As the video of George Floyd's death circulated the globe by social and traditional media, protests erupted.[10]

The top layer contains the most celebrated cases, the most notorious, and therefore, the most interesting to the average viewer. So, where's the harm in that? These cases are rare examples from the criminal justice system. Because they feature celebrities or heinous crimes or in some cases, both, they capture the most attention. Here is where some confusion comes in: it is not a one-sided decision by media outlets to keep these stories under our gaze for often months at a time; if the viewers or readers or listeners were not captivated by these stories, the media would not continue to run them.

This is sometimes a point of confusion for students when learning about the criminal justice wedding cake. Students may believe that the media set out to lure unsuspecting consumers into being transfixed by whatever story them deem the most newsworthy. There are two obvious reasons why this is not the case:

1. If these stories were manufactured in some way, all of the various media outlets would not have the same story at the same time.
2. If viewers did not watch these stories in record numbers when crimes like these arise, media outlets would stop running the stories.

Now that we have established the symbiotic nature of these celebrated cases (in sum, they keep viewers satisfied and they make money for media outlets), let's go back to the question—where's the harm in that? The harm comes from the skewed view of the criminal justice system that results from these high-profile cases capturing our collection attention.

FULL COURT PRESS

Most of these celebrated cases go to trial (for that matter, all the cases on *Law & Order* go to trial, but that is the stuff of a different chapter). The Bureau of Justice Statistics estimates that only 5 percent of all felony cases go to trial; the other 95 percent are settled by plea bargaining. O. J. Simpson's trial lasted for months and featured an entire defense *team*; this is just not a reality for most defendants. The Bureau of Justice Statistics conducted a study of the 75 most populous counties in the United States and found that 82 percent of state defendants had a court-appointed attorney.[11] In a trial we get to see the fundamental issues contested in public view—the sanity of the defendant, the inadmissibility of the evidence, the credibility of the witnesses, the competence of the prosecutor and defense attorney, and the fairness of the judge.[12] Glimpses of trials on the news bring the viewer into the most exciting yet most rare events of the criminal justice system, the trial.

Here is where the tricky part comes in—understanding how this happens. While it is true that the news business is a business, the consumers also play a part in the types of crimes they find compelling. If the news organizations ran the actual routine crime cases that make up the majority of police business, viewers might not tune in, in droves. One station in Florida attempted to run all "positive" stories on the air and the idea was met with some enthusiasm. When viewership dropped, however, the traditional news format was reinstalled.

It is not just the negative vs. positive news that is at issue; as the Criminal Justice Wedding Cake shows, the celebrated cases give the idea that the criminal justice system is far more exciting than it is. Routine crime is far less titillating, does not often include wealthy or powerful people, and is usually a result of social ills. It is important to note, too, that celebrated cases are not just those involving celebrities or particularly odious crimes. The top layer of the CJ Wedding Cake includes cases that become landmark decisions and therefore influence policy and law—*Miranda v. Arizona* is one of these cases.

The upshot of the "murder in the first block" syndrome is that it distorts public perception of the criminal justice system. It puts an unwarranted focus on homicide that is echoed in fictional media and makes people believe that the world is a much scarier place than it really is. Most Americans would be surprised, for example, to learn that crime has been dropping since 1993! Also, the idea that you would get a trial if you were involved in a criminal offense is just not true, as the percentages are against it. Another important aspect of this focus on the top layer is the kinds of prison terms that celebrities receive do not mirror the terms that an average, non-famous person would receive. In the case of the college admissions scandal, while both actresses faced years of prison, one received months and the other was sentenced to two weeks. There is nothing normal or routine about this layer of the cake.

REST OF THE CAKE

The second and third layers of the "cake" include serious felonies. If we take the eight index crimes and divide them into crime against property and crimes against the person, we have felony crimes, but the more "serious" would obviously be those against the person. Crimes against property include larceny-theft, arson, burglary, and motor vehicle theft. Obviously, these crimes carry prison sentences, but not as severe as the punishment for homicide, rape, felonious assault, and robbery. Of course, these crimes are often top stories and would be considered "top layer," but usually because of the nature of the case. Criminal justice professor, Samuel Walker, contends that there is a "courtroom work group"—a group that put the system in the criminal justice system.[13] We asked Officer John Swiderski for his take *From the Field*.

From the Field: A Police Officer Explains Relationships with Prosecutors

As a police officer, I have little interaction with judges and defense attorneys. Mostly, I and my fellow officers have interactions with prosecutors. We may be asked to meet the prosecutor in person to discuss the events of a case, ranging from a traffic stop to a more serious criminal case. For traffic stops, the officer may be asked to explain what happened, what the infraction(s) was, how the driver responded to being pulled over, and if the officer wants to pursue the case in court. The prosecutor will also review footage from the officer's body camera and/or the dashboard camera on the police vehicle. For a non-serious traffic offense, the prosecutor and representative of the driver may come to an agreement to pay a fine and reduce points on the license. Sometimes, drivers have to both pay a fine and deal with added points on their license. For criminal cases, we may get called in to testify for the prosecution. We will also be cross-examined by the defense attorney. In a grand jury, most officers are asked mostly yes or no questions. The grand jury really just wants the officer's perspective on what happened after the officer arrived to the scene. Overall, the working relationship between police officers and the prosecutor is positive. This may be different in other cities depending on the conduct of one or more officers, but I have only had positive experiences.

—John Swiderski

This group, also known as "local legal culture" consists of a group of professionals who decide how cases are handled. These groups include prosecutors, judges, defense attorneys, and police officers. When these groups process a case from the beginning, they decide its worth. They determine whether the case is "worth" putting in the time and the full strength of the law or it is not. Walker[14] states that research suggests criminal justice officials consistently use several factors to define the seriousness of an offense:

1. The nature of the crime
2. Whether a weapon was used
3. Whether the victim was injured
4. The suspect's prior record
5. The relationship between the victim and the offender

Members of the media make these same distinctions—from a different viewpoint. Remember the example from earlier in the chapter about the car crash? Reporters out in the field covering a story on school children falling ill from the food in their cafeteria will drive by a seven-car crash with the passengers all standing around to continue on to their story. These same reporters will stop if a school bus crashed because a driver of an 18-wheeler came down off a drug-induced high and ran the bus off the road. While they would never admit it, the police and the media both employ an unwritten code of where on the layer cake a sexy story sits. Police refer to these crimes as "heavy" or "real." A crime that is not worth full pursuit would be called "garbage" or "bullshit."[15] A reporter would call it a "non-story" or a "nothing" story. Put into this framework, it is apparent why third-layer crimes will not be watched on the news—they are not "worth" it because they are not serious enough or interesting enough.

The fourth layer is the layer you will never see on the news in a big city or on national news; that is unless, as denoted at the beginning of this chapter, it is a "dumb criminal story." Outside of this kind of entertaining offense, the majority of crime sits in this layer. Misdemeanors are the most commonly committed crime and will only make it to the news in the smallest of towns with very small populations and no crime to speak of. Television markets will be explained in chapter 5, but suffice it to say that approximately 83 percent of all arrests across the country each year will never make it from that wedding cake plate to the living room console.

IS BLEEDING STILL LEADING?

It is important to emphasize that not only crime stories dominate the first news block. As mentioned, a terrible highway accident or plane crash—which may or may not have criminal attachments—can take that top spot. Natural disasters also will populate Block #1 of a newscast. Terrible accidents and natural disasters occur less frequently than serious or celebrated crimes. Crime is the "go-to," first block story.

As we discussed in chapter 2, crime cultivation theory includes the notion that how you see the world depends on what you watch. Gerbner developed this theory in 1972 and countless research teams have explored the concept. We wanted to know if all of that research has made a difference; for example, would we find less titillating, more instructive news in the first block? In order to study this, we watched 434 TV news broadcasts between January 2018 and November 2019. We divided the observations into international, national, and local news. We also looked at newspaper stories and social media, but let's talk about television news first.

DIVIDING THE NEWS INTO THE FOLLOWING CATEGORIES—

- International Cable News
- National Cable News
- National Nightly Network News (ABC, CBS, and NBC)
- Local Affiliate Newscasts (in other words, local news, non-cable . . . in other words, "free")
- Local 24-hour Cable News

Table 3.1 below provides a splattering of the top crime stories, by news outlet, we observed between January 2018 and November 2019. If crime was included in the top story, we list the crime(s) discussed in the top story in the middle column. If one or more crime stories was included in the first block, a brief description of the crime(s), as it was displayed on TV, is included in the right column.

ANALYSIS

It would be impossible to list the thousands of stories we cataloged, but this gives some insight into the kinds of top stories across media outlets. We

Table 3.1 Top Stories from Media Outlets January 2018–November 2019

News Outlet	Crime as Top Story	Crime in the 1st Block
CNN	*Impeachment (more than 40 times) *Iraq withdrawal *Trump/Putin	John Bolton agrees to testify in Trump impeachment
CNN International	Killing of Soleimani+ *Flu deaths *Kenya attack	
BBC	*Australian Bushfires *Poison Rivers *Harvey Weinstein *Olympian murdered	
Fox News	*Impeachment *Jeffrey Epstein suicide? *Trump/Putin	*North Korean Kim calls for phased synchronized moves to denuclearize his country
MSBNC	*DV—against Heather Locklear's boyfriend *Three Americans killed in Kenya *Border officers detaining Iranian immigrants *Suicide bombers—brothers—attempt in Brussels airport *Stephen Hawking death *Spy poisoning in the UK	*Harvey Weinstein *Trump wants teachers to carry guns *Trump/Putin *Trump jokes that guns are not the problem *Trump declares Palestinian city of Jerusalem as Israeli capital
National Nightly News (ABC, CBS, and NBC combined)	*Florida School shooting+ (3 consecutive nights) *Florida students go back to school after massacre *Mini-van rammed into the White House—white female+ *Dorm shooting *Deadly bridge collapse at FIU+ *Porn star vs. POTUS *Cambridge Analytica misused data	*NRA backlash x2 *TV series to focus on unsolved murders of Tupac Shakur and Biggie Smalls *Jared Kushner doesn't have proper clearance *Rick Gates accused funneling $75 million into off-shore accounts+ *FBI Director under threat from Pres. Trump

New York Market Local News	*Shark bite *Nurse strangled by date *School shooting in Maryland *Helicopter crash+ *Dow plunges *Students chant to end gun violence *Baby found alone on subway platform *Corrections officer attacked at Rikers+ *Cirque du Soleil death+ *Fire in train station	*Crash in Queens—jaws of life *Thieves attack a 79-year-old male *Bus driver fired for mooning
New Jersey/New York 24-hour Cable News	*Police stand-off (no details on race gender, or age) Gunman shot by *police *Governor unveils budget	*Ex-teacher pleads guilty to taking video up the skirts of Medford, NJ, students

+Denotes all stations in this category carried this story

Source: Table created by author based on author study

observed and analyzed 434 social media stories, 130 newspaper entries, and 434 TV news programs from January 2018 through November 2019. As you can see, the international and national cable stations tend to air stories that affect greater numbers of people. It absolutely comports with the Criminal Justice Wedding Cake in that the top stories involve celebrated cases.

According to the Department of Justice, over 15,000 Americans were killed in both 2018 and 2019—the time period of our observational study—but single murders do not make it into the top story on CNN or Fox. CNN International and BBC also did not have one story of a single, non-celebrity homicide as a top story. Does that mean "if it bleeds, it leads" is not true? That depends on the level of media coverage and that brings us to more of the analysis—the CJ Wedding Cake may be sharing tabletop space with the Media Pineapple Upside Down Cake.

MEDIA PINEAPPLE UPSIDE DOWN CAKE

The hierarchy of media coverage from international to national cable to national network to local affiliate to local cable is inverted in its coverage—in other words, the higher up, the broader the coverage; hence this idea of the upside-down cake. While we still see celebrated cases in the top story slot, we do not see all of the "every day" criminal event. Yes, if it bleeds, it leads, but only if there are far more people affected.

As you can see from the chart, as you go from the broader news organizations to the local, the emphasis changes. While local news will definitely lead with a national or global top story, local news will switch the focus to the viewers' concerns in their areas. Local crimes of unknown people will populate the top story slot and as much of the first block as necessary. One can absolutely depend on the bleeding and leading in local news coverage. The differences among the strata of news hierarchy must be acknowledged.

The Criminal Justice Wedding Cake is a useful and accurate way of determining how much information people will glean about the criminal justice system from watching the news, but the *category* of news watching is additional factor that must be considered. An interesting future study could be a nationwide survey of the combination of news that people watch and how that affects their view of the innerworkings of the criminal justice system. Just as people watch ESPN for national sports, but will watch their local news on Friday nights for high school football results, perhaps people pick and choose? This addition to the cake metaphor may give us a clearer picture of news consumption.

INTERNATIONAL CABLE NEWS

(CNN INTERNATIONAL, BBC, AL JAZEERA)

↓

NATIONAL CABLE NEWS

(CNN, Fox, MSNBC)

↓

NATIONAL NETWORK NEWS

↓

LOCAL AFFILIATE NEWS

↓

LOCAL CABLE

Figure 3.1. Media Pineapple Upside Down News Chart. *Created by author.*

ONE LAST WORD ON BLEEDING AND LEADING

Psychologist Deborah Serani says that watching the news is a "psychologically risky pursuit."[16] Her contention is that the overwhelming nature of this focus on traumatic crime events—and natural disasters, too—exploits people's vulnerabilities. She says "gone are the days" of tuning in for information and that this focus on the tragic and horror is damaging. She cites many studies that indicate the observation of such horror leads to the increased likelihood of depressive orders, anxiety disorders, and post-traumatic stress disorders for adults and children. This is important to consider for members of the media and even for the public information officers who give crime accounts to the media. From the viewpoint of news makers, however, one could counter this with the idea that no one is forcing people to watch the news.

While psychologists may be much more studied in this regard than those involved in news production, what Serani and her many colleagues describe as being technologically influenced and post 9/11 in nature, is really not so different from various forms of media throughout known history. There is obviously an audience for this kind of news coverage, which is inextricably linked to the criminal justice system. It is important to be aware of the negative impact on viewers. It is not uncommon nowadays to have the anchor state at the top of the newscast that violent video will be shown and children should perhaps be shielded. Equally common is a "trigger warning" on a news story that may involve violence and tragedy targeting specific survivors of crime.

This fairly recent use of the warning provides not only a chance for viewers to turn off the broadcast but also could give viewers the impetus to find a broadcast on a different layer of the cake.

CHAPTER SUMMARY

In this chapter, we learned about the building blocks of a newscast—literally broken down into what we call "blocks." What goes in the first news block is the most titillating news possible. In that same vein, we discussed the concept of a "top story": what makes a good top story and how connected is the top story with the workings of the criminal justice system. We included a "*From the Field*" report to illustrate the making of a top story.

Putting these ideas into criminological contexts, we looked at the Criminal Justice Wedding Cake, an idea that uses a wedding cake metaphor to explain the media/crime connection. It is a theory that has been revamped—an oldie, but still a goodie. Criminal justice work groups are another important concept to understand, clarifying the everyday workings of police. We include another *From the Field* to help understand this concept. Finally, we explore new research that could perhaps show a more recent way we construct a newscast—have we cut down on our reliance on racist tropes in the news or have we only just begun?

NOTES

1. Criss, Doug. "25 years ago today, America stopped to watch the cops chase O.J. in a white Ford Bronco." CNN, 17 June 2019, https://www.cnn.com/2019/06/17/us/oj-simpson-car-chase-anniversary-trnd.
2. Reider, Rem. "O.J. Simpson's Huge Impact on the News Media." *USA Today*, 16 June, 2014, https://www.usatoday.com/story/money/columnist/rieder/2014/06/16/oj-saga-ushered-in-new-media-era/10574759/.
3. *Law & Order*, https://www.imdb.com/title/tt0098844/.
4. Walker, Samuel. *Sense and Nonsense about Crime, Drugs, and Communities*, eighth ed., Stamford, CT, Cengage Learning, 2015, pp. 43–53.
5. Ibid.
6. Chavez, Nicole. "Lori Loughlin and Felicity Huffman Are Two Contrasting Faces in the College Admissions Scam." CNN, 23 October 2019, Retrieved from: https://www.cnn.com/2019/10/22/us/lori-loughlin-felicity-huffman-fallout.
7. Salam, Maya. "The Unraveling of Jeffrey Epstein: The Story Line Is Moving Quickly. Here's What to Know." *New York Times*, 16 July 2019, Retrieved from: https://www.nytimes.com/2019/07/16/us/jeffrey-epstein-what-to-know.html?searchResultPosition=7.
8. Levenson, Michael. "Harvey Weinstein Faces Six Additional Sex Charges in Los Angeles." *New York Times*, 27 January 2021.
9. Pogrebin, Robin. "Amy Sherald Directs Her Breonna Taylor Painting Toward Justice." *New York Times*, 7 March 2021, https://www.nytimes.com/2021/03/07/arts/design/amy-sherald-breonna-taylor-painting.html?searchResultPosition=1.
10. New York Times. "What to Know About the Death of George Floyd in Minneapolis." 10 March 2021, https://www.nytimes.com/article/george-floyd.html?name=styln-floyd-trial&region=TOP_BANNER&block=storyline_menu_recirc&action=click&pgtype=Article&impression_id=&variant=show.
11. Wolf Harlow, Caroline, BJS Statistician. "Defense Counsel in Criminal Cases." U.S. Department of Justice, Bureau of Justice Statistics, Special Report, November 2000.
12. Surette, Ray. *Media, Crime and Criminal Justice: Images, Realities, and Policies*. Belmont, CA, Cengage Learning, 2011.
13. Op cit., Walker.
14. Ibid., p. 67.
15. Ibid., p. 47.
16. Serani, Deborah. "If It Bleeds, It Leads: The Clinical Implications of Fear-Based Programming in News Media." *Psychoanalysis & Psychotherapy*, vol. 238, Winter 2008, Retrieved from: https://www.researchgate.net/profile/Deborah-Serani/publication/247898920_If_It_Bleeds_It_Leads_The_Clinical_Implications_of_Fear-Based_Programming_in_News_Media/links/5a91f67c0f7e9ba4296db443/If-It-Bleeds-It-Leads-The-Clinical-Implications-of-Fear-Based-Programming-in-News-Media.pdf.

Chapter 4

"True" Crime Shows

Frank Columbo. William "Bunk" Moreland. Andy Sipowicz. Sonny Crockett. Rico Tubbs. Starsky and Hutch. Andy Taylor. Frank Pembleton. Joe Friday. Kate Beckett. Cagney and Lacey. Danny Reagan. Leroy Jethro Gibbs. Derek Morgan. Spencer Reid. Penelope Garcia. Olivia Benson. Elliot Stabler. Lenny Briscoe. Jake Peralta. Perry Mason. John Nolan. Ben Sherman. Erin Lindsay. Elizabeth Keen. Maybe you have heard some of these names, and maybe one or more of these men and women has become a favorite of yours on TV. These individuals all represent law enforcement officers in popular crime dramas like *Criminal Minds, Blue Bloods, Miami Vice, NCIS, The Blacklist, Law & Order, The Wire, Chicago PD, Brooklyn Nine-Nine,* and *NYPD Blue.*

Law enforcement operates at the local, state, and federal levels. Most municipalities have police departments. These are the police that patrol your neighborhoods daily. And some local police are designated as special jurisdiction, meaning they serve a specific area, like a park, university, or hospital. Police can also be found at the county and state levels. They may be referred to as sheriffs (county level) and/or troopers (state level). At the federal level, law enforcement officers may work for agencies like U.S. Customs and Border Protection, the FBI, Immigration and Customs Enforcement, or the Federal Bureau of Prisons.[1] There are close to 18,000 state and local law enforcement agencies in the U.S. In 2019, there were just under 700,000 full-time law enforcement officers employed in the U.S.; nearly 90 percent of these officers are male.[2]

FROM THE FIELD: THE TYPICAL SHIFT OF A PATROL OFFICER

A typical day starts with me waking up early in the morning (if working the day shift) or waking up late afternoon (if working the night shift). The sound of coffee brewing is one way I know my day is about to begin. I relax and eat before prepping for work. As I begin to get ready, I do a quick shave with my Gillette razor, going from peach fuzz to clean shaven. I shower and head to work.

The funny, reserved, and easygoing "me" transforms once my vest, uniform, and belt are put on. The officer-me is now stern, firm, and my overall demeanor changes. My shift begins with line-up; this can take up to 20 minutes. During line-up, I am briefed on what had occurred on other shifts (like previous arrests or criminal incidents), what I should be looking for (like missing persons or stolen motor vehicles), and what my assignment is (my district to patrol). After, I inspect my vehicle, making sure the medical supplies are replaced, oxygen is filled, and other miscellaneous items are in the vehicle. In this profession, the unexpected occurs, and my typical days is always different from the last.

In service and ready to start the shift, I take a ride around the business district to see if the town is busy; I see packed restaurants, music in the air, and kids playing on the sidewalk. At night, I get to see the sunset, light blue skies, radiating orange and red, indicating that the nightshift is fast approaching and the criminal element (like delinquency or motor vehicle thefts) is slowly coming out. After I get my second coffee at the local coffee shop, my awareness increases, the extra kick to my step starts settling in and the music in the patrol vehicle gets slowly louder.

Parked on the side of the road (a main artery roadway), I observe a motor vehicle speeding through town. The vehicle passes, and the night begins with a quick, sharp U-turn, and the speed odometer needle moves clockwise quickly, in the attempt to close the gap between the violator and myself. I do a quick inquiry of the vehicle's registration, giving me some background information on the driver's pedigree and previous violations (known as driver's abstract). I activate the red and blue lights and the motor vehicle slowly pulls over. I introduce myself and inform the driver that I pulled him over because he was speeding. I also let him know that it's a potential safety hazard because other children, bicyclists, joggers and motorists always use the roadway. In any event, while conversing with the driver, I notice other violations, such as a hanging air freshener, past due inspection sticker, missing headlight, and not wearing a seatbelt. Usually, I would issue a warning or write a citation for a headlamp missing in lieu of writing the driver a speeding ticket (which carries points on his license and fines up to two hundred dollars). With the authority as a police officer, I can really put a damper on someone's day. However, it's more rewarding and satisfying when it comes to addressing public safety, and to inform the driver to slow down.

For domestic violence calls, usually the dispatcher calls my patrol vehicle number, and I respond with my number, awaiting the nature of the call. The dispatcher tells me to respond to X location—the caller is currently arguing with her husband, and it appears strictly verbal. However, I never know what I am responding to, what weapons are in the residence (like firearms), or whether the situation had escalated prior to my arrival. Upon arrival, my backup officer and supervisor are normally right behind me. Once I enter the residence, I immediately separate both parties and start my investigation. Usually, partners only argue; some experience marital issues that remain verbal, but in other cases it can get physical. During my initial investigation, I take out my notepad and write down the people's names and list the events that had occurred. I then fill out paperwork, including a domestic violence packet, and try to find a solution for both parties. It's best to have one party leave the residence for the night to prevent further arguing. In some other cases, the male or female party (or both) is arrested for simple assault due to visible signs of marks or bruises. Domestic calls that you observe in *COPS* or *Live PD* usually give you glimpses of what's going on. But, in person, it's totally real, and it's one of officers' least favorite calls to respond to.

I am back in my patrol vehicle, finishing up from the previous call. A drive around my district is peaceful. It's time to reset and await the next call. In the meantime, the dispatcher immediately advises that there is a "10–17" (motor vehicle accident) with possible injuries. I inform and acknowledge the dispatcher that I am en route to the said location. I activate the red and blue lights and the screaming sirens to warn other motorists to stay on the side of the roadway. Upon arrival, at times you are surrounded by concerned residents, and you can smell the coolant and oil burning prior to speaking with the drivers involved in the accident. A typical scene is twisted metal, followed by debris all over the scene, the driver is bloodied, and the paramedics and firefighters work hard to cut into the vehicle. You do everything you can to make the scene safe, knowing persons involved are still alive. During my investigation, I gather witness statements, brief the supervisor, take photographs, and try to ascertain what had occurred prior to the crash. There is a sigh of relief that no one was killed.

Stolen vehicle pursuits are one of my favorite details on the job. Pursuits occur at random times, typically between the hours of 2 a.m. to 5 a.m. Usually, juveniles or young adults take part in this operation and they usually gravitate toward residential areas. Many residents leave their key fobs in their personal vehicle, or leave their vehicle unlocked, increasing opportunities for motor vehicle thefts or burglaries. The job also entails random preventive patrol, also known as cruising your beat. While cruising the neighborhood, I observed a dark color sedan traveling at a high rate of speed. Next, a quick U-turn is conducted and then I follow the vehicle, seeing that the vehicle is only traveling faster. I attempt to close the gap and then advise dispatch of the vehicle description (its make, model, and license plate). The dispatcher then replies, "The vehicle is stolen." It's on. The chase ensues; however, given the appropriate conditions (no traffic, fair weather, and speed), the supervisor will let me follow the vehicle. At times I have been lucky to apprehend the suspects. There are other nights when they are long gone.

   Toward the end of my shift, a lot of times I catch up on reports. Reports are essential in policing, and they're important because every single detail needs to be in them. Narratives are written and testimonies are also included. A thorough, well-written report is important. It often gives the readers (supervisors, lawyers, and judges) the facts that are needed for a rightful conviction or the release of a guilty person. Reports are also written in regard to arrest reports, evidence collection, crime reports, DUI reports, and other crime-related offenses. Report writing is one of the most important aspects of the job.

OFFICERS ON DUTY

Let's face it—much of a patrol officer's time is spent on the road looking for, or responding to, crime, and writing reports. In a ten- or eleven-hour shift, some officers may respond to as little as one, or even no, calls (depending on the hours of their shift and the jurisdiction they serve). But where is the glamour in that? Sure, police walk away with exciting tales of foot or vehicle pursuits and discoveries of bricks of heroin from time to time, but most of their work is monotonous and not nearly as thrilling as we may expect (think: writing parking tickets, pulling someone over for running a stop sign, responding to a medical call, checking on a house alarm). This may be especially true for suburban and rural officers, who tend to be exposed to less serious crimes daily and overall compared to urban officers.

   Other law enforcement officers, like detectives, state troopers, and federal investigators, are likely to encounter more serious criminal activity compared to patrol officers. While patrol officers may be those who arrive first to a crime scene and who conduct an initial investigation, it is typically the detectives in a police department who will collect evidence and more thoroughly investigate a crime. This is especially true for juvenile crimes and other serious offenses, like rape, robbery, or homicide. Patrol officers typically have the option, after gaining some time and experience in their department, to move to their department's detective bureau. Patrol officers may also apply for other specialized groups, like K-9 or SWAT (depending on what the department offers).

   While state troopers do patrol highways, some are more likely to be involved in operations that uncover more serious crimes, like drug trafficking rings, child pornography rings, and carjacking rings. So, there may be the opportunity for some hired by state law enforcement agencies to be involved in investigative work from the start. Federal agents or investigators do not necessarily need any prior patrol experience. Instead, many federal agencies will require training for their special agents or investigators specific to the position. Federal agents may conduct surveillance, investigate drug or firearm violations, deal with white-collar crime, fraud, or embezzlement, protect government officials, and uncover terrorist activities. These law enforcement officers may see more action, or deal with more serious crimes, compared to the average patrol officer (hence why characters in these roles tend to be featured most in crime dramas).

Regardless of what law enforcement officers *actually* do on a typical shift, we, as TV viewers, want to see the exciting stuff—the hot pursuits, the identification of a suspect before he or she can commit the next crime, the takedown of multiple suspects singlehandedly, the shots fired that never seem to miss their target, the talking down of a dangerous suspect holding a gun to a hostage's head. *This* is what excites viewers. *This* is what gets a series nominated for a coveted Emmy award. Does this portrayal of law enforcement officers affect our perceptions of police or crime? And how accurate are shows that feature police? We explore these questions below.

POLICE DEPICTION IN CRIME DRAMAS

In the U.S., *Stand By for Crime* was the first televised police drama, airing in 1949.[3] Since that time, police dramas have been some of the most popular shows on primetime television. The number of crime dramas on broadcast networks was at a high during the 2014–2015 season, at twenty-nine dramas. In 2019–2020, nineteen crime dramas were on broadcast networks. While the number of crime dramas today may seem much lower than five years ago, they still accounted for nearly one-fifth of all scripted shows on these networks.[4]

Before reading on, we want you to think of your favorite crime drama. Now, think of the law enforcement officers who are on the show. Who is your favorite? What are some of the qualities or characteristics of this person? Is he/she very athletic? Stoic? Does he/she run into a dangerous situation without backup? Does this person always catch the "bad guy"? How is his or her personal life? Do you think, if you were in this person's position, that you could do the same job just as effectively? Or is the person an unrealistic version of a law enforcement officer? We explore how police have been and are portrayed on TV below, beginning with police in crime (or police) dramas.

Scharrer provides some insight into how police officers were portrayed in TV crime dramas. She explored characteristics of "good guys" (mostly police) in crime dramas from the 1970s through 1990s, specifically surrounding hypermasculinity. In other words, were the "good guys" demonstrating exaggerated stereotypes of males, like acting macho and not showing emotion? In short, the answer is yes. The "good guys" were more likely to act tough and stoic than show emotion, and were drawn to danger because of the excitement and thrill it generated. Such depictions of police were more prominent in crime dramas in the 1970s. Police in crime dramas in the 1990s were less hypermasculine, meaning that the depiction of police as über-macho is occurring less as time goes on.[5]

Dowler provides additional background on how police were portrayed in crime dramas throughout the decades. In the 1970s, police were portrayed as "super-cops" who sought justice for victims. This fits Scharrer's findings of the hypermasculine officer running toward danger.[6] Crime dramas in the 1980s, however, featured police with true emotions and vulnerabilities fighting crimes rooted in systemic racism and social inequality. Nowadays, Dowler argues that primetime television dramas will feature police who act on the belief of law and order, while cable dramas are more likely to detail the personal struggles of officers in an effort to humanize police.[7] No matter how police are depicted, we are typically only exposed to White officers.

In 2020, Color of Change and the University of Southern California Annenberg Norman Lear Center published a report titled *Normalizing Injustice* to highlight the lack of representation of People of Color as crime show writers and as showrunners (the lead people) in crime dramas. The report looked at crime dramas on primetime networks and on subscription networks (Netflix and Amazon Prime) in 2017–2018, finding that over 80 percent of lead actors in crime shows were White.[8] And these "good guy" actors were committing more acts of misconduct compared to the "bad guys" on these shows, suggesting that police misconduct and ethical violations are normal and acceptable.[9] In the episodes examined, racial bias displayed by officers was not addressed much, the use of excessive force was rare, and, if problems within police departments or the criminal justice system were highlighted, the problems were positioned as a result of police not having enough power.[10] Thus, this report suggests that police in crime dramas, and police behavior in crime dramas, do not accurately reflect the police who patrol our streets daily.

Because of the time constraints on TV episodes, we often see law enforcement officers solving complex crimes in one hour or less. Clearance rates refer to the number of criminal incidents that result in arrest. Police in crime dramas have much higher clearance rates compared to police in the real world.[11] Indeed, Reiner argues that the crime solving efforts by police in crime dramas are oversimplified and not representative of real police investigations.[12] He warns that this can send the message to viewers that solving crimes is easy, when in reality it is not. Given the misrepresentation of police and their work in crime dramas, how do people view everyday officers?

Donovan and Klahm found that people who watched one or more hours of crime dramas each week had more positive views of police, such that they perceived police as effective crime solvers whose misconduct does not result in false confessions.[13] And participants felt that police use of force was necessary, and police do not use force too often.[14] Dowler and Zawilski found that frequent viewers of police dramas believed that wealthier people receive preferential treatment by police.[15] Conversely, in another study by Dowler, it was found that people's perception of police effectiveness was *not* influenced by regular viewing of crime dramas.[16] Instead, other factors, like age, race, prior police contact, fear of crime, income, education level, and neighborhood problems influenced people's perceptions of police.[17] Taken together, it appears that TV crime dramas affect people and their perceptions of police differently, whereby some viewers see police in a more positive light and others are not affected by crime dramas at all.

POLICE DEPICTION IN NONFICTION CRIME SHOWS

True crime shows are those that expose the details of one or more past crimes that happened in real-life. Such series may focus on a single case, like *Tiger King, The Trials of Gabriel Fernandez, Killer Inside: The Mind of Aaron Hernandez, McMillions,* and *Dirty John*. Or, some series may focus on a new crime or criminal in each episode, like in *American Justice, The First 48, Cold Case Files, American Greed,* and *Snapped*. Like police dramas, true crime shows have been met with positive ratings and high viewership. It seems that nearly every month Netflix releases one or more of these shows.

How do police in true crime shows differ from those in crime dramas? Police in true crime shows may be represented as themselves (if still alive and willing to be on TV). And the show will detail the actions of officers as they have been recorded or documented, reflecting the actual events that occurred. Police on true crime shows may discuss the obstacles encountered in a case, their interviews with suspects, the evidence they uncovered, their thoughts on the suspect, and more. While we do not know much about how police are portrayed on these shows, or the effects (if any) true crime shows have on viewers' perceptions of police, we do have information on how reality police shows, also a type of nonfiction police show, depict police.

FROM *COPS* TO *LIVE PD*: REALITY POLICE SHOWS (AND THEIR CANCELLATION)

COPS

Chances are, if you grew up in the late 1980s and 1990s and heard the lyrics to *Bad Boys* by Inner Circle, you would immediately think of the TV show *COPS*. *COPS* is perhaps the most well-known reality, or live action, TV show featuring police. On *COPS*, cameras follow officers during their patrol shifts. Police are filmed talking in their patrol cars about their jobs in general, why they became a police officer, a call they are going to or a call they just left, and/or crime news in the neighborhood. Viewers get to see the officers interact with citizens, and get a firsthand look at the discretion police exercise on a case-by-case basis. For example, a police officer may be seen pulling over a car on the show, and viewers will get to see if the officer writes the driver a ticket, lets him or her go with a warning, or takes some other action (like performing a search of the car or driver).

First airing in 1989, *COPS* quickly gained popularity and maintained that popularity in the years that followed. The show was often on TV multiple hours each week; Doyle states that the show helped TV networks fill increasing slots (as more channels become available to viewers) and helped police improve their public image. But how much of *COPS* truly reflected reality?[18] The creator of the show notes that footage was edited down (e.g., an hour-long police-citizen interaction was cut to ten minutes or less); producers chose material most likely to interest viewers and evoke emotions or thought from the audience.[19]

Given the above, it should come as no surprise that *COPS* has influenced public opinion and criminal justice discourse since its initial airings. The show highlights the law and order ideology, which involves a tough on crime approach and a clear distinction between police and the public.[20] Focus is on the officers, as the names of the officers are displayed in episodes, and the cameras are positioned in the car to transport viewers into the passenger seat of a patrol officer's vehicle. Names of suspects or civilians are not listed, and sometimes faces of people are blurred for those who did not agree to be filmed. When officers arrive at a scene, only their point of view is shown; very little background information, if any, is provided to viewers about the call for service. Police are portrayed as the experts, and it is their lead we follow through the show. Police officers are rarely portrayed negatively on *COPS*, instead being depicted as swift and effective problem solvers.[21]

While *COPS* is meant to focus on more mundane crimes encountered by police, Oliver finds that the show overrepresents violent crime (about 60 percent of suspects were associated with violent crime) and suggests that more cases are cleared than in reality.[22] This is likely because the footage chosen for airing contains interactions that tell a complete story—from an officer arriving on-scene to an arrest being made. Indeed, nearly 70 percent of suspects on *COPS* were arrested, which is much higher than the national clearance rate of law enforcement officers (which was less than 20 percent during the time of Oliver's study). As far as *who* is shown on *COPS*, Oliver notes that Black and Hispanic officers of Color are underrepresented (9 percent and less than 3 percent of total officers, respectively), while their suspect counterparts (30 percent Black, 16 percent Hispanic) are overrepresented.[23]

Oliver and Armstrong found that those who viewed *COPS* (and other reality-based police shows) felt the programming was more authentic than crime dramas.[24] They also found that those who view and enjoy *COPS* the most are those who favor a tough on crime approach, those who demonstrate higher levels of racial prejudice, a younger audience, people with lower education levels, and those who watch TV more often in general.[25] And people who view police reality shows consider the footage as informational; they feel as if they are watching the news versus a fictional drama.[26] That said, Curry conducted focus groups of criminal justice students who watched *COPS*.[27] These students recognized that *COPS* focused more on crimes committed by disadvantaged people, notably People of Color, and largely excluded white-collar crimes and offenders. That said, the participants also stated that the violence in *COPS* is what drew them (and likely others) to watch.[28]

COPS remained on-air for twenty-five seasons before being cancelled the first time. The show was then picked up again in 2013 by what is now Paramount Network, running for another seven seasons. Paramount Network officially cancelled *COPS* and pulled the show entirely from its airing schedule after the death of George Floyd in 2020. That said, it appears that filming for *COPS* has again re-started in Washington state, but episodes will be available to viewers outside of the U.S. only.[29]

Live PD

Live PD first aired in 2016 on A&E Network and depicted on-duty police officers in locations around the U.S., including (but not limited to): Richland County, South Carolina, Franklin County, Ohio, Williamson County, Texas, Tulsa (Oklahoma) Police Department, Bridgeport (Connecticut) Police Department, Berkeley County (South Carolina) Sheriff's Department, and Homestead (Florida) Police Department. Episodes spanned several hours on Friday and Saturday evenings. The show was hosted by Dan Abrams and included two primary commentators, Tom Morris Jr. (retired Washington, D.C. special police officer) and Sergeant Sean "Sticks" Larkin (Tulsa Police Department). The show would switch from live officer footage to commentary. During commentary the host and commentators would ask viewers to interact with them on Twitter using the hashtag #LivePD and would read viewers' tweets during the show. The #LivePD hashtag would normally be in the top trending hashtags on Twitter during the time in which the show was airing, speaking to its popularity.

During "live" blocks, *Live PD* would jump from location to location based on when officers were dispatched to a scene or radioed in dispatch to pull over a vehicle. Because the footage was as close to real-time as possible, when an investigation or scene became 'stale,' the host would redirect viewers to a different pursuit or case. Typically, the show would return to a previous location to show viewers how an investigation or vehicle stop was resolved.

Just how "live" was *Live PD*? Footage included broadcasting delays of seconds to minutes to seemingly provide producers time to censor foul language. But reports claim that these delays also allowed for officers to review the "live" footage before airing and allowed agencies to request that footage not be aired. Indeed, the Marshall Project reports that thirteen of forty-seven agencies featured on the show asked that certain incidents not make it to TV. Many of these incidents involved officer misconduct or officer violation of department policies.[30]

While the above report from the Marshall Project suggests that police are not accurately portrayed on *Live PD*, given the recency of the show there is little to no empirical research on the series surrounding how police are featured. Anecdotal evidence from the authors' personal viewership of *Live PD* is that the show may have represented a more diverse group of officers compared to others they have watched, as it featured a number of Black and Latinx officers, and a couple of female officers. And, it is likely that, like *COPS*, *Live PD* showed more violent and drug crimes, and more foot and vehicle pursuits, than what is experienced nationally. Officers on *Live PD* also regularly deployed K-9 units to scenes to pursue fleeing suspects or search for drugs. Thus, the show portrays officers as those who are constantly involved in active investigations and exciting police work, which is not consistent with the day-to-day actions of most officers.[31]

Prior to its cancellation, *Live PD* was A&E Network's highest-rated television show.[32] And *Live PD* was the most-watched show in the Friday night primetime time slot.[33] Despite its obvious success, in June 2020 it was announced that *Live PD* was being cancelled as a result of the recent death of George Floyd, and because news unearthed that *Live PD* producers did not air and destroyed all footage of the 2019 death of Javier Ambler.[34] Javier Ambler was a Black man, diagnosed with congestive heart failure, who was tased several times for not complying with police; the multiple tasings affected his heart and led to his death.[35] Today, *Live Rescue*, a new television series featuring firemen and Emergency Medical Technicians, has replaced *Live PD*.

Police Body Cameras and Citizen Videos on Social Media

Despite the cancellation of reality police shows, actions of police officers are still recorded formally and informally, by police-worn body cameras and by citizen-captured videos, respectively. Police worn body cameras became popular after Michael Brown's death, in which a White police officer shot Brown, an unarmed African American teen. The officer was not wearing a body camera, and as a result the actual circumstances leading up to Brown's death remain unclear.[36] Police may wear body cameras on their chest or hat. The goal of these cameras is to capture the complete interaction between an officer and citizen, from the time an officer steps out of his or her vehicle to approach a citizen to the time the officer returns to his or her car to leave a scene. Body camera footage is recorded and stored so that officers and/or their supervisors can review footage. This can be helpful in writing detailed reports, in educating future officers on right versus wrong actions, and in court, as prosecutors can use this footage as evidence in convicting (or acquitting) a suspect.[37] Additional benefits of body cameras are the protection of officers (from false claims and noncomplying citizens) and the public (from excessive use of force).[38]

While the intent of body cameras was to increase transparency by and accountability of law enforcement officers, some criticize this practice for imposing on officers' and the public's privacy, for allowing officers discretion on when to turn cameras on and off, and for providing only the officer's point of view.[39] That is, we cannot see the officer and his or her body language in the body camera footage. Because of this, we have seen more and more people videoing their or others' interactions with officers.

In addition to body cameras, it is becoming increasingly commonplace for citizens to record interactions either they, or someone else, have with police. Many have the ability to record such interactions on their cell phones and upload these videos simultaneously onto social media sites via Facebook or Instagram stories, IGTV, Snapchat, or YouTube. Many times, we will see footage captured by citizens before any footage from body cameras is released. For example, in 2020, many bystander videos of officer Derek Chauvin kneeling on George Floyd for over eight minutes were uploaded to and shared by major media and news sites.

As the medium by which we view real-life police interactions changes, we should pay attention to the representation and portrayal of police via these sources. In recent years, news coverage of police has shifted almost exclusively to police brutality. Such news coverage may even use a citizen's footage in their coverage of police (like in Floyd's case). But this practice can be deceiving, as footage can be edited or cut, thus giving viewers a false or incomplete picture of events. Research on civilians' filming and posting of police-citizen interactions is ongoing. What we currently know is that the public's attitudes toward law enforcement officers have become increasingly negative as a result of news coverage of high profile cases of police excessive use of force and other negative coverage of police, including non-force misconduct.[40] Awareness of such police misconduct is related to negative perceptions of police (e.g., distrust in officers), and increased public perception that police misconduct occurs more often than in actuality.[41] What happens when the public do not trust or have confidence in police? We briefly discuss police legitimacy and procedural justice below.

POLICING AND THE IMPORTANCE OF PROCEDURAL JUSTICE

We would be remiss if we did not touch on police legitimacy and procedural justice in our discussion on police officers. Police legitimacy refers to the belief that police have the authority to exercise discretion and that police should be obeyed.[42] What factors affect whether the public views police as legitimate? One, if not *the*, main factor is procedural justice, which refers to officers going through the proper steps, or procedures, when dealing with citizens. This includes treating all people respectfully and fairly, hearing people out during an interaction, and making decisions based on facts. When people view police as high in procedural justice and police legitimacy, they are more willing to cooperate with police, report crime, and obey the law.[43,44]

FROM THE FIELD: A LOCAL POLICE OFFICER EXPLAINS BODY CAMERAS AND EFFORTS TO ENGAGE WITH THE COMMUNITY

In the wake of Ferguson, many policy makers, criminal justice advocates, and then-Attorney General of the U.S., Eric Holder, agreed that the utilization of body cameras by police may improve community policing and police accountability. Many police departments in the U.S. have adopted the use of body cameras. Body cameras record every interaction between citizens and the police. Today, my peers and I believe that body cameras are important. Supervisors review our recordings and, at times, officers are counseled to improve their tactics in resolving issues. Regardless, body worn cameras are important because police-citizen encounters are recorded. It is beneficial to record such interactions because officers have been accused of wrongdoing, even though wrongdoing has not occurred during the encounter. Second, transparency and accountability is essential—it limits racial profiling, it increases police legitimacy, and it increases procedural justice.

In current times, we can assume that procedural justice and police legitimacy are low. Will police be able to regain a more positive status among the public? As we have seen, this will depend on a number of factors, especially revolving around how police (and how police-related TV shows) address racial bias and excessive force.

CHAPTER SUMMARY

TV crime dramas make officers' jobs seem more exciting, and portray officers as more effective crime stoppers and case solvers. Indeed, even reality TV programs focus on more interesting cases when, in actuality, the daily responsibilities of police officers may be less exciting and more focused on report writing. This creates false perceptions of police officers—the public may set unrealistic expectations for and have unrealistic perceptions of local, state, and federal officers.

A couple decades ago police were portrayed as hypermasculine super-cops who lacked emotion and ran into danger. In more recent decades, and even today, the human side of officers is portrayed in crime dramas (problems and all!). While crime dramas seem to have changed their portrayal of officers as everyday people with the same struggles as everyone, and also portray more instances of police use of force, reality programs continue to downplay (or fail to show altogether) police misconduct or excessive force. In lieu of reality shows, police body cameras and citizen videos provide real-life footage of police-citizen interactions.

NOTES

1. "Types of Law Enforcement Agencies." *International Association of Chiefs of Police*, 2018, https://www.discoverpolicing.org/explore-the-field/types-of-law-enforcement-agencies/.
2. "Table 74." *Federal Bureau of Investigation (FBI)*, 2020, https://ucr.fbi.gov/crime-in-the-u.s/2019/crime-in-the-u.s.-2019/tables/table-74/table-74.xls#overview.
3. Dowler, Ken. "Police Dramas on Television." *Oxford Research Encyclopedia of Criminology and Criminal Justice*. Oxford, 2016.
4. Porter, Rick. "TV Long View: How Much Network TV Depends on Cop Shows." *The Hollywood Reporter*, 20 June 2020, https://www.hollywoodreporter.com/live-feed/heres-how-network-tv-depends-cop-shows-1299504. Accessed 27 Feb. 2021.

5. Scharrer, Erica. "Tough Guys: The Portrayal of Hypermasculinity and Aggression in Televised Police Dramas." *Journal of Broadcasting & Electronic Media*, vol. 45, no. 4, Fall 2001, pp. 615–634.

6. Dowler, "Police Dramas on Television," p. 1.

7. Ibid.

8. Color of Change and The University of Southern California Annenberg Norman Lear Center. *Normalizing Injustice*. 2020, https://hollywood.colorofchange.org//wp-content/uploads/2020/02/Normalizing-Injustice_Abridged-1.pdf.

9. Ibid, p. 18.

10. Ibid, p. 17.

11. Rhineberger-dunn et al. "Clearing Crime in Prime-Time: The Disjuncture Between Fiction and Reality." *American Journal of Criminal Justice*, vol. 41, no. 2, June 2016, pp. 255–278.

12. Reiner, Robert. "Policing and the Media." *Handbook of Policing*, 2008, pp. 313–335.

13. Donovan, Kathleen M., and Charles F. Klahm IV. "The Role of Entertainment Media in Perceptions of Police Use of Force." *Criminal Justice and Behavior*, vol. 42, no. 12, December 2015, pp. 1261–1281.

14. Ibid, p. 1273.

15. Dowler, Kenneth, and Valerie Zawilski. "Public perceptions of police misconduct and discrimination: Examining the Impact of Media Consumption." *Journal of Criminal Justice*, vol. 35, 2007, 193–203.

16. Dowler, Kenneth. "Media Influence on Citizen Attitudes Toward Police Effectiveness." *Policing and Society*, vol. 12, no. 3, 2002, pp. 227–238.

17. Ibid, p. 232.

18. Doyle, Aaron. "'Cops': Television Policing as Policing Reality." *Entertaining Crime: Television Reality Programs*. Aldine de Gruyter, 1998, pp. 95–116.

19. Ibid.

20. Ibid.

21. Ibid.

22. Oliver, Mary Beth. "Portrayals of Crime, Race, and Aggression in 'Reality-Based' Police Shows: A Content Analysis." *Journal of Broadcasting & Electronic Media*, vol. 28, no. 2, Spring 1994, pp. 179–192.

23. Ibid.

24. Oliver, Mary Beth, and G. Blake Armstrong. "Predictors of Viewing and Enjoyment of Reality-Based and Fictional Crime Shows." *Journalism and Mass Communication Quarterly*, vol. 72, no. 3, January 1995, pp. 559–570.

25. Ibid, p. 559.

26. Andersen, Robin. *Consumer Culture and TV Programming (Critical Studies in Communication and in the Cultural Industries)*. Westview Press, 1995.

27. Curry, Kathleen. "Mediating *COPS*: An Analysis of Viewer Reaction to Reality TV." *Journal of Criminal Justice and Popular Culture*, vol. 8, no. 3, 2001, pp. 169–185.

28. Ibid, p. 180.

29. Andreeva, Nellie. "COPS Back In Production On New Episodes Following Cancellation." *Deadline*, 1 October 2020, https://deadline.com/2020/10/cops-back-in-production-new-episodes-following-cancellation-1234590025/.

30. Aspinwall, Cary, and Sachi McClendon. "Did Live PD Let Police Censor Footage?" *The Marshall Project*. 2020, https://www.themarshallproject.org/2020/07/01/did-live-pd-let-police-censor-footage.

31. Brenner, Emily. "Justifying Force: Police Procedurals and the Normalization of Violence." *Faculty Curated Undergraduate Works*, 2020, no. 69.

32. Porter, "TV Long View: How Much Network TV Depends on Cop Shows," *The Hollywood Reporter*.

33. Petski, Denise. "Live PD Hits Series Ratings High in Live+Same Day." *Deadline*. 2019, https://deadline.com/2019/06/live-pd-series-ratings-highs-livesame-day-ae-dan-abrams-1202637653/.

34. Walther, Joseph B. "Social Media and Intergroup Encounters with 'Cops': Biased Samples, Echo Chambers, and Research Opportunities." *The Rowman & Littlefield Handbook of Policing, Communication, and Society*, Rowman & Littlefield, 2021.

35. Ibid, p. 242.

36. Kampfe, Karson. "Police-Worn Body Cameras: Balancing Privacy and Accountability Through State and Police Department Action." *Ohio State Law Journal*, vol. 76, no. 5, 2015, pp. 1153–1200.

37. Ibid, p. 1165.

38. Ibid, p. 1162.

39. Ibid, p. 1175.

40. Graziano, Lisa M. "News Media and Perceptions of Police: A State-of-the-Art Review." *Policing: An International Journal*, vol. 42, no. 2, 2019, pp. 209–225.

41. Ibid, p. 216.

42. Tankebe, Justice. "Viewing Things Differently: The Dimensions of Public Perceptions of Police Legitimacy. *Criminology*, vol. 51, no. 1, 2013, pp. 103–135.

43. Ibid, p. 113.

44. Tyler, Tom R. "Viewing CSI and the Threshold of Guilt: Managing Truth and Justice in Reality and Fiction." *The Yale Law Journal*, vol. 115, no. 5, March 2006, pp.1050–1085.

Chapter 5

News You Can't Use

FROM THE FIELD: NO MORE GRATUITOUS VIOLENCE

News reporters move around from station to station, across the country. At one point, I was working as the morning anchor in a midwestern TV station, which is an NBC affiliate. Morning news has become a popular news slot and usually the broadcasts are longer than perhaps the 5:00 p.m. or 11:00 p.m., half-hour shows. It is also quiet in the newsroom at that time, because the crew is small. There is usually the "over-night photog," who has been there since midnight, in case there is breaking news, some camera operators, and the morning producers. The anchor is perhaps even more involved in the content of the newscast, just because there are so few people in the newsroom.

So, there are fewer people adding to the newscast and nothing has really happened since the 11:00 broadcast. Some stories carry over from the 11:00 news, but the morning newscast relies heavily on "what comes down from the network." The morning producer and I were planning the first block of the news, which as we discussed in chapter 3, is replete with the most serious and most frightening news stories. The shape of the news goes from any important national story that affects the whole country to local news.

As we were building the first block, we included a horrible story of a young girl who had been murdered in Oregon. I will not give the details of the murder here, because that is precisely the point of this story. I said to my producer at the time that this was the third horrific murder of a child we were putting in our newscast over the course of the previous few weeks and why, exactly, were we doing it?

We talked it over and we realized that we had been combing the available stories from around the country and finding the truly frightening ones because . . . well . . . that's what you do. I remember asking him, "Does anyone in our viewer area benefit from knowing the details of this story?" And he agreed that no one did. He and I made a pact that morning to never include gratuitous violence in our morning news. We would obviously include stories that were in our TV market or stories that could prevent people from falling victim in some way, but we were not going to show images of young children who succumbed to a tragic end just to keep people watching our show. We could keep our audience by showing them stories that has an impact on their lives and we would have to rely on our ability to please an audience without the exploitation of children.

That young producer in his first TV job is now working as a reporter in the field and is a shining example of integrity in his work. We also maintained our status as "number one" in our time slot and did not have to depend on unspeakable devastation

—Beth Adubato

One of the concepts bandying about in local news stations is "news you can use." It makes good sense. This probably influenced the increase in the number of weather reports in a single newscast and the addition of traffic reporters in some markets. Other examples of news you can use might be a story about a school bus strike, because you would need to find a way to get your children to school. News you can use could include bridge repairs on your route to work. News you can use is useful; news you can use does not scare you, it informs you, so why isn't there more news that you can use? One important aspect of news you can use is that it most likely should be local. A bridge out in Pittsburgh will not affect your morning commute in Tampa Bay. It is important that we clear up the differences among the categories of news markets.

TELEVISION MARKETS

Wherever you grow up in the United States, it is in a television market. (It is also a radio market and there are newspaper markets, but this discussion will be focused on television.) The market designation indicates the size of the population in the viewing area. Some of the market cities may surprise you, because their geographical location may include sections of another state or there may be more than one large market close to another. Cleveland, Pittsburgh, and Buffalo are relatively close to each other and therefore, take viewers from the other markets. There are 210 Designated Market Areas (DMAs) in the United States, according to Neilsen Media Research. Neilsen is a company that monitors the size of a TV-watching audience. Neilsen looms large in the world of commercial television for both news and entertainment. Here are the Top Forty television markets:[1]

- New York (#1)
- Los Angeles (#2)
- Chicago (#3)
- Philadelphia (#4)
- Dallas-Fort Worth (#5)
- San Francisco-Oakland-San Jose (#6)
- Atlanta (#7)
- Houston (#8)
- Washington, D.C. (Hagerstown) (#9)
- Boston (Manchester) (#10)
- Phoenix (Prescott) (#11)
- Seattle-Tacoma (#12)
- Tampa-St. Petersburg (Sarasota) (#13)
- Minneapolis-St. Paul (#14)
- Detroit (#15)
- Denver (#16)
- Orlando-Daytona Beach-Melbourne (#17)
- Miami-Fort Lauderdale (#18)
- Cleveland-Akron (Canton) (#19)
- Sacramento-Stockton-Modesto (#20)
- Portland, OR (#21)
- Charlotte (#22)
- St. Louis (#23)
- Raleigh-Durham (Fayetteville) (#24)
- Indianapolis (#25)
- Pittsburgh (#26)
- San Diego (#27)
- Baltimore (#28)
- Nashville (#29)
- Salt Lake City (#30)
- San Antonio (#31)
- Hartford & New Haven (#32)
- Columbus, OH (#33)
- Kansas City (#34)
- Greenville-Spartanburg-Asheville-Anderson (#35)
- Cincinnati (#36)
- Milwaukee (#37)
- Austin (#38)

- West Palm Beach-Fort Pierce (#39)
- Las Vegas (#40)

If you are wondering why market-size has anything to do with crime and criminal justice, you have to start from the basics. Basically, news is a business. More specifically, commercial news is a business. Public television and radio are funded by the government and by fundraising efforts and private donations. Commercial television is paid for by commercials. Even cable television is paid for by commercials, although you pay extra to have cable. Even streaming services have some commercials, if you pay less to have the service. The intricacies of how this all works may belong in a book on business and marketing, but it really does play a major role in why crime coverage is the staple of television news.

COMMERCIALS

If commercial television is called that because it is paid for by commercials, we have to learn a bit about those quick little stories that sell us products. A large beverage corporation or car company wants consumers to know about its latest and greatest soda or SUV. The company hires an advertising agency to design a "campaign" that will highlight the product. After the campaign is constructed, the style of the commercial and the on-air talent must be chosen. Shooting a car commercial, for example, could cost millions of dollars. After the commercial is shot and edited and ready for air, there must be an outlet for the ad. There is obviously more than just television advertising, but TV is the most expeditious route to sell one's wares.

The car company wants the most "bang for its buck," so it wants to air its commercials during a show that many people watch. On the network level, this "air time" also costs millions. A commercial shown during the Super Bowl, for example, cost a company approximately $5.6 million for 30 seconds.[2] The Super Bowl is an extreme case, but does illustrate the lengths that companies will go to obtain your business.

NETWORKS VS. CABLE

Think about the commercials you see when you are watching the news—during cable news shows, you may see the same commercials over and over. On cable news shows, you will see more Public Service Announcements (PSAs) and more "advertisements" for nonprofit organizations. This is because overall airtime is much less expensive on cable. When you consider the commercials you see during the "network nightly news," you may recall seeing highly styled commercials that appear to be upscale productions—many car commercials and many pharmaceutical commercials. These are in the top echelon of commercials as far as cost and production value.

How do these companies that devote such a large portion of their budgets to commercials decide when to have their commercials play? They decide to go for the shows with the highest ratings in their time slots and that brings us back to our "bang for the buck" litmus test. There are still only three major network news programs (the same three for decades). Just to be clear what newscasts are considered network news, they are:

- ABC—*World News Tonight*
- CBS—*CBS Evening News*
- NBC—*Nightly News*

The difference between these programs and your local news programs is that these three shows are the same for everyone in the country. The anchor who hosts *World News Tonight* will appear on the television screen of a person in Anchorage and a person in Alpena.

This is the same for the major cable news outlets:

- CNN
- Fox News Network
- MSNBC

Important differences between these cable news outlets and the network evening news are that the network evening news is only ONE HALF HOUR of programming per evening, whereas the cable news outlets run programming 24-hours a day, seven days a week. Also, if you have a television and you plug it in, you can watch the network evening news shows, but without cable, you cannot watch the cable news shows. (The reception on your television may not be great without cable, but you do not have to pay an additional fee over the cost of your TV and your electricity.)

It is an advantage to advertise on television—in any capacity—rather than relying on print advertisements or radio ads or ads on social media. The reason that it is an advantage is the size of the viewing audience.

AUDIENCE SIZE

Here is the heart of the matter—audience size:

> Audience size = more viewers who are influenced by the commercials → sales increase → profits increase

Hearken back to the introduction, when we discussed how "fear sells." Fear will lead people to turn on the television to see what could be lurking out in the world that could harm them or their family members. Fear brings viewers to a television program. Viewers bring companies to advertise on that station, during that time slot, therefore . . . fear can bring in money.

How does a station pay for the production of the news? Money. You can see where this is going. It is important to remember that the news business is not an altruistic entity that informs you every evening or throughout the day. It is a business and one that pays many people and some of those people are paid very well.

LOCAL MARKETS AND MORE BREAKDOWN (AFFILIATES VS. LOCAL CABLE)

In chapter 3, we gave you the results of recent research from over a two-year time period, conducted by students at Saint Peter's University in Jersey City, and Rutgers-Newark, both in New Jersey. Table 3.1 showed how the international cable news networks, while sometimes running fear-inducing stories at the top of the newscast, were more likely to take on larger subjects in import; larger meaning having a greater effect on a greater number of people. The top stories on the three nightly news stations were essentially the same stories. Even two of the three major cable news outlets run stories with the same focus. It is important to note, however, that many of the programs on Fox News and MSBNC are highly opinionated and politically slanted. That does not mean that they will not use fear to appeal to an audience, but they cater to specific and philosophically opposed audiences. This brings us to the crux of the fear sells issue—local news.

If you love the show Grey's Anatomy, you have to watch network programming to see it, ABC, in fact. If the show starts at 9:00 p.m. and ends at 10:00 p.m. and you live in the Midwest, your local news on the ABC affiliate will begin immediately afterward. This is called a "lead-in," it is the show that comes right before a newscast. An extremely popular show often leads to a popular newscast because people are likely to stay on the channel they were already watching. Networks not only compete for commercial income; they also compete for popular scripted shows! This complicates our newscast lesson even more. If, for example, you are a news director of a CBS affiliate in Houston (#8 market) and you are competing for "ad buys" with the ABC affiliate for the best-in-the-market rating, you need to persuade those viewers of *Grey's Anatomy* that there is a reason to turn that channel. Why is this competition for viewers so dire? People's jobs depend on it.

COMPETITION AS A CATALYST FOR SELLING FEAR

This lesson is not designed to blame local news outlets, but it is designed to inform about the level and intensity of crime news in our country. To be clear, we have a good deal of crime in our country, but not to the extent one could imagine from watching crime dramas on TV. As we learned in chapter 2, murder is the most common offense on a crime show. Imagine if there was really this much murder and mayhem in our society!

Does this make you wonder why we do not have a national, commercial-free news source, so we can rest assured that our news content is not influenced by the whims of the marketplace? There is public television in our country—Public Broadcasting System or PBS. They do not have to depend on advertising, but they do have to fundraise in order to make ends meet. Additionally, not all of the 210 markets have their own PBS station, so if you want to know about those school bus strikes and which bridges are out, you may not be able to find that information on what serves as your local station.

"We've Got the Exclusive!"

Can competition be a positive thing? Of course it can! Competition can ensure that reporters are on their toes and working their contacts for the best stories. Competition for stories drives news crews to edit their stories and report them faster, which leaves time for more up-to-date news. Competition spurs on reporters to be the most accurate, to continuously polish their writing, to gamble and try to reach the unreachable source; it pushed news videographers to capture the scenes through an artistic and compassionate lens and to edit the stories in a compelling manner. Competition has its place.

Competition becomes a negative entity when it drives a news station to go beyond boundaries of good taste or even ethical standards. It is understandable that executive producers and news directors feel pressure for higher ratings, but there are also times when they push for news you cannot use. The following two stories From the Field illustrate the negative and positive aspects of competition in the market and the emphasis on crime stories.

FROM THE FIELD: SCHOOL SHOOTING

In the last years of the 1990s, there was a spate of school shootings—within a few months there were school shootings in Jonesboro, Arkansas; West Paducah, Kentucky; and Pearl, Mississippi. This is not to say that school shootings in the United States have stopped, but it seemed at the time they were coming all too regularly. In April 1998, in Edinboro, Pennsylvania, a 14-year-old middle school student named Andrew Wurst took a Raven MP-25 to an 8th grade dinner dance and shot a 48-year-old teacher, John Gillette.[3] A Raven MP-25 is a .25-calibre, semi-automatic pistol; a "Saturday night special."[4] Wurst shot another teacher and two students. John Gillette succumbed to his wounds and died.

National news crews descended upon our television market. We were told to answer to the network news directors and let the national reporters take the lead on this story. This may have been a source of frustration for our news director. I have to admit, I was quite thankful that I was not put on this particular story.

The morning of the funeral, many of us were sitting in the newsroom, working on various projects. Our news director chose a young woman who was not a regular news reporter—she was the weekend weather anchor—to go out into the field and cover the funeral.

It was a tense morning because we had more than one news crew covering the story, but the weekend weather anchor was ordered to go to the funeral and "grab someone from the family" for an interview. We could hear her speaking with the news director as her call came into the newsroom. She told him that the police were not allowing anyone to go near the family of the victim. He answered that she'd better get someone to talk. Again, she informed him that police were not permitting anyone to go past the "police caution" tape. Finally, he yelled and told her that if she did not get an interview from someone in the family, she need not bother coming back to the station, because she'd be fired.

We all felt for her that morning. It was an impossible situation. She did not get an interview. She was not fired. She did, however, leave the station a few months later.

This is the kind of tragic story that comes from a terrible crime. It should be covered—that is not in doubt—we as a society need to know about these events that put our children at risk. We do not, however, need to overstep a decent boundary for the sake of the story. That is not news you can use.

FROM THE FIELD: NON-COMPETE FOR THE GREATER GOOD

In 1963, images of "snarling police dogs unleashed against non-violent protesters and of children being sprayed with high-pressured hoses appeared in print and television news around the world."[5] These dramatic scenes were emblematic of treatment of protesters during segregation and the fight for civil rights. A statue was erected to commemorate the photograph taken in Kelly Ingram Park. In 2017, President Barack Obama declared the area from the A.G. Gaston Motel, where Martin Luther King and other civil rights leaders planned their civil rights campaign through the location of the Sixteenth Street Baptist Church, to be a national monument, under the auspices of the National Park Service.

The Sixteenth Street Baptist Church Bombing was an act of white supremacist terrorism[6] on September 15, 1963. Four members of the Ku Klux Klan planted 15 sticks of dynamite under the steps of the church. Just before 11:00 that morning, when the congregation rose to pray, the dynamite exploded, killing four little girls.[7]

This From the Field event happened four decades after the Birmingham Church Bombing, a decade before the #BlackLivesMatter movement and a decade after the bombing of the Alfred P. Murrah Building in Oklahoma City, Oklahoma. On April 19, 1995, hundreds of people were hurt and 168 people lost their lives, including nineteen children.[8] One of the convicted co-conspirators, Timothy McVeigh, had formerly been a member of the "Michigan Militia."[9]

The background for this story is crucial. It became known that the Michigan Militia (presumably operating out of Michigan) contacted the city of Birmingham, Alabama, for a permit for a parade. They had also contacted the local chapter of the Ku Klux Klan to take part in this parade.

According to the United States Census Bureau, the Black population of Birmingham is approximately 65 percent.[10] While neither the KKK nor the Michigan Militia limit their hate to only Black people, they were most likely aware of the particularly pointed message this parade would send. It would be a source of sadness and terror to all people who are anti-hate, but it would be excruciatingly painful for the Black population. The parade permit was in fact granted.

Something unusual happened that week leading up to the day of the parade. The general managers of the four affiliates in Birmingham (ABC, CBS, FOX, and NBC) held a meeting. While these stations were in sharp competition, this was to be a troubling event for all. When the general manager from our station returned from the meeting, he called all of the members of the news team and gave us the results of the conclave: all four stations agreed that these hate groups wanted publicity for their march and we were not going to give it to them.

It was a bold move because any one of the stations could renege on its pledge and that station would have the exclusive, yet they all promised.

On the day of the parade/rally, all four stations did send a news crew to the site—in case some kind of violence broke out that would have to be covered. Our crew sent the live feed back to our station. I was covering sports that day and was in the newsroom for the event. Those of us who were there stood silently watching the monitors. Hardly anyone showed up for the parade. Few people stood by the side as the marchers walked by. It was a flop.

As the afternoon unfolded, we learned of another story—some ministers had organized a peace march at the same time. About a mile away, around 3,000 people gathered for peace. That became the day's top story.

—Beth Adubato

DRAWING THE LINE

What is the line? Does every American need to know about all the crimes that are happening across the country? Does every person in every market deserve to know what kinds of crimes are being committed in their neighborhoods? Those questions may not be that hard to answer—if it will help the viewer in some way, it fits the notion of news you can use.

Who sets the standard on crime coverage? Should it be the police who makes the decision or reporters? Police and reporters do not have the same agendas when it comes to crime stories given to the public. Police departments utilize public information officers to control the release of stories. This may delay the public's awareness of a story until police decide when it should be published. Adubato, Sachs, and Fizzinoglia conducted a study on this exact subject—who controls the message in a time of crisis?

The study surveyed three groups of people—those who work in police administration, those who work in the news business, and those who do neither. The assumption was that the police would believe they had the right to control the story and the news professionals would believe they did. These hypotheses were supported in the study. What was surprising was that the "others" or those who were considered the consumers of news believed that the police should hold on to information in a time of crisis, even if media outlets were ready to release the stories earlier.

MEDIA LITERACY—BUZZWORD FOR THE BUZZFEED GENERATION OR CRUCIAL CONSTRUCT?

As defined by the participants of the 1992 Aspen Media Literacy Leadership Institute, Media Literacy is the ability to access, analyze, evaluate and create media in a variety of forms.[11]

The Center for Media Literacy recently expanded the definition: "Media Literacy is a 21st century approach to education. It provides a framework to access, analyze, evaluate, create and participate with messages in a variety of forms—from print to video to the Internet. Media literacy builds an understanding of the role of media in society as well as essential skills of inquiry and self-expression necessary for citizens of a democracy."[12]

The word "literacy" is nominally a reference to the ability to "read," but in the 21st century world of media and the multiplicity of mega- and micro-media at hand, the ability to "read" the myriad sources of information (or misinformation) has become a most important skill for citizens who expect to make informed choices in a complex participatory democracy.

It is now far from a single source that creates a belief system. If a Paul Revere rides through town calling "the British are coming, the British are coming," it's easy to make a choice to believe him and take to the parapets or not! Today it's beyond newspapers or TV or even websites—social media is a seemingly unending source of information, often displaying Fake News in the garb of the truth.

Climate change . . . Critical Race Theory . . . The 1/6 Insurrection . . . The 2020 election results! These are topics that have drawn controversial responses, including radical right conspiracy theories from the Web and the Dark Web, some slipping through the self-policing of the social media giants, Facebook, Twitter, and Google.

How can you ascertain what's true and what isn't? Let's take climate change as an example. Unless you are a meteorologist or climate scientist, you have no first-hand knowledge of the veracity of this subject, and certainly not the nuances of relevant reporting. You will need to take a multi-layered approach to have the wherewithal to assign a belief, an approach like the one suggested by Michelle Ciulla Lipkin, Executive Director of NAMLE, the National Association for Media Literacy, who writes in her blog, 4 Essential Skills for Media Literacy, "Whether it's through social media, blogs, advertising, or the nightly news, all aspects of media cumulatively affect our perception of the world and what is happening in it. With such an incredible impact on our daily lives, the ability to navigate, verify, and trust information is vital for everyone."[13]

"4 ESSENTIAL SKILLS FOR MEDIA LITERACY"

Skill #1: Slowing Down in a Fast-Paced World

The speed with which news and information travel can overwhelm the consumer faced with trying to keep up. Because sometimes a news outlet (or any other information source) may value speed of reportage over accuracy, it's up to the consumer to develop the patience to stop and verify a source, and then back that up with three credible sources.

> "By doing so, and by taking time to understand the information we receive, we can start to break the bad habits of our rapid-fire media consumption and sharing."

Skill #2: Finding the Source(s)

While in the past the sources of news may have been relatively easy to determine, in today's online world, the consumer should start by following the links to find out where the information originated. If it started in a personal blog, for instance, your confidence in sharing that news might be wobbled.

> "For all media, backing up a source by comparing the information on several different media networks is always a good idea. Are there noticeable differences between the facts that are being shared? What bias is there? Using multiple reputable national news sources as a reference is always a good idea."

Skill #3: Exploring Media as a Creator

Recently, the definition of Media Literacy was expanded to include media creation. Since media consumers are now no longer mere passive receivers of information, but "active content creators as well, via online sharing, posting and commenting . . . contributing to the media landscape," it has become important to train young consumers, students who can garner communication skills and at the same time understand that media landscape through critical thinking about "what they are consuming, and what they choose to share."

Skill #4: Understanding Bias

"Evaluating the media for bias includes asking questions about news sources, point of view, stereotypes, loaded language, etc." These are tools for the consumer of news and information to sharpen for critical analysis of information but it's also important to also take stock of personal bias:

"With the vast amounts of information we receive today, it's critical that we . . . understand where our own values, beliefs, and experience come in when assessing media."

—Michelle Ciulla Lipkin, Executive Director of NAMLE[14]

NOT USER FRIENDLY

One could make the supposition that if you do not like the way your local station covers news, you could change the channel and watch another one. As you may have gathered from this chapter, there could be very little difference among the stations' coverage decisions. You could get your news from another source—perhaps a newspaper or radio broadcast? Even so, there is pressure on all media to gather news stories, churn them out as quickly as possible, and grab the most viewers. Not watching sends a strong message to a station that may be too aggressive or invasive into people's private trauma. Taking a stand gives power to the viewers to decide which news you can use and which news you cannot.

CHAPTER SUMMARY

In chapter 5, we took on gratuitous violence. How much violent news content is necessary for people to function in their everyday lives? Are stories of violence and tragedy from a different region of the country important to know? And on the topic of regions, we broke down how local television markets work and how the news differs from market to market and certainly from local news to national news. We consider the notion that some local stories should make national headlines and that some violent stories can be warnings or show patterns that create a shared importance. Finally, we discuss "media literary," a concept that guides us to become better consumers of news.

NOTES

1. TVJobs.com. "Master Station Index." http://msi.tvjobs.com/.

2. Statista. "Super Bowl average costs of a 30-second TV advertisement from 2002 to 2021." Retrieved from: https://www.statista.com/statistics/217134/total-advertisement-revenue-of-super-bowls/#:~:text=In%202021%2C%20advertisers%20had%20to,the%20Super%20Bowl%20LV%20broadcast.

3. Hays, Kristen. "Edinboro Teen Killer Sentenced." *Pittsburgh Post-Gazette*. September 10, 1999.

4. The Specialists LTD. Catalogue.

5. National Park Service. "Birmingham Civil Rights Monument." Retrieved from: https://www.nps.gov/bicr/learn/historyculture.htm.

6. Ibid.

7. The History Channel. This Day in History September 15, 1963, https://www.history.com/this-day-in-history/four-black-schoolgirls-killed-in-birmingham.

8. Federal Bureau of Investigation. "Oklahoma City" Famous Cases and Criminal, History Page. Retrieved from: https://www.fbi.gov/history/famous-cases/oklahoma-city-bombing.

9. United States Census Bureau. "Race." https://www.census.gov/topics/population/race.html.

10. Beth Adubato, Nicole M. Sachs, and Donald F. Fizzinoglia (2020). Gatekeepers: Controlling Communication in a Time of Crisis, *Atlantic Journal of Communication*, DOI: 10.1080/15456870.2020.1779724.

11. The Center for Media Literacy. "Media Literacy: A Definition and More." https://www.medialit.org/media-literacy-definition-and-more.

12. Ibid.

13. Michelle Ciulla Lipkin, "4 essential skills for media literacy." https://www.renaissance.com/2018/07/26/blog-4-essential-skills-media-literacy/.

14. Ibid.

Chapter 6

It's All in the Genes

A man, barely out of his teenage years, runs unclothed through the Las Vegas desert at night, scared of whatever, or whoever, is pursuing him. While we do not see what causes his untimely death, the scene fast forwards to a bright, sunny day in the desert, the man's decomposed body now being photographed by a forensic scientist. Maggots are seen on the body, suggesting the man has been dead for some time. No gunshot wounds are present, and there are no signs of strangulation or stab wounds. The forensic team identifies correctly that the man was running before death. They note that, given the footprint pattern, the man was looking back as he ran. Is there any evidence that points to the cause of death?

The body is transferred to the morgue for an autopsy. The medical examiner and forensic scientists are discussing the body's skin samples. The skin is bone dry—not surprising for being left in the desert. Seeing this as a dead end (no pun intended), the forensic scientist suggests taking a sample from the maggots that were pulled from the body. Another scientist runs a maggot through the mass spectrometer and within 15 seconds (yes, 15 seconds) it is determined that jimsonweed, a plant known to cause hallucinations, was absorbed by the maggot. What was that doing in the dead man's body?

The forensic scientist and homicide detective question a friend of the dead man who comes forth to report the dead man as missing. The friend says they were raving the night his friend went missing. Though initially denying that any drugs were ingested, upon further questioning the friend admits to taking jimsonweed tea with the dead man. The team asks for the dealer of the tea, but the friend does not know his name. One forensic scientist asks if the friend was stamped at the rave and, using a black light, discovers the stamp on the friend's skin. The forensic scientist identified the stamp as belonging to a "hot" DJ in Vegas.

Lab samples come back, finding that aluminum was found in the dead man's nose and mouth. How does that apply to the investigation? The scientists do not know (yet). In the meantime, they and the homicide detective attend a rave with the friend of the dead man. They find the dealer of the jimsonweed tea who allows the team to search his car. The forensic scientist finds plant seeds in the dealer's car. The dealer is taken into custody for further questioning.

It seems easy . . . the dealer of the tea is the killer, right? Maybe so. The investigators return to the morgue and find jimsonweed seeds, the most dangerous part of the plant, in the body's intestines. But this is not enough to conclude the dealer is to blame. The team needs more evidence. They return to the friend of the dead man. The friend has pain in his arm, and shows the scientist a wound. The scientist thinks the wound was caused by a human bite and requests an impression be taken. At the same time, more lab results come in on the aluminum—it's from fireworks. The friend of the dead man conveniently happens to work at a store that sells fireworks . . . the case is starting to come together!

The lead scientist lays out the scene . . . After taking the jimsonweed, the dead man's body was overheated, and as a result of the hallucinations from the plant, he became scared of the lights at the rave. The dead man stripped and started running. His friend, who followed him, instead experienced auditory hallucinations. In an attempt to get rid of the noise, the friend suffocated the dead man. During the suffocation, the dead man bit his friend and at the same time, the friend left firework residue from his hands on the dead man's mouth. The friend, who could not remember any of these events, sat stunned.

"Who Are You" is the name of the song and question asked by The Who, which is perhaps most well-known for its placement in the opening credits for *CSI*. Indeed, the scene above is from the series' first season, titled "Friends and Lovers."[1] As a result of this series, researchers have introduced what is known as the *CSI* Effect, or the idea that people who watch *CSI* believe that forensic evidence is regularly collected at crime scenes and have unrealistic expectations about DNA evidence presented in jury trials.[2] Returning to cultivation theory from chapter 2, we may expect that the technology available to police departments and forensic laboratories on TV is also readily available to local, state, and/or federal departments. However, as we will see, this is often not the case. How then, do TV crime dramas influence our expectations of police investigations? And how may this negatively impact jury decisions?

FORENSIC INVESTIGATIVE TECHNOLOGIES

If *CSI* taught us anything, it is that there are a number of tools available to identify a suspect based on only a trace amount of evidence left at a crime scene. We typically call the people who analyze crime scene evidence forensic investigators. In recent decades, we have seen the advancement of investigative technology available to these investigators. But this technology is expensive and out of reach of many departmental budgets. Below we discuss some of these technologies, associated costs, and other pros and cons that have been identified.

FINGERPRINT ANALYSIS

You may know by now that everyone has a different fingerprint—even identical twins! Fingerprints do not change as we age and are extremely hard to change. Fingerprint analysis has been utilized in forensic investigations since the late 1800s. Our fingerprints consist of a pattern of ridges and grooves. Most times when we touch something, our fingerprint is left behind, but we may not be able to see the fingerprint; this is called a latent fingerprint. To see such fingerprints left behind at a crime scene, investigators rely on different fingerprint powders (on non-porous objects) or chemical solutions, like ninhydrin spray (on porous objects).[3] Fingerprints that we can see with the naked eye are patent or plastic fingerprints, depending on the what the finger was coated in when the fingerprint was left behind. For example, a fingerprint of blood is a patent print, which a fingerprint of wax is a plastic print.[4]

When we touch objects, we do not only leave our fingerprint behind. The pores on our skin, in this case the pores on our fingers, secrete three different types of sweat. While we will not get into the specifics of each type of sweat secreted, it is important to note that something other than the ridge and loop patterns are left behind for further analysis. And it is through sweat left behind that forensic investigators can now determine whether someone has touched explosive materials, has consumed marijuana, cocaine, or methadone, or has smoked cigarettes via fingerprints![5] Forensic investigators can also determine whether someone had blood on their finger through fingerprint analysis.[6]

When a suspect is arrested, his or her fingerprints are taken by police during the booking phase. This practice has been established for centuries, as law enforcement officers would take the fingerprints of arrested people during the time of King Hammurabi in 1700 BC.[7] While original fingerprinting during King Hammurabi's days were captured on clay, fingerprints are now captured digitally in police departments (and even when processing suspects or convicted offenders in jails) and are stored in a fingerprint database. In the U.S., the FBI manages our national fingerprint database, or the Integrated Automated Fingerprint Identification System (IAFIS).[8] There are over 64 million fingerprints in this database, with the number of fingerprints added growing daily.[9] A crime scene fingerprint can be captured and uploaded to the database, which can then accurately identify any matches to known criminals, other crimes scenes, and/or unsolved cases/prints. It is estimated that 50,000 suspects each year are identified by the IAFIS.[10] The IAFIS can provide results in as a little as twenty minutes, but most results come through in about two hours.[11]

BALLISTICS IDENTIFICATION

Like fingerprints, guns transfer unique scratches and dents to the bullets fired from them. When bullets and casings are recovered from a crime scene, forensic investigators can take digital images of them and run the images through the Integrated Ballistics Identification System (IBIS), a database developed in the 1990s by Forensic Technologies, Inc.[12] The IBIS has two parts, the first of which is the Data Acquisition Station, where a forensic or firearm examiner will enter data gathered from the bullet or casing into the system. The second part of the IBIS is the Signature Analysis Station, which compares images and identifies potential matches through a scoring system.[13] Ultimately, a firearms examiner has to compare images to determine if they were indeed fired from the same weapon.[14]

In 1997, the Bureau of Alcohol, Tobacco, Firearms and Explosives implemented the National Integrated Ballistics Information Network (NIBIN) whereby automated ballistics images are compared to bullet and casing images from other crime scenes.[15] NIBIN is a nationally networked system and IBIS is the collection of ballistics images, thus NIBIN uses IBIS technology.[16] NIBIN allows law enforcement agencies to connect crime scenes and cases, identify new suspects, connect one crime scene to a cold case, and connect organized crime events.[17] There are over 45 million ballistic images stored in the system, and in the past twenty-plus years NIBIN has identified over 220,00 leads and over 125,000 hits.[18]

Initially, bullet images were in 2D format; however, BulletTrax-3-D now allows for 3D images of bullets, which has greatly improved ballistics matches.[19] While such technological advancements can clearly assist law enforcement agencies in solving crime, they come at a high cost. The NIBIN machines cost over $150,000; the BulletTrax-3-D machines cost $360,000.[20] Given these high costs, it is not unusual for multiple municipalities to share one system.

DNA ANALYSIS AND CODIS

All of our body's cells carry our DNA (deoxyribonucleic acid), or our unique genetic makeup. Half of our DNA comes from our mothers (or a female egg) and half from our fathers (or a male sperm). Everyone's DNA is different, *except* for identical twins. If anything from our body is left behind at a crime scene, so too is our DNA. Forensic investigators may test skin flakes or scrapes, hair, blood, and other bodily fluids for DNA.

DNA testing has been around since the 1980s.[21] DNA obtained from a crime scene is sent out to a forensic laboratory for analysis. Then, the unknown person's DNA profile is entered into a national DNA database to determine if there is a match to another DNA profile already in the database. The national database containing DNA profiles, created by the FBI in 1998, is known as NDIS—National DNA Index System. NDIS is part of the Combined DNA Index System (CODIS) which is the term the FBI gives to the software used to run DNA databases.[22] Not only can NDIS search for DNA matches to a specific person, but because of who contributes to our DNA biological relatives may also be identified through NDIS. If a match is identified, forensic investigators will first confirm the match, and only then can information (e.g., name) on the unknown person be obtained.[23]

All states require DNA to be collected by people who are convicted of certain crimes, and some allow DNA collection by people arrested for certain crimes. Such crimes include sex crimes, all other violent crime (homicide, assault, robbery), other felony offenses, and burglary.[24] DNA of missing persons may also be entered into CODIS; if no DNA of the missing person is available, the biological parents or child(ren) of the missing person may submit their DNA.[25]

Lately, many people have been voluntarily sending in saliva samples to AncestryDNA and 23andMe companies to trace their lineage. Questions are now arising as to whether law enforcement should have access to these databases, which have millions of DNA profiles, to aid investigations. In 2019, a judge allowed police to search the database of GEDmatch, which is a smaller company with far less samples than Ancestry or 23andMe.[26] GEDmatch consumers did not consent for their DNA to be shared. One year earlier, investigators submitted crime scene DNA to GEDmatch and identified the elusive Golden State Killer.[27] The GEDmatch case led to new policies stating that only profiles of people who consent to law enforcement searches can be searched. As of the writing of this text, law enforcement is *not* permitted to access these databases. And 23andMe stated that they would take whatever legal action is necessary to fight against law enforcement tapping into their databases.[28]

THE *CSI* EFFECT

Imagine you are selected to serve on the jury of a homicide case. It is your task to determine whether the defendant is guilty or innocent. What evidence, if any, would convince you that the defendant is guilty? What evidence would you *expect* the prosecution to produce?

At the beginning of this chapter you read a summary of the plot of one episode of *CSI: Crime Scene Investigation (CSI)*. Generally, each episode of *CSI* follows a similar format: a dead body (or bodies) is discovered, a team of forensic investigators comb the crime scene for evidence while law enforcement officers simultaneously interview suspects, witnesses, and/or family and friends of the deceased. Sometimes, the forensic team returns to a crime scene multiple times to uncover previously unfound evidence. Ultimately, the science used by the forensic investigators, whether fingerprint, ballistics, DNA analysis, or some combination of these techniques (and others, like blood splatter analysis), coupled with information gained by law enforcement officials, leads to the identification of the offender(s), who is then arrested and charged for the crime(s).

Because forensic evidence is present in every *CSI* episode, viewers may believe that such evidence is regularly collected at crime scenes and is present during criminal trials. And, as one forensic scientist points out, around 40 percent of the technology we see on *CSI* and similar shows does not even exist![29] These false perceptions about forensic evidence stemming from crime dramas are collectively referred to as the *CSI* Effect.

The *CSI* Effect produces several hypotheses related to juror decision-making. First, it hypothesizes that jurors expect the prosecution to produce forensic evidence and, if they do not, they will find the defendant not guilty.[30] Similarly, the *CSI* Effect theorizes that if evidence presented is not enough in quantity nor as "sexy" as it is on TV, jurors are left unimpressed by the prosecution's case and acquit the defendant.[31] Tyler additionally posited that the *CSI* Effect may lead people to believe that forensic evidence is more accurate, thus jurors will accept whatever results are presented without question and be *more likely* to convict.[32]

As a reminder, the burden of proof required in a criminal trial is beyond a reasonable doubt. For a jury to find a defendant guilty this means that, after all evidence is presented and testimony given, there is no other reasonable explanation for the crime—the defendant was the person who committed the crime. If even a small amount of doubt exists, meaning there is a slight chance, based on the evidence, that the defendant did *not* commit the crime, then a no guilty verdict should be rendered. You can see now that, depending on the forensic evidence presented, this can affect the doubt aspect of a criminal trial, and ultimately the verdict, if the *CSI* Effect hypotheses are confirmed.

Several researchers have tested the above *CSI* Effect hypotheses; overall, there is mixed support for its hypotheses.[33,34] We first discuss studies finding support of one or more *CSI* Effect hypotheses. Shelton et al. found that jurors who watched *CSI* were more likely to expect scientific evidence in serious criminal cases, like homicide, rape, and assault.[35] And *CSI*-watching jurors were more likely to expect DNA evidence, fingerprint evidence, and ballistics evidence in assault and rape, burglary and theft, and gun cases, respectively, compared to those who did not watch *CSI*.[36] In general, jurors were more likely to expect scientific evidence, especially in rape cases.[37] That said, in most cases scientific evidence did not seem to make jurors less likely to convict someone, with the exception of rape. Jurors reported they would be more likely to acquit defendants in rape trials if no scientific evidence was presented.[38] Also, Baskin and Sommers discovered, in their telephone study of over 1,200 registered voters (i.e., those people who are eligible for jury duty), that people felt scientific evidence (like DNA and fingerprints) was more accurate than other types of evidence, like eyewitness testimony.[39] Further, participants who watched three or more hours of crime programs per week were less inclined to convict defendants if no scientific evidence was available.[40]

Schweitzer and Saks presented a mock jury with a fictitious transcript of a criminal trial, which included a forensic-science component of microscopic hair analysis. Participants who watched forensic-science TV shows were more critical of the evidence, and were *less* likely to believe what was presented.[41] And participants who viewed forensic TV shows and crime dramas felt like they had a greater level of understanding of the job of a forensic scientist or investigator compared to those who did not view such shows. These findings supported the authors' hypothesis that jurors have high expectations of forensic evidence as a result of watching shows like *CSI*.[42]

Cather writes that prosecutors report different experiences regarding the *CSI* Effect on jurors; some say the *CSI* Effect has no impact on juror decisions, while others report that jurors are acquitting defendants when no forensic evidence is present.[43] Both Watkins and Podlas found that prosecutors believed in the *CSI* Effect. Although a small study and sample, prosecutors in Watkins's study felt that jurors' high expectations of evidence were attributed to shows like *CSI*.[44] Of course, we do not know for certain if it is *CSI* shaping jurors' expectations, but such perceptions on the part of prosecutors suggest that the *CSI* Effect is believed by this group.

Podlas demonstrates that prosecutors believe in the *CSI* Effect. She asked prosecutors to identify cases where they believed the *CSI* Effect was present.

After being forwarded the names of these cases, Podlas concluded that the memories of prosecutors were faulty, as many of the cases they identified resulted in convictions (which goes against the traditional *CSI* Effect hypotheses, but is in line with Tyler's hypothesis above).[45] Similarly, the Maricopa County Prosecuting Attorney's Office found that nearly 40 percent of prosecutors reported losing cases as a result of the *CSI* Effect, reported that jurors in their trials expected more scientific evidence, and reported that jurors in their trials who watched *CSI* would share their knowledge with other jurors.[46]

Despite some support for the *CSI* Effect, other researchers find no support at all.[47,48] Podlas explored the *CSI* Effect on a mock jury, finding that possible jurors who heavily watched *CSI* did not rely more on *CSI* factors in determining guilt or innocence than those who did not watch *CSI*.[49] And Tyler argues that there are several other reasons to explain juries' decision to acquit besides the *CSI* Effect, like sympathy for the defendant, different thresholds for conviction, and lack of trust in legal authorities.[50]

Before moving on, think back to the questions we asked you in the beginning of this section. Now that you have read more about the *CSI* Effect, do you think that watching crime shows like *CSI* affected your answers? If you were sitting on a jury and no scientific evidence were present, would you immediately see the defendant as not guilty, or would you weigh the other evidence presented before making a decision?

RAPE KITS

Imagine this: a woman is violently raped. She calls the police, who arrive at the scene. The police call for an ambulance to take the woman, who has just suffered an extreme trauma, to the hospital for a rape kit. Upon arriving at the hospital, the woman meets a forensic nurse. The nurse explains that she needs to take the woman's clothes, including undergarments, as evidence. She also informs the woman that she needs to check her body for any signs of cuts, scrapes, gashes, or bruises; anything found needs to be documented. Then, she also needs to take blood, urine, hair, and DNA (via cheek swab) samples from the woman. This is all the "easy" part of the exam. What comes next is a collection of the woman's pubic hair, and then a swab of the woman's cervix, vaginal, and rectal areas. The woman, who was just violated against her will, is being subject to further penetration to *hopefully* collect a DNA sample of the offender that will uncover his identity. The hair and clothing samples, and all of the body fluid swabs, are what is included in a rape kit (note that rape kits are also conducted on men, which include a penile swab in place of the cervix and vaginal swabs of females). Now imagine you are this same woman and, six months after the rape you check in with your local police department, only to be told that they have not sent out your rape kit for testing. You check in another six months, and then a year after that, and five years after that, only to be told the same thing over and over: your rape kit has not yet been tested. How would you feel?

In her TED Talk, Kym Worthy spoke about the 2009 discovery of 11,341 rape kits (also known as sexual assault kits) in Detroit, hidden in trash bags and barrels in an abandoned warehouse. Some of the rape kits sat for over 40 years without being tested.[51] To work through the analyses of these old, and any new incoming, rape kits (which cost between $1,000 and $2,000 per kit) the City of Detroit partnered with the United Parcel Service of America (better known as UPS) to number and track rape kits as they were processed, so stakeholders could know where a rape kit was located at any given time.[52] Worthy reported that, after implementing this system, no new rape kits were lost.[53] And after seeing this system, Michigan dedicated funds to develop a state-wide rape kit tracking system. As for the 11,000-plus untested rape kits, Worthy reported that after analyzing almost 90 percent of them, CODIS identified 2,600 suspects, over 850 of which were serial rapists—people committing more than one rape.[54] And CODIS linked DNA samples to crime scenes in forty other states. Imagine how many rapes or sexual assaults might have been prevented had these rape kits been tested quickly![55]

Certainly, Detroit is not the only city where rape kits have not received proper attention and analysis. The Joyful Heart Project, a nonprofit founded by *Law & Order: SVU* showrunner Mariska Hargitay, includes the End the Backlog program, which seeks to identify the number of untested rape kits nationally. The goal of this project is to ensure all rape kits are tested. Of the states where the number of untested rape kits is known, California, North Carolina, Oklahoma, and Missouri lead with the highest number of rape kits untested (about 14,000 untested rape kits in CA, 9,000 in NC, and 7,000 in OK and MO).[56] And, in New Jersey, where the authors of this text reside and/ or work, legislation *failed* to pass in 2020 that would require police departments to send rape kits to state forensic labs within ten business days, and require the labs to process rape kits within six months of receipt.[57]

Why are rape kits ignored, sitting on shelves for days, weeks, months, or years before they are submitted to state forensic labs for testing? Put simply, why don't police submit rape kits? Perhaps the most obvious answer is lack of resources, namely funding. Rape kits are expensive to test, at over $1,000 per kit (and states are required to cover the cost of rape kits). To determine if cost was one factor explaining rape kits were not being submitted, Campbell et al. examined reasons why rape kits go untested, and identified four primary reasons: (1) victims did not provide written consent to have their rape kits tested, (2) police do not believe DNA testing would be helpful because they did not identify a suspect or a potential suspect had already been adjudicated,

(3) lack of resources (funding and staff), and (4) if it is understood in a jurisdiction that not all rape kits can be tested, police consider the credibility of the victim and nature of the assault in determining what kits are submitted for testing.[58] Similarly, in a study of Detroit's rape kit backlog, Campbell and Fehler-Cabral found that the reasons for the city's backlog were because: (1) some cases were too weak to warrant a rape kit submission, (2) there was an overall lack of resources and staffing, (3) there was an intersectionality of sexism, racism, and classism that led to cases being disregarded (and some victims being deemed not credible), and (4) some victims were uncooperative (so police did not pursue the case).[59]

Based on the above, it is clear that more work needs to be done to address the current rape kit backlog, and policies need to be updated and introduced that prevent this backlog from worsening in the future. We write this text during a time when the Violence Against Women Act Reauthorization Act of 2021 (VAWA 2021) has been passed by the House but is awaiting vote in the Senate. This piece of legislation is important for a number of reasons, but as it applies to the current discussion, VAWA 2021 supports Sexual Assault Nurse Examiner (SANE) medical forensic exams and adds language to the existing sexual assault survivors' rights piece that states survivors, "be informed of the status and location of a sexual assault evidence collection kit."[60] This will allow victims to continue to receive forensic exams at little to no cost to them and be able to track their rape kits as they are processed.

RAPE KITS ON TV

Given the importance of rape kits, we looked at existing research to see whether rape kits are represented in TV crime dramas or on other TV shows. Levin selected four crime shows, and thirteen episodes of these shows, at random and analyzed whether rape kits were performed; in just over one-third of episodes, rape kits were collected.[61] Perhaps unsurprisingly, rape kits have been featured on *Law & Order: SVU*. And a search on IMdb reveals additional crime or police dramas that featured a rape kit in at least one episode: *Rizzoli & Isles, Cracked, Two Sentence Horror Stories, Cracker, Born to Kill?, Good Girls, Southland, CSI,* and *Miami Vice*.[62] Further, true crime shows have addressed rape kits, and the rape kit backlog. In the first episode of Netflix's *Unbelievable*, a true crime series, viewers see the process of a young woman going through the steps to complete a rape kit.[63] And the Flint, Michigan, police department agreed to provide information on TNT's show, *Cold Justice*.[64] Other documentaries addressing rape kits and/or their backlog are *I Am Evidence, Battling the Backlog,* and *Weaponizing Women*.[65]

CHAPTER SUMMARY

The *CSI* Effect refers to the idea that people who watch *CSI* or related shows believe that forensic evidence is abundant, and jurors expect this evidence during criminal trials. When forensic evident is not present, or not what the jurors expect it to be, the *CSI* Effect predicts that jurors will be more likely to acquit a defendant. Forensic evidence includes fingerprint, ballistics, and DNA analyses. The fingerprint database is IAFIS, ballistics database is NIBIN, and DNA database is CODIS. Forensic evidence is not common and overall expensive to analyze.

Overall, there are mixed findings regarding the *CSI* Effect, but most prosecutors do believe it exists.

Rape kits are analyzed for DNA. Any DNA found is run through CODIS to determine if there is a match. Many rape kits were and remain untested, mostly due to lack of resources, but also because there is not a strong enough case, victims may not cooperate or may be deemed not credible, or because of underlying racism, sexism, and classism. End the Backlog seeks to identify states with rape kit backlogs and influence policy so that all rape kits are tested, and tested in a timely manner. Rape kits have been featured on TV, both in crime dramas and true crime documentaries.

NOTES

1. "Friends and Lovers." CSI: Crime Scene Investigation, created by Anthony E. Zuiker, season 1, episode 5, Jerry Bruckheimer Television, 2000.
2. Podlas, Kimberlianne. "The CSI Effect and Other Forensic Fictions." *Loyola of Los Angeles Entertainment Law Review*, vol. 27, 2006, pp. 87–125.
3. Hazarika, Pompi, and David A. Russell. "Advances in Fingerprint Analysis." *Angewandte Chemie International Edition*, vol. 51, no. 15, 2012, pp. 3524–3531.
4. Bose, Palash Kumar, and Mohammad Jubaidul Kabir. "Fingerprint: A Unique and Reliable Method for Identification." *Journal of Enam Medical College*, vol. 7, no. 1, January 2017, pp. 29–34.
5. Hazarika and Russell, "Advances in Fingerprint Analysis," p. 3524.
6. Ibid, p. 3527.
7. Bose and Kabir, "Fingerprint: A Unique and Reliable Method for Identification," p. 29.
8. Ibid, p. 31.
9. Moses, Kenneth R., et al. "Automated Fingerprint Identification System (AFIS)." Scientific Working Group on Friction Ridge Analysis Study and Technology and National institute of Justice (eds.) SWGFAST-The fingerprint sourcebook, 2011, pp. 1–33.
10. Ibid, p. 11.

11. Ibid, p. 12.

12. Braga, Anthony A., and Glenn L. Pierce. "Linking Crime Guns: The Impact of Ballistics Imaging Technology on the Productivity of the Boston Police Department's Ballistics Unit." *Journal of Forensic Science*, vol. 49, no. 4, 2004, pp. 1–6.

13. "Automated Firearms Ballistic Technology." Bureau of Alcohol, Tobacco, Firearms and Explosives (ATF), 2016, https://www.atf.gov/firearms/automated-firearms-ballistics technology.

14. Ibid.

15. "NIBIN." Bureau of Alcohol, Tobacco, Firearms and Explosives (ATF), 2019, https://www.atf.gov/resource-center/docs/undefined/nibin-fact-sheet-june-2020/download.

16. "ATF's NIBIN Program." Bureau of Alcohol, Tobacco, Firearms and Explosives (ATF), 2011, https://www.atf.gov/file/3826/download.

17. Morgan, Anthony, and Penny Jorna. "Impact of Ballistic Evidence on Criminal Investigations." *Trends and Issues in Crime and Criminal Justice*, vol. 28, 2018, pp. 1–16.

18. "NIBIN." Bureau of Alcohol, Tobacco, Firearms and Explosives (ATF).

19. Braga, Anthony A., and Glenn L. Pierce. "Reconsidering the Ballistic Imaging of Crime Bullets in Gun Law Enforcement Operations." *Forensic Science Policy & Management*, vol. 2, 2011, 105–117.

20. Beth Schwartzapfel, "This Machine Could Prevent Gun Violence—If Only Cops Used It," The Marshall Project, 2016, https://www.themarshallproject.org/2016/10/06/this-machine-could-prevent-gun-violence-if-only-copsusedit#:~:text=This%20number%20is%20not%20likely,to%20pick%20up%20the%20cost; "Justification for Non-Competitive Procurement," City of Chicago, 2012, https://www.chicago.gov/content/dam/city/depts/dps/SoleSource/NCRB2012/ForensicTechnologyApproved.pdf.

21. Butler, John M. "The Future of Forensic DNA Analysis." *Philosophical Transactions*, vol. 370, 2015, pp. 1–10.

22. "Frequently Asked Questions on CODIS and NDIS." Federal Bureau of Investigation (FBI), 2021, https://www.fbi.gov/services/laboratory/biometric-analysis/codis/codis-and-ndis-factsheet#:~:text=CODIS%20is%20the%20acronym%20for,used%20to%20run%20these%20databases.

23. Ibid.

24. Butler, "The Future of Forensic DNA Analysis," p. 4.

25. "Frequently Asked Questions on CODIS and NDIS." Federal Bureau of Investigation (FBI).

26. Kaiser, Jocelyn. "A Judge Said Police Can Search the DNA Database of 1 Million Americans without Their Consent. What's next?" *Science*, 2019, https://www.sciencemag.org/news/2019/11/judge-said-police-can-search-dna-millions-americans-without-their-consent-what-s-next.

27. Ibid.

28. Ibid.

29. Cole, Simon, and Rachel Dioso. "Law and the Lab." *The Wall Street Journal*, 2005, https://www.wsj.com/articles/SB111594466027532447.

30. Podlas, "The CSI Effect and Other Forensic Fictions," p. 90.

31. Schweitzer, N. J., and Michael J. Saks. "The CSI Effect: Popular Fiction about Forensic Science Affects the Publics Expectations about Real Forensic Science." *Jurimetrics*, vol. 4, pp. 357–364.

32. Tyler, Tom R. "Viewing CSI and the Threshold of Guilt: Managing Truth and Justice in Reality and Fiction." *The Yale Law Journal*, vol. 115, no. 5, March 2006, pp. 1050–1085.

33. Kim, Young S., et al. "Examining the CSI Effect in the Cases of Circumstantial Evidence and Eyewitness Testimony: Multivariate and Path Analyses." *Journal of Criminal Justice*, vol. 37, no. 5, September–October 2009, pp. 452–460.

34. Podlas, "The CSI Effect and Other Forensic Fictions," p. 120.

35. Shelton, Hon. Donald E., et al. "A Study of Juror Expectations and Demands Concerning Scientific Evidence: Does the CSI Effect Exist?" *Vanderbilt Journal of Entertainment and Technology Law*, vol. 9, no. 2, 2006, pp. 331–368.

36. Ibid, p. 358.

37. Ibid, p. 359.

38. Ibid, p. 360.

39. Baskin, Deborah R., and Ira B. Sommers. "Crime-Show-Viewing Habits and Public Attitudes Toward Forensic Evidence: The 'CSI Effect' Revisited." *The Justice System Journal*, vol. 31, no. 1, 2010, pp. 97–113.

40. Ibid, p. 106.

41. Schweitzer and Saks, "The CSI Effect: Popular Fiction about Forensic Science Affects the Public's Expectations about Real Forensic Science," p. 352.

42. Ibid, p. 353.

43. Cather, Karin H. "The CSI Effect: Fake TV and its Impact on Jurors in Criminal Cases," *The Prosecutor*, vol. 34, 2004, pp. 9–16.

44. Watkins, Michael J. "Forensics in the Media: Have Attorneys Reacted to the Growing Popularity of Forensic Crime Dramas?" Unpublished MA, Florida State University, Tallahassee, FL, 2004.

45. Podlas, "The CSI Effect and Other Forensic Fictions," p. 107.

46. "CSI: Maricopa County: The CSI Effect and Its Real-Life Impact on Justice." Maricopa County Attorney's Office. 2005, http://www.ce9.uscourts.gov/jc2008/references/csi/CSI_Effect_report.pdf.

47. Kim et al., "Examining the CSI Effect in the Cases of Circumstantial Evidence and Eyewitness Testimony: Multivariate and Path Analyses," p. 452.

48. Podlas, "The CSI Effect and Other Forensic Fictions," p. 120.

49. Ibid, p. 119.

50. Tyler, "Viewing CSI and the Threshold of Guilt: Managing Truth and Justice in Reality and Fiction," p. 1084.

51. Worthy, Kym. "What Happened When We Tested Thousands of Abandoned Rape Kits in Detroit." TED: Ideas Worth Spreading, 2018, https://www.ted.com/talks/kym_worthy_what_happened_when_we_tested_thousands_of_abandoned_rape_kits_in_detroit/transcript?language=en#t-180943.

52. Ibid.

53. Ibid.

54. Ibid.

55. Ibid.

56. "End the Backlog." Joyful Heart Foundation, 2021, https://www.endthebacklog.org/.

57. Ibid.

58. Campbell, Rebecca, et al. "The National Problem of Untested Sexual Assault Kits (SAKs): Scope, Causes, Future Directions for Research, Policy, and Practice." *Trauma, Violence, & Abuse*, vol. 18, no. 4, 2017, pp. 363–376.

59. Campbell, Rebecca, and Giannina Fehler-Cabral. "Why Police 'Couldn't or Wouldn't' Submit Sexual Assault Kits for DNA Testing: A Focal Concerns Theory Analysis of Untested Rape Kits." *Law & Society Review*, vol. 52, no. 1, 2018, pp. 73–105.

60. "H.R. 1620 – Violence Against Women Act Reauthorization Act of 2021." Library of Congress, 2021, https://www.congress.gov/bill/117th-congress/house-bill/1620/text.

61. Levin, Jessica. "Representations of Victims, Suspects and Offenders: A Content Analysis of Four Television Crime Shows." Spring 2013. Undergraduate Honors Theses, University of Colorado, Boulder, student paper.

62. "Sort by Popularity - Most Popular Movies and TV Shows Tagged with Keyword 'Rape Kit.'" IMdb, 2021, https://www.imdb.com/search/keyword/?keywords=rape-kit.

63. Smith, Erika W. "What Netflix's Unbelievable Gets Right About Rape Kits." Refinery29, 2019, https://www.refinery29.com/en-us/rape-kit-exam#:~:text=In%20the%20first%20episode%20of,immediately%20after%20reporting%20her%20rape.&text=The%20process%20of%20getting%20a,is%20another%20trauma%20in%20itself.

64. "Police Get Help from TV Show to Test Unprocessed Rape Kits." *The Press of Atlantic City*, 2015, https://pressofatlanticcity.com/life/police-get-help-from-tv-show-to-test-unprocessed-rape-kits/article_cafe760c-8a95-5462-9e3b-3ca93a946cba.html.

65. "Sort by Popularity - Most Popular Movies and TV Shows Tagged with Keyword 'Rape-Kit,'" IMdb.

Chapter 7

The Unbearable Weight of Being Black

A young Black man is running through a run-down neighborhood. He is speeding down an alley, a brick building on his left and a not-so-sturdy fence on his right, when a German Shepherd appears, barking. He pauses, gathering himself, and then continues on running through a broken fence and empty lot. Two people, armed, are following him. He finds a loitered rag and twists it around his hand, using it to bust the window of an abandoned warehouse. The two people continue to pursue him. In the warehouse, he is able to hide from the followers at first, but eventually is spotted, and shot at. He pulls a gun, shooting back. Seeing his pursuers down, he reveals himself, gun in hand and at the ready. One pursuer is sitting up against a wall, red paint ball splatter on his abdomen and hands. He asks the young man what is next. The young man responds, saying, "a bullet to the head." The second pursuer comes around, critiquing the young man's shooting skills (or lack thereof). This is a lesson in dealing with rivals, in survival . . .

This scene, often used by criminology professors to exemplify differential association theory, is from *The Wire*.[1] In our classes we have students go through an exercise, whereby we ask the following: close your eyes, and think of the first image that comes to mind when I say the word "criminal." Perhaps unsurprisingly, most students report that a Black male is the first image that comes to mind. This phenomenon is not limited to students, however. Many people will conjure the same profile. In fact, we urge you to give this exercise a try with your family and friends.

Arguably one of the most persistent stereotypes in today's society is that of Black people as criminals. How did this happen? How has media played a role in perpetuating these stereotypes? Below we explore the media's depiction of Black people as criminals on the news. Then, we turn to the portrayal of Black people in TV crime dramas. Do news sources and crime dramas portray Black people in a similar manner? And how do these portrayals match up to official statistics? We answer all of these questions below.

RACE, CRIME, AND MEDIA

It is well known by now that African Americans have received differential and discriminatory treatment by the criminal justice system throughout the history of the United States. For example, slave patrols in the early 1700s were meant to find and punish escaped slaves, slaves suspected of causing an uprising, or slaves who did not follow the rules of their plantation owners.[2] Since these times, Blacks have been perceived and labeled as criminals, and this has been confirmed by many researchers. For example, MacLin and Herrera asked participants about their perceptions of the prevalence of offenders of different races. After analyzing the responses, it was determined that participants thought Blacks made up the majority of the criminal population at 40 percent (versus 30 percent Hispanic, 20 percent White, and 10 percent Asian).[3] And Madriz found in her interviews that participants were aware of the media's stereotypical portrayal of the Black criminal, but nevertheless stated that that image was the first that came to mind when asked to think about a criminal.[4] Interestingly, this image of the stereotypical Black offender was described by most women in the study, regardless of their own race or income status.[5]

Returning to more modern times, when crime was spiking in the 1980s and 1990s, politicians and policymakers blamed "superpredators," or violent juveniles whose criminal impulses could not be controlled. Implicit in this discussion was that superpredators were *Black* juveniles. Similarly, when the War on Drugs was in full swing, attention was focused on the dangers of crack (versus powder) cocaine, a drug that was associated with lower-class Black use.[6] And Welch reminds us that during this same time, Willie Horton, a Black man who committed rape and murder during a prison furlough, was used in President George H. W. Bush's campaign to push for tough-on-crime policies.[7] His face, popping up on televisions regularly in a campaign commercial, reinforced the Black man as violent stereotype.[8] While these examples are only the tip of the iceberg, they demonstrate that the media's narrative of crime is that most crime is committed by People of Color, namely Black people.

PORTRAYAL OF BLACK PEOPLE ON THE NEWS

Think of the last time you watched the news on TV. Do you remember a story about crime? If so, do you remember the race of the offender? Of the victim? Chances are you recall a news story about a Black person, or Black man specifically, committing some heinous offense against some White person, perhaps a White woman.

Entman argues that news stations perpetuate racism via their portrayal of Black individuals.[9] He studied local Chicago television news for one week, viewing three hours of news programming each day, and recorded all stories that involved Black people. Of these news stories, nearly 40 percent were of violent crimes committed by Black individuals.[10] And a mugshot, or a live shot of the Black suspect in handcuffs, was displayed; the same imagery was not shown for White suspects in the news programs under study.[11] In the week of TV news studied, one particular story received the most attention—a crime committed by Black juveniles against White girls. And the "side" of the White girls was featured more heavily.[12] Entman followed up this work with another study, this time looking at the representation of Black people in TV news stories on three different stations. After analyzing 30 hours of coverage of stories featuring Black individuals, he concluded that crime was the most common story. Entman notes that in nearly half of the crime stories, Black individuals are either portrayed as criminals or as victims of misfortune—thus, they are either a threat to society or not contributing to society (i.e., both negative depictions).[13]

Findings like Entman's are not limited to one city, region, or news station. Sheley and Ashkins found that Black individuals were portrayed as robbery suspects most often (in 67 percent of news reports on one station and 83 percent and 100 percent on two others) in their analysis of three New Orleans news stations over a three-month period in 1981.[14] Gilliam et al. analyzed TV news in Los Angeles between 1993 and 1994. Their findings indicated that media substantially overrepresented Black violent crime, but underrepresented Black nonviolent crime.[15] A couple years later, Dixon and Linz found that Whites are overrepresented as victims and Blacks are overrepresented as perpetrators, compared to arrest reports.[16] The authors examined a total of 200 news programs in Los Angeles and Orange Counties (in California) from 1995 to 1997; they also discovered that Blacks were underrepresented as victims of crime compared to official reports.[17] Another study by Dixon et al. found similar results in regard to Black victims—they were significantly underrepresented on local news (as were Black police officers!)[18]

More recent studies of local news reports suggest that the portrayal of Blacks as criminals may be changing. For example, Dixon and Williams viewed nearly 150 hours of cable and network news that aired between 2008 and 2012. They found that Black people were actually underrepresented as violent suspects and homicide victims.[19] Similarly, Chiricos and Eschholz found in Orlando that Black suspects were not overrepresented in local TV news; however, Black suspects were featured in more threatening crime stories, and Black people were more likely to be featured as suspects than victims or some other positive role model.[20]

When we consider all of the research above, it seems that Black individuals were disproportionately portrayed as suspects in local news during the 1980s and 1990s, but are represented somewhat more accurately in the 2000s and 2010s. Still, there is a tendency to portray Black individuals as violent. Keep in mind that news channels are more likely to cover crime stories on violent or particularly egregious offenses, as these continue to receive the greatest interest and bring in a greater number of viewers. That said, it does seem that Black victims have received little attention throughout these decades. Does this affect our perceptions of Black people? Are we supposed to feel less sympathy for a Black victim as a result of their invisibility as victims on the news?

We would be remiss if we did not acknowledge that in 2021, people are receiving news information from sources other than their local TV news stations. Cable TV news has grown, with popular stations like CNN, MSNBC, FOX News, and One America News. And social media sites like Twitter are often consulted and viewed by users several times daily for the latest headlines. Do these sources of news paint Black individuals in the same light? Are people who view Internet or social media news likely to stereotype Black people as criminals?

Intravia and Pickett provide some insight to the latter question, examining the relation between Internet and social media news consumption and engagement, and criminal stereotypes. In other words, do people who view and interact with Internet and social media news channels stereotype criminals as Black? The findings are mixed: people who consume Internet news are less likely to engage in criminal stereotyping, while people who consume social media news are more likely to engage in criminal stereotyping.[21] Further confounding results are that people who *engage* with social media news outlets are less likely to engage in criminal stereotyping. The authors suggest that it could be the influence of social movements, like #BlackLivesMatter, #HandsUp, or #JusticeforGeorgeFloyd (note: George Floyd's death occurred after the publication of this study) that cause people to take action and change their views, that could explain their interesting results.[22] We will discuss television crime dramas and news' impact on criminal stereotypes later in this chapter.

It is possible, given recent events surrounding the unjustified deaths of Black individuals by police, that the depiction of Black people on the news will change, and will change in a way that is more positive for the Black community. We are writing this book during the one-year anniversary of the death of Breonna Taylor. In 2020, Breonna Taylor, a Black female EMT living with her boyfriend, was killed by police while sleeping when they entered her home to conduct an investigation. Breonna's boyfriend, who says he did not hear the officers identify themselves, fired a warning shot. In return, officers fired dozens of bullets, six of which hit and fatally wounded Breonna. Just over two months later, video surfaced around the nation of White officers who kneeled on the neck of George Floyd for about eight minutes, causing Floyd to die. Floyd was accused of paying for cigarettes with a $20 counterfeit bill. These deaths, occurring so close together, and in the middle of a pandemic, sparked outrage throughout the nation. Media outlets focused on the short-lived lives of these individuals, the wrongfulness of these acts, the protests they sparked, and the collective efforts of businesses, celebrities, and the like to provide more support to the Black community. And they also brought in experts to discuss systemic racism in the U.S. and the mishandling of Black people by the criminal justice system. The Black Lives Matter movement has grown since these untimely deaths, and it seems a tide is turning in the media, and in crime dramas, to more accurately depict the experiences of Black Americans. Will this change last? We will have to wait and see . . .

BLACKS AS PERPETRATORS AND VICTIMS IN CRIME DRAMAS

In their content analysis of *Law & Order*, *Law & Order: Criminal Intent*, and *Law & Order: Special Victims Unit* episodes, Sood and Trielli find that Black people as victims and offenders are underrepresented, meaning they are not depicted in crime dramas to the extent that they experience or perpetrate crime in the real world.[23] We found these same results in our analysis of television crime drama episodes that featured homicides. In a similar analysis of *Law & Order: SVU*, Britto and colleagues note that people of color, especially Hispanics and Blacks, are underrepresented as victims.[24] And when people of color are victims in some episodes, the victim is shown in a photo, rather than in physical form, which depersonalizes (i.e., to take away one's personal identity or individuality) the victim.[25]

During the fall 1997, Mastro and Robinson analyzed representation of People of Color in 336 hours of primetime television. They focused on police and perpetrators in these shows, finding that 19 percent of cops were Blacks and 5 percent of criminals were Black. Thus, Black people were overrepresented as police officers and underrepresented as criminals.[26] However, the authors also found that when it came to police use of force on TV crime dramas, police were most likely to use excessive force on young, Black males.[27] They warn that such depictions imply that the behavior of Black people is so bad that police must use whatever means necessary to control them, which can be a dangerous implication if this were to play out in the real world (as it has publicly since the publication of their article.[28]

Parrott and Parrott found that Black and White men were equally as likely to perpetrate violence in their analysis of 65 crime dramas aired between 2010 and 2013.[29] Black men were also no more likely to be portrayed as criminals compared to White women.[30] However, Black females and Black males were less likely to be portrayed as victims compared to their White counterparts, and Black females especially made up the smallest percentage of victims of violence.[31]

FINDINGS FROM OUR TV CRIME DRAMA ANALYSES

Black Perpetrators

In two of our datasets we looked at Black perpetrators and victims. Our first data set includes 169 episodes of television crime dramas (including dramas featuring homicides). Of these, 143 (84.6 percent) episodes included either a Black perpetrator only, White perpetrator only, or both (we compare Black versus White perpetrators only here, as White people make up the majority of perps in the crime dramas we examined). One hundred nineteen (83.2 percent) episodes featured White perpetrators only, 17 (11.9 percent) featured Black perpetrators, and seven (4.9 percent) episodes featured Black and White co-perpetrators.

We further analyzed the 17 episodes featuring Black perpetrators only. Because four episodes featured two Black perpetrators, we have a total of 21 Black perpetrators. Of these perpetrators, 12 (57.1 percent) were male, one (4.8 percent) was female, and gender was not recorded for another eight (38.1 percent) perpetrators. Most Black perpetrators were young adults, with nine (42.8 percent) in the 19–30 age category and two (9.5 percent) age 18 or younger. Another six (28.6 percent) Black perps were in the 31–45 age category, and three (14.3 percent) were in the 46–65 age range; data on age was missing for one (4.8 percent) perpetrator. No Black perpetrators over age 65 were shown. The crimes committed by Black perpetrators only in crime dramas were both violent (homicide, aggravated assault, kidnapping, robbery, rape) and nonviolent (conspiracy, drug distribution, possession, and smuggling, theft, bribery, extortion, insurance fraud, and adultery). And the shows featuring Black perpetrators only were *Blue Bloods, Law & Order: SVU, Murder in the Thirst, Orange is the New Black, The First 48,* and *The Wire.*

Our second data set includes aggregate data from 280 hours of television crime dramas. Of these 280 hours, we are missing offender data from only one hour (episode). Here we have frequencies of Black perpetrators, but are unable to identify what specific crimes these individuals committed. Race was identified for 380 perpetrators; only 66 (17.4 percent) perpetrators were Black.

Black Victims

In our dataset of 169 episodes of crime dramas, 127 (75.1 percent) episodes included either a Black victim only, White victim only, or both Black and White victims. Specifically, 105 (82.7 percent) episodes featured White victims only, 17 (13.4 percent) featured Black victims only, and five (3.9 percent) featured both Black and White victims. In the 17 episodes that featured Black victims only, there were a total of 21 victims. Of these, 15 (71.4 percent) victims were male and six (28.6 percent) were female. Most victims were young adults, with ten (47.6 percent) ages 19–30 and three (14.3 percent) under age 18. Another six (28.6 percent) Black victims were between ages 46–65, one (4.8 percent) was between 31–45, and age data for one (4.8 percent) victim was missing. And, in eight (47 percent) of these episodes, Black victims were wronged by Black perpetrators (all nine other episodes featured perps of a different race, or Black and White co-perpetrators). Finally, in our aggregate dataset of 280 crime drama episodes, race was identified for 632 victims. Of these, 83 (13.1 percent) victims were Black.

WHAT DO THE OFFICIAL STATISTICS SAY?

Black Perpetrators

Most crime is committed by White people, and White males in particular; however, Black people, and Black men in particular, are *disproportionately* represented in the criminal justice system. That is, while Black or African Americans make up about 13 percent of the U.S. population, they make up approximately 27 percent of total people arrested in 2019, according to the UCR.[32] But this statistic takes many violent and property offenses into account. If we look further at individual crimes, we see the following: Black people make up about 51 percent of those arrested for murder, 27 percent of those arrested for rape, 52 percent of those arrested for robbery, 33 percent of those arrested for aggravated assault, 28 percent of those arrested for burglary,

30 percent of those arrested for theft, 29 percent of those arrested for motor vehicle theft, and 25 percent of those arrested for arson.[33] They further make up about 30 percent of those arrested for forgery, fraud, disorderly conduct and curfew and loitering violations, 36 percent of those arrested for embezzlement, 35 percent of those arrested for receiving or selling stolen property, 27 percent of those arrested for vandalism, 26 percent of those arrested for drug abuse violations, and 28 percent of those arrested for vagrancy and offenses against the family and children.[34] Taken together, the percentage of Black people arrested for violent and property offenses is approximately double (or more than double) their percent makeup in the U.S. population.

Black offenders make up approximately 39 percent of the U.S. prison population.[35] As of 2019, the rate of incarceration for Black males is nearly six times higher than that of White males.[36] For further comparison, White, non-Hispanic persons comprise about 60 percent of the U.S. population, and just under 58 percent of the U.S. prison population.[37] Such disproportionate representation of Black people, namely Black men, encountering the criminal justice system may lead some to perceive Black people as those who make up the majority of criminals.

Black Victims

Percentages of Black people as victims are more proportionate to the percentage of Black people in the general population. According to the 2019 NCVS, Black people comprised about 11 percent of violent crime victims (including simple assault). Broken down further, Black individuals make up about 6 percent of rape victims, 11 percent of simple assault victims, 12 percent of aggravated assault victims, and 18 percent of robbery victims. And Black people make up slightly over 11 percent of personal theft victims.[38]

DO CRIME DRAMAS MIRROR OFFICIAL STATISTICS?

Our data suggest that Black perpetrators are underrepresented in crime dramas when compared to the percentage of Black arrestees in official statistics. That said, in one of our datasets (where we have specific perpetrator information for 169 episodes of crime dramas) the percentage of Black perpetrators is slightly less than the percentage of Black individuals in the U.S. population. But in the other dataset (of aggregate data from 280 crime drama episodes), the percentage of Black offenders is greater than the percentage of Black individuals in the U.S. population. As for victims, in the crime dramas we examined the percentage of Black victims was nearly equal their makeup in the general population, and slightly higher than the percentage of Black violent crime and personal theft victims from official reports. So, there is a marginal overrepresentation of Black victims in crime dramas.

In the Academy Award–winning documentary, Bowling for Columbine, *Michael Moore strolls down a street in a quiet section of South Central, L.A. He is joined by Professor Barry Glassner, author of* Culture of Fear.
  Glassner says to Moore: If you turn on TV, what are you gonna hear about? Dangerous Black guys.
  As the two men continue their stroll, we see video cut after cut, with anchor voice-overs and Black men being pat down by police or taken away in handcuffs.
  The ensuing dialogue of the montage sounds like this:

Voice-over: Now the suspect is a Black male in his 20s, we are told large afro, sideburns, he was wearing a silver chain at the time

Voice-over: Police say the suspect is a Black man, six-foot-one inches tall, 180 pounds, about 35 years of age

Voice-over: The suspect is a Black male about 16 to 18

Voice-over: The suspect is African-American

Voice-over: Black man

Voice-over: Suspect . . . Suspect . . . Black Male . . . Black . . . Black . . . Black . . . Black . . . Black man . . .

Glassner: Susan Smith drowns her two children and she tells people a Black guy stole the car and stole the kids and everyone, at first, bought it.

9-1-1 Call: Some guy jumped at a red light with her car with her two kids in it and he took off with them. Black male.

Black Male?

Yes, ma'am.

Susan Smith: And I told 'em I loved him. I hollered I loved 'em. It's just a tragedy.

Glassner: The anonymous, urban—which means usually Black, male—comes by and does this. It's the excuse for all kinds of things.

Moore: Charles Stewart, the lawyer in Boston.

Glassner: Right. Exactly.

Moore: Kills his pregnant wife, says a Black guy did it, everyone buys it.

Anchor: The suspect described as a Black male, about six feet tall. Chuck and Carol Stewart were robbed at gun point, as they left a Lamaze class. It seemed the ultimate urban nightmare.

Moore: The thing I love about my country is whether you're a psychotic killer or running for president of the United States, the one thing you always count on is white America's fear of the Black man.

A RETURN TO CULTIVATION THEORY, AND MEDIA-PRIMING THEORY

In chapter 2 we spoke in detail about cultivation theory, or the idea that what we see on TV helps us construct our social reality. Taking this one step further, Shrum argued that people who watch television often use what they see on television as a cognitive shortcut when evaluating the world around them.[39] What this means is that we use what the media tells us to form our assumptions about what is going on in the world around us.

Think back to the thought exercise we gave you previously, where we asked you to think about a crime story you saw on the news and the suspect in that story. That suspect was, more likely than not, Black. How do these stories affect our perceptions of Black people as a whole? If the media is continuously displaying criminals as Blacks, notably Black men, we begin to make an association cognitively between criminal and Black. Associations between criminal and Black can occur explicitly, or consciously, or implicitly, or nonconsciously or automatically. An explicit association between criminal and Black would occur if we watched crime on the news and said, either outwardly or to ourselves, "The criminal they are showing is Black." You are aware of the race of the perpetrator shown and are making a connection between race and crime. An implicit association between criminal and Black may occur if you watched the news while completing homework. You are paying attention to the news and may glimpse an image of a Black criminal on the screen, but you do not consciously acknowledge it. Rather, the image of a Black criminal is stored in your mind, and a connection is made between criminal and Black without your conscious knowledge! (An implicit association can also be formed at the same time an explicit association is formed, just not with your knowledge.)

If presented with similar news accounts frequently, that criminal-Black association becomes stronger and more accessible. Shrum argues, then, that we use this criminal-Black association as a mental shortcut.[40] Indeed, Anderson notes that crime news has led to an automatic association of Blacks and crime.[41] For example, if you are asked about what people commit the most crime in your neighborhood, you may answer Black men without giving the question much thought. Other research has confirmed this hypothesis, and adds that as a result of being exposed to Black people as violent offenders on local news, White people tend to be more supportive of harsher criminal penalties and tend to have less favorable attitudes toward Black people as a whole.[42] We discuss further implications below, but first turn to a related theory, that of media-priming.

Why do these associations between criminal and Black matter? One answer comes from media-priming theory. Media-priming theory says that, because we have made associations between concepts (like Black and criminal) in our memory, being reminded of one of these concepts will activate the other.[43] So, if you have made a cognitive association between Black and criminal in your memory, when you see the image of a Black person on the local news or on a TV crime drama (i.e., the media prime), that image should activate other concepts associated with Black in your memory, like criminal. If the concepts Black and criminal are frequently activated, they become more accessible to us (hence, the cognitive shortcut discussion above), and we are *primed* to now apply this association to situations in the real world.[44] Thus, the activation of the concepts Black or criminal can affect our beliefs, judgments, and behavior. How does this play out exactly?

Dixon and Maddox conducted an experiment in which participants viewed news stories of perpetrators and victims of different skin colors. The skin colors of perpetrators shown were either White, light-skinned Black, medium-skinned Black, and dark-skinned Black. Results of this study showed that people who reported watching the news heavily expressed more concern over dark-skinned Black compared to White perpetrators.[45] And no matter how much news a person reported watching, participants rated dark-skinned Black (versus White) perpetrators as more memorable.[46] Finally, those who more frequently watched the news rated victims of all Black perpetrators more positively, suggesting some bias against Black offenders.[47]

Dixon and Maddox argued in their study that it was frequent priming, and thus a stronger association between Black and criminal, that led heavy television viewers to recall dark-skinned perpetrators more easily and to report more discomfort when a dark-skinned Black perpetrator was featured. Related to their findings, Lipschultz and Hilt argue that the stereotypes we hold of Black people, many of these perpetuated by media, may inform our perceptions of neighborhoods.[48] For example, if we believe that a neighborhood consists of mostly Black people, we may actively avoid it, thinking it is unsafe. They also make the point that, months after viewing a White perpetrator on the news, some people may think back to the story and misidentify the suspect as Black: "In other words, viewers who associate crime with minorities . . . will misperceive news in order to remain consistent."[49] As you might imagine, this can have serious implications related to false accusation or misidentification of suspects.

If you recall, in chapter 2 we mentioned that our student research assistants recorded their *perceptions* of perpetrator and victims' races if race was not explicitly stated in the episode. That is, they relied on skin color and other contextual cues to record the race of an offender or victim. Now that we know about the potential effect of media on stereotyping Black individuals as criminal, could this have influenced our research assistants' recording of data? While we do not like to think so, the theories we have covered might suggest otherwise.

CHAPTER SUMMARY

Black men have been, and continue to be, stereotyped as criminals. And Black people are disproportionately represented in the U.S. criminal justice system. In our data, we find that Black perpetrators are slightly underrepresented in crime dramas when compared to the percentage of Black arrestees in official statistics. We also find that there is a marginal overrepresentation of Black victims in crime dramas compared to Black victims in official statistics.

Even as the image of the Black man, or Black person, changes in crime dramas and on the news, many still associate Black people with criminals. When the media portray Black people as criminals, viewers form both conscious (explicit) and nonconscious (implicit) associations between the concepts. The Black-criminal association that is activated then affects how we make sense of the world around us. This has strong implications for our behavior and actions toward Black people as a social group.

NOTES

1. Pelecanos, George, writer. *The Wire*. Season 4, episode 12, "That's Got His Own." Directed by Joe Chappelle, featuring Wendell Pierce, Dominic West, Lance Reddick, Michael K. Williams, and Felicia Pearson. Aired on December 3, 2006, in broadcast syndication.
2. Waxman, Olivia B. "How the U.S. Got Its Police Force." *Time*, 2020, https://time.com/4779112/police-history-origins/.
3. MacLin, M. Kimberly, and Vivian Herrera. "The Criminal Stereotype." *North American Journal of Psychology*, vol. 8, no. 2, Jun/Jul 2006, pp. 197–207.
4. Madriz, Esther I. "Images of Criminals and Victims: A Study on Women's Fear and Social Control." *Gender & Society*, vol. 11, no. 3, 1997, pp. 342–356.
5. Ibid, p. 345.

6. Welch, Kelly. "Black Criminal Stereotypes and Racial Profiling." *Journal of Contemporary Criminal Justice*, vol. 23, no. 3, August 2007, pp. 276–288.

7. Ibid, p. 282.

8. Ibid.

9. Entman, Robert M. "Modern Racism and the Images of Blacks in Local Television News." *Critical Studies in Mass Communication*, vol. 7, 1990, pp. 332–345.

10. Ibid, p. 336.

11. Ibid, p. 337.

12. Ibid.

13. Entman, Robert M. "Representation and Reality in the Portrayal of Blacks on Network Television News." *Journalism Quarterly*, vol. 71, no. 3, Fall 1994, pp. 509–520.

14. heley, Joseph F., and Cindy D. Ashkins. "Crime, Crime News, and Crime Views." *The Public Opinion Quarterly*, vol. 45, no. 4, Winter 1981, pp. 492–506.

15. Gilliam Jr., Franklin D., et al. "Crime in Black and White: The Violent, Scary World of Local News." *Press/Politics*, vol. 1, no. 3, 1996, pp. 6–23.

16. Dixon, Travis L., and Daniel Linz. "Race and the Misrepresentation of Victimization on Local Television News." *Communication Research*, vol. 27, no 5., October 2000, pp. 547–573.

17. Ibid, pp. 555–556.

18. Dixon et al. "The Portrayal of Race and Crime on Television Network News." *Journal of Broadcasting & Electronic Media*, vol. 47, no. 4, December 2003, pp. 498–523.

19. Dixon, Travis L., and Charlotte L. Williams. "The Changing Misrepresentation of Race and Crime on Network and Cable News." *Journal of Communication*, vol. 65, 2015, pp. 24–39.

20. Chiricos, Ted, and Sarah Eschholz. "The Racial and Ethnic Typification of Crime and the Criminal Typification of Race and Ethnicity in Local Television News." *Journal of Research in Crime and Delinquency*, vol. 39, no. 4, November 2002, pp. 400–420.

21. Intravia, Jonathan, and Justin T. Pickett. "Stereotyping Online? Internet News, Social Media, and the Racial Typification of Crime." *Sociological Forum*, vol. 34, no. 3, September 2019, pp. 616–642.

22. Ibid, p. 636.

23. Sood, Gaurav, and Daniel Trielli. "The Face of Crime in Prime Time: Evidence from Law and Order." *SSRN Electronic Journal*, 2017, pp. 1–30.

24. Britto, Sarah, et al. "Does 'Special' Mean Young, White, and Female? Deconstructing the Meaning of 'Special' in Law & Order: Special Victims Unit." *Journal of Criminal Justice and Popular Culture*, vol. 14, no. 1, 2007, pp. 39–56.

25. Ibid, p. 50.

26. Mastro, Dana E., and Amanda L. Robinson. "Cops and Crooks: Images of Minorities on Primetime Television." *Journal of Criminal Justice*, vol. 28, no. 5, September–October 2000, pp. 385–396.

27. Ibid, p. 394.

28. Ibid.

29. Parrott, Scott, and Caroline Titcomb Parrott. "U.S. Television's 'Mean World' for White Women: The Portrayal of Gender and Race on Fictional Crime Dramas." *Sex Roles*, vol. 73, no. 1–2, s2015, pp. 70–82.

30. Ibid, p. 74.

31. Ibid.

32. "Quick Facts." United States Census Bureau, July 2019, https://www.census.gov/quickfacts/fact/table/US/PST045219.

33. Table 43A." Federal Bureau of Investigation (FBI), 2019, https://ucr.fbi.gov/crime-in-the-u.s/2019/crime-in-the-u.s.-2019/tables/table-43.

34. Ibid.

35. "Inmate Race." Federal Bureau of Prisons, March 2021, https://www.bop.gov/about/statistics/statistics_inmate_race.jsp.

36. Carson, E. Ann. "Prisoners in 2019." Bureau of Justice Statistics (BJS), October 2020, https://www.bjs.gov/content/pub/pdf/p19.pdf.

37. "Quick Facts," United States Census Bureau; "Inmate Race," Federal Bureau of Prisons.

38. "NCVS Victimization Analysis Tool (NVAT) Report." Bureau of Justice Statistics, 9 March 2021, https://www.bjs.gov/index.cfm?ty=nvat.

39. Shrum, L. J. "The Role of Source Confusion in Cultivation Effects May Depend on Processing Strategy: A Comment on Mares (1996)." *Human Communication Research*, vol. 24, no. 2, December 1997, pp. 349–358.

40. Ibid.

41. Anderson, D. C. *Crime & the Politics of Hysteria*. Random House, 1995.

42. Gilliam Jr., Franklin D., and Shanto Iyengar. "Prime Suspects: The Influence of Local Television News on the Viewing Public." *American Journal of Political Science*, vol. 44, no. 3, July 2000, pp. 560–573.

43. Iyengar, Shanto, and Donald R. Kinder. *News that Matters: Television and American Opinion*. University of Chicago Press, 2010.

44. Moy, Patricia et al. "Agenda-Setting, Priming, and Framing." *The International Encyclopedia of Communication Theory and Philosophy*, John Wiley & Sons, Inc., 2016, pp. 1–13.

45. Dixon, Travis L., and Keith B. Maddox. "Skin Tone, Crime News, and Social Reality Judgments: Priming the Stereotype of the Dark and Dangerous Black Criminal." *Journal of Applied Social Psychology*, vol. 35, no. 8, 2005, pp. 1555–1570.

46. Ibid, p. 1564.

47. Ibid, p. 1563.

48. Lipschultz, Jeremy Harris, and Michael L. Hilt. "Race and Local Television News Crime Coverage." *Studies in Media & Information Literacy Education*, vol. 3, no. 4, November 2003, pp. 1–10.

49. Ibid, p. 7.

Chapter 8

Damsels in Distress

Girl meets boy. Boy asks her out on a date. She agrees, and we see her spending time perfecting her makeup for a night of dinner and drinks. Dinner could not be better. He makes her laugh, and they spend hours talking about life. He asks her to come to his place afterward, and she agrees, not wanting the night to end. They hold hands and when they get to his place, they sit close to one another on the couch. He makes the first move, kissing her, and she kisses him back. He begins to lift her shirt, and she stops him. She tells him it's only the first date and this is moving too fast. He does not listen and continues, becoming aggressive. She tries to get up and leave, but he forces her down on the couch. Her perfect night is now a nightmare.

Two college women go to a fraternity party, excited to be done with final exams. They just want to have a fun night out, mingle with friends, and drink. They arrive at the party and hug their friends. Soon, they walk over to a keg and fill their red cups with cheap alcohol. Their friends wave them over to play a game of beer pong. They get into the game, playing several rounds. At one point, a fraternity brother approaches one of the women, asking if she wants a stronger drink. She agrees, but walks over to the jungle juice with him, not trusting anyone to pour a drink for her. The two get into talking, and at one point the women rests her drink on a bar ledge. She looks away for a split second, as her friend is nearing her, and the fraternity brother takes the opportunity to slip a pill in her drink. We see the scene cut to the morning after, when the woman wakes up alone, in a bed that is not her own, with a splitting headache, unable to ascertain where she is or what happened the night before. She tries sitting up and is met with unbearable pain in her groin region. Something is not right . . .

It's 6:00 a.m. and a young, urban man goes jogging in his neighborhood park before work. As he rounds a corner, he notices a black stiletto by a tree. Finding this unusual, he walks over to the shoe to investigate. He is shocked at what he finds—a woman, half naked, skin paper white and lips blue, is dead behind the tree. Investigators arrive at the scene and determine the woman was killed overnight. She has what looks like rope barks around her wrists and ankles. An autopsy report concludes she was first bound, and then raped, before being killed. After speaking with friends and family, investigators are nowhere closer to naming a suspect; they suspect this crime was committed by a stranger. DNA from the victims' body pulls up the profile of a middle-aged man with a prior record for stalking. Investigators track down the man, interrogate him, and determine he is the rapist/killer. The case is solved.

You may have seen similar storylines to the above in *Law & Order: Special Victims Unit (SVU)*, perhaps the most renowned drama featuring female victims of sexual assault and rape. While the two terms are sometimes used interchangeably, there is a difference between rape and sexual assault. As of 2013, the FBI defines rape as, "Penetration, no matter how slight, of the vagina or anus with any body part or object, or oral penetration by a sex organ of another person, without the consent of the victim."[1] In contrast, sexual assault is defined by the Bureau of Justice Statistics (publisher of the National Crime Victimization Survey) as, "A wide range of victimizations, separate from rape or attempted rape. These crimes include attacks or attempted attacks generally involving unwanted sexual contact between victim and offender. Sexual assaults may or may not involve force and include such things as grabbing or fondling. It also includes verbal threats."[2] Sexual assault and rape are mostly experienced by female victims.

In this chapter we will explore why females (versus men) are associated with the social group victims, and victimization, more so than men. We also explore why women are often blamed for the victimization(s) they experience, especially as it applies to rape, sexual assault, and domestic violence. We present official statistics of female victims and perpetrators, and data on the representation of female perpetrators and victims in crime dramas. As in previous chapters, we examine whether TV crime dramas accurately depict females as offenders and victims.

GENDER STEREOTYPES AND FEMALES AS VICTIMS

Traditional gender stereotypes hold that males are the powerful, aggressive gender who do not show signs of weakness. In contrast, females are nurturing, passive, and weak. These stereotypes inform our perceptions of which gender should make up a majority of perpetrators (male) and which should make up a majority of victims (female).[3] In a number of studies, participants were asked to imagine or describe a criminal; most described criminals as male.[4] Conversely, when participants were asked to imagine victims, most described them as female.[5,] The result of Madriz's study, in which the author interviewed female participants, further detailed the stereotypical criminal as a poor man of color and the stereotypical (or ideal) victim as a White, middle-class woman.[6] In line with gender stereotypes, men are more likely to stereotype women as weak and vulnerable and, indeed, women do associate themselves with these stereotypes (compared to men).[7] Similarly, women are more likely to stereotype men as aggressive, and men do associate themselves with the aggressive stereotype (compared to women).[8,]

THE FEMINIST PERSPECTIVE

The feminist perspective emerged to highlight the unique experiences of female offenders and victims. There are several branches of feminism, each of which provide a different explanation as to why women have not been properly represented in society, and in research. Liberal feminism, for example, posit the gender inequality is due to the different roles prescribed to women in society. Radical feminism takes this a step further and blames gender inequality on males' aggressiveness and their control of female sexuality. Underlying this supposition is patriarchy. Patriarchy refers to a male-dominated society that often excludes women altogether, or at least from positions of power. Indeed, socialist feminism cites patriarchy, and capitalism, and the source of gender inequality.[9]

Feminist perspectives help to explain female crime and victimization. Liberal feminists argued that, because of females' changing roles in the 1950s (i.e., they started to work outside of the home), we should expect to see females committing many of the same crimes as men, and committing crimes in greater numbers. However, this perspective did not receive much evidentiary support. As it pertains to victims, radical feminists provided an explanation of rape that defined it as a crime of male power and control (versus sex). This perspective expanded to other crimes, and many now view women as victims of control or social dominance; this fits with nearly all feminist perspectives outlined above.[10] For example, a husband may abuse his breadwinning wife as a means of exerting control.[11] While this may have softened treatment of female victims, it has done so more for White women, suggesting that race also plays a factor in how we view and treat female victims of crime.[12]

Feminist theory is also present in communication. We focus specifically on media in our discussion, as this is the main focus of the text. Women have historically been underrepresented in media (Sink and Mastro 1), perhaps due to their unequal status in society and in media more generally.[13,] Indeed, feminist scholars suggest that male dominance and female subordination are present in media.[14] Nearly four-fifths of people featured on the news are men.[15] More male sports are featured on television (and major channels) compared to female sports. When females are featured on television and political candidates, they receive more coverage on their personal lives, which fits with the stereotypical role of female as homemaker.[16] Female actors are typically paid less and featured as the lead role less often compared to men.[17] And, in many instances, females are depicted generally as sex objects, whether on television, in video games, or in music (both within lyrics and in music videos). It should come as no surprise, then, that females are most often featured as victims of sex crimes in the media. Cuklanz sums it up best, "when represented in scenes of criminal assault including sexual assault, female characters are most often featured as victims and very seldom as perpetrators. When female characters are presented as physically capable of violent action, they are often presented either as evil or unfeminine (Maleficent), they are highly sexualized (Lara Croft), or they are unhappy or uncomfortable with their superhero-type role (Buffy the Vampire Slayer)."[18]

CULTIVATION THEORY, REVISITED (AGAIN)

Returning to cultivation theory from chapter 2, the theory posits that television shapes culture; but television is controlled by those in power, or men.[19] This can affect the way that heavy television viewers shape reality. If television shows are portraying women in ways that are consistent with traditional gender stereotypes, then this reinforces the stereotypes people hold of women in society. Portraying women as weak, submissive, innocent, and vulnerable suggests that they cannot protect themselves during a victimization event. And when women are shown as victims of rape or sexual assault on television, this could signify that violence against women, or violence as a way of subduing or controlling women, is okay.[20]

As some people's worldviews are shaped by television, the question then becomes what happens when they see a real-life female victim who does not match the stereotype? For example, how would people view a poor, Black woman raped by an ex-boyfriend? This victim does not fit the stereotypical White, middle-class woman assaulted by a stranger. Chances are, this victim will be met with even more hostility and blame from the public and criminal justice actors for the victimization she suffered.

FEMALES AS VICTIMS

Official Statistics: Rape, Sexual Assault, and Domestic Violence

Females make up the majority of victims of rape, sexual assault, and domestic violence. While we have previously defined rape and sexual assault, we have yet to define domestic violence. Domestic violence refers to violent and nonviolent acts between current or former spouses, romantic partners (boyfriends or girlfriends), civil union partners, parents and children, siblings, other blood relatives, and those who share child. Intimate partner violence is a subcategory of domestic violence that refers to violent and nonviolent acts between current or former spouses, romantic partners (boyfriends or girlfriends), and civil union partners only. Intimate relationships consist of heterosexual relationships, homosexual relationships, and relationships between members of the LGBTQIA+ community. And while violent acts may be more obvious (hitting, punching, kicking, slapping, etc.), nonviolent acts are less so. Nonviolent acts of domestic violence may include economic (e.g., not allowing the person to work, not allowing access to a shared bank account), emotional (e.g., calling the person names, threatening suicide if the person leaves you), and/or psychological (e.g., threatening to kill the person, saying you will take the children away, not allowing the person to work or communicate with friends and family) manipulation, with the intent to gain power or control over another person.

Both the Uniform Crime Report (UCR) and National Crime Victimization Survey (NCVS) provide data on these crimes. However, the UCR does not provide information on the victims of these crimes. In other words, it does not tell us how many victims of rape, sexual assault, and domestic violence were female. The NCVS provides data on victims of rape or sexual assault (the report groups these categories together); of the 459,306 rapes or sexual assaults in 2019, females were victims in 406,970 (88.6 percent) cases.[21] As for domestic violence, we look at the relationship between victims and offenders, which the NCVS provides. Relationships that would fall under the domestic violence umbrella include those labeled intimates or other relatives. With that, there were 695,059 intimate partner violence incidents in 2019; females were victims in 627,635 (90.3 percent) of these events. And there were 469,476 domestic violence incidents where the victim-offender relationship was noted as other relatives in 2019, of which 386,424 (82.3 percent) involved females as victims.[22]

Official Statistics: Females as Victims of Other Crimes

While the above discussion focuses on sexual or domestic violence, females are victims of nearly all crimes. If you recall from chapter 2, females comprise about one-fifth of murder victims. For other violent crimes, however, there seem to be a near equal number of female and male victims. The 2019 NCVS report states that 1.6 million men and 1.5 million women were victims of at least one violent crime in that reporting year.[23] In the NCVS, violent crime consists of rape or sexual assault (grouped together), robbery, and aggravated and simple assault (grouped separately). Data on property crime victims are not as readily available.

WHY DO WE BLAME WOMEN FOR THEIR VICTIMIZATIONS?

Just World Hypothesis

The just world hypothesis was first introduced by Lerner.[24] It describes the way in which people make sense of the world and its injustices—for example, poverty and victimization. The just world hypothesis states that people are deserving of what they get (or what happens to them), and they get what they deserve.[25] Thus, if you are a good person, good things will happen to you (and we all tend to view ourselves as good people). If you are a bad person, however, bad things will happen to you.[26]

As it applies to victims of crime, those who believe in the just world hypothesis might react to victims in one of two ways: either by scorning them, or by blaming them.[27] Scorning victims allows people to attribute a person's victimization to some character flaw. Blaming victims allows people to attribute a person's victimization to some behavior or act a person inflicted upon him or herself.[28] To some, this sounds an awful lot like karma—the idea that what goes around, comes around.

What does the research say about belief in a just world, and rape victims? Some do not find any relation.[29] More researchers tend to find that those who demonstrate belief in a just world are more likely to blame rape victims and accept rape myths.[30,] Others find more nuanced results, such that men with high belief in a just world view rape victims more negatively, or that female participants with high belief in a just world assign more blame to victims of stranger rape.[31,] Hayes and colleagues find that when people apply just world beliefs more to themselves and their lives, they are less accepting of rape myths.[32] However, when people apply just world beliefs more to others, they are more accepting of rape myths. This means that if we believe that good things happen will happen to us because we are good, then if we are raped we do not believe that we could possibly be responsible for our own suffering. It is, essentially, a way of protecting ourselves and our psychological well-being.[33]

Rape Myths

The just world hypothesis is related to rape myths, as people may utilize rape myths to justify (or make sense of) the victimization of a person. Rape myths are false beliefs of rape perpetrators and victims that result in blaming the victim. Rape myths, it is argued, are a result of our patriarchal society in the United States (see our discussion of radical feminism, above). Thus, the blame is placed on the *female* victim of rape while the *male* perpetrator is excused of responsibility. Perhaps you have heard some of these myths; we provide some examples below:

- "Her skirt was too short; she was asking to be raped."
- "She drank too much; she was looking to have sex."
- "She was dressed so provocatively; he couldn't resist her temptation."
- "She never said no. That means she consented."
- "She said no, but I know she really means yes."
- "She didn't fight back; therefore, she wanted it."
- "She didn't tell me to stop. That means she wanted me to continue."
- "We had sex before, so that means she consented to all (future) sexual encounters."
- "She came to my place; she wanted to have sex."
- "She was so beautiful; he could not control himself around her."
- "She is my wife; she can't be raped by me! She agreed to sex when she married me!"
- "We were already in the middle of fooling around; I couldn't stop myself."

While not an exhaustive list of rape myths, those listed are some of the most common. Such myths suggest that there is a certain type of woman—beautiful, seductive, careless—who deserves to be raped. As you may have known or guessed, *anyone* can be raped. And it is important to note that victims are not responsible for any rape that is imposed on them. That said, there are some scholars who suggest otherwise; that for rape, and other types of crime, victims may be, at least in part, responsible for their own victimization.

Those who watch television in general, and especially those who watch soap operas, tend to believe traditional rape myths. Traditional rape myths include beliefs like, "She was asking to be raped because her skirt was short," "She is a promiscuous woman as it is," or "She didn't tell him to stop, so that doesn't count as rape." And those who watch television in general (and soap operas) also tend to believe that there are more false accusations of rape than in reality. In other words, such viewers believe women "cry wolf" about rape more so than they actually do. Interestingly, those who watched one to two hours per week, on average, of crime dramas were *less* likely to accept rape myths. And there was no effect of viewing crime dramas on people's estimations of false accusations of rape.[34]

Victim Precipitation

In 1957, Marvin Wolfgang introduced the idea of victim precipitation in his article investigating homicides in Philadelphia. Wolfgang suggested that in at least one-quarter of the homicides he studied, the victim(s) provoked the incident that led to his or her (or their) death.[35] Before Wolfgang, in 1948 von Hentig introduced the criminal-victim dyad, which argued that we need to focus on the dynamic that led to a victimization, including a victim's contribution to the event leading to his or her victimization.[36] Mendelsohn, the father of victimology, provided typologies (or categories) of victims, ranging from the completely innocent to the most guilty victim.[37] Taken together, these ideas suggest that victims are in part responsible for what happens to them. Coupled with the just world hypothesis and rape myths, we are provided with many an opportunity to blame victims, notably female victims, for any sexual violence they experience.

FEMALE-DOMINATED CRIMES

Official Statistics: Females as Perpetrators

In general, it is males (compared to females) who make up a greater number and overall percentage of perpetrators for crimes. The UCR lists the number of male and female offenders of violent and property crimes in 2018 and 2019. The number of male offenders exceeds women for nearly all crimes in both years except for prostitution and commercialized vice, and embezzlement.[38] The NCVS provides additional information on female offenders of violent crime. In 2019, females made up 21 percent of all violent offenders. Female offenders were more likely to perpetrate violent crimes against other females (28 percent) compared to males (14 percent).[39]

Females in Prison

Less than 250,000 women are under correctional supervision in the United States. Approximately 107,000 women are in state and federal prisons, and another 114,000 are incarcerated in jails.[40] A greater percentage of women than men are in state prisons for property (24 percent versus 16 percent) and drug offenses (26 percent versus 13 percent).[41] And while females make up less than 13 percent of the federal prison population, most are incarcerated for drug trafficking, immigration, or fraud offenses. While a smaller percentage of women commit these crimes compared to men, it is nevertheless worth understanding for what crimes females land in prison.[42]

FEMALES IN CRIME DRAMAS

Female Perps

In two of our datasets we looked at female perpetrators. Our first data set includes 169 episodes of television crime dramas (including dramas featuring homicides). In this data set we had complete offender information for 161 episodes. Females were featured as perpetrators in 44 (27.3 percent) episodes. And, of the 44 episodes featuring female perpetrators, 26 (59 percent) episodes portrayed females as co-perpetrators with other male offenders. Eighteen (40.9 percent) episodes featured female-only perpetrators, with 17 (94.4 percent) of these episodes showing a single female perpetrator and one (5.5 percent) showing two female perpetrators.

We further analyzed the 18 episodes featuring female perpetrators only. Because one episode featured two female perpetrators, we have a total of nineteen female perpetrators. Of these perpetrators, 15 (78.9 percent) were White, two (10.5 percent) were Hispanic, one (5.3 percent) was Black, and another one (5.3 percent) was Asian. Most female perpetrators were young adults, with 10 (52.6 percent) in the 19–30 age category and two (10.5 percent) age 18 or younger. Another three (15.8 percent) female perpetrators were in the 31–45 age range and four (21 percent) were in the 46–65 age range. No female perpetrators over age 65 were shown. The crimes committed by female-only perpetrators were: murder (8 episodes), attempted murder (2 episodes), aggravated assault (2 episodes), arson, child pornography, felony murder, insider trading, terrorism, hate crime, child sexual assault, extortion, and theft (all of these crimes were shown in one episode). And, of the television shows viewed, those that displayed female offenders only were: *How to Get Away with Murder, Orange Is the New Black, Castle, CSI: NY, Law & Order: SVU, Psych, Criminals Minds,* and *The Blacklist.*

Our second data set includes aggregate data from 280 hours of television crime dramas. Of these 280 hours, we are missing offender data from only one hour (episode). Here we have frequencies of female perpetrators, but are unable to identify what specific crimes these women committed. A total of 397 perpetrators were identified in all episodes; only 77 (19.4 percent) perpetrators were female. Taken together, our data suggest that females may be slightly overrepresented as perpetrators in crime dramas when compared to the percentage of women who perpetrate violent crime according to the official statistics. And by portraying females as mostly co-perps, crime dramas may be helping to perpetuate the stereotype of females as weak by suggesting they need help from another male offender to complete a crime.

Female Victims

Parrott and Parrott conducted a content analysis of 65 television crime dramas on major networks from 2010 to 2013, including *Blue Bloods*, *Bones*, *Castle*, *NCIS*, *Criminal Minds*, *Lie to Me*, and *The Mentalist*.[43] They found that White women were most likely to be featured as victims in these crime shows, compared to White men, Black men, and Black women. And they were more likely to be victims in crimes of murder and rape, crimes perpetrated by strangers, and crimes resulting in serious physical injury.[44] This is consistent with gender stereotypes that females are the weaker gender, and official statistics that females are more likely to be victims of sex crimes.

Sood and Trielli find, in their content analysis of all *Law & Order: SVU* episodes from 1999 to 2015, that females were underrepresented as victims of rape.[45] While the percentage of female victims of rape in official data is around 90 percent, in *SVU* females were victims in only 60 percent of the episodes analyzed.[46] Britto and colleagues come to the same conclusion in their content analysis of the same crime drama, also adding that most *SVU* victims are White and younger in age (around 18) than their perpetrators, who are typically around their 30s.[47] Returning to the higher percentage of male victims in *SVU*, Britto and colleagues suggest that when males are portrayed as victims of rape at higher rates than what official statistics reflect, we begin to believe that female sex offenders are more prevalent in society.[48]

Law & Order: SVU tends to focus on brutal rapes perpetrated by strangers. This is problematic for two reasons. First, by only portraying rapes in a way that emphasizes physical injuries, the drama fails to acknowledge (in many episodes) the fact that there may be no obvious physical injuries resulting from rape or sexual assault. This can lead viewers to downplay or deny someone who claims to have been raped by has no physical injuries to show for it. Second, most rapes and sexual assaults are committed by someone known to the victim. *SVU* does not portray spousal rape or acquaintance rape (date rape) to the extent it is found in official statistics. Again, this can skew viewers' opinions of what types of incidents count as actual rapes or sexual assaults, and again they may minimize rapes committed by a person previously known to a victim.[49]

Given the above, what *SVU* does depict correctly, as per Britto and colleagues, is the innocence of victims.[50] The question then becomes, does the innocence of victims garner more attention than the overrepresented female sexual offenders in this show? And with female victims still mostly portrayed as victims of sexual assault and rape, is focusing on their innocence enough to reverse or alter the pervasive rape myths and stereotypes of females, and female victims, discussed above? Only time will tell.

RAPE AND SEXUAL ASSAULT IN CRIME DRAMAS

In our own data, of the 169 hours of crime show data collected that identified type(s) of crime and perpetrator and victim demographics, 20 hours of crime shows featured a rape or sexual assault in the episodes. Specifically, the television dramas featuring rape were *Blue Bloods*, *Criminal Minds*, *Law & Order: SVU*, and *Mindhunter* with *Law & Order: SVU* comprising 12 (60 percent) of the hours. In all twenty episodes, males were the perpetrators of the rape or sexual assaults, and females were the victims. Ninety percent of perpetrators and victims were perceived as White; one Hispanic perpetrator and victim, and one Black perpetrator and victim were also featured. Most rape victims were perceived to be in the 19–30 (45 percent) or 31–45 (45 percent) age range. The same applied to perpetrators, with a majority (55 percent) categorized in the 31–45 age range. The victim profile in our subset of crime dramas matches Madriz's ideal victim discussed earlier in the chapter. While our data only contain a small number of episodes, our data overrepresent females as victims compared to official statistics. This begs the question, are crime dramas featuring *more* women as victims of rape and sexual assault to better reflect official data? More research, specifically on more recent crime dramas, is needed to answer this question.

CHAPTER SUMMARY

Women make up the majority of victims of sexual assault, rape, and domestic violence. Traditional gender stereotypes dictate that females are the weaker, more vulnerable gender, so females tend to be more associated with crime victims than men (even though this is largely not the case). As it pertains to crime, females are more likely to be perpetrators in crimes of prostitution and embezzlement, according to official data sources. In our data, females are rarely depicted as offenders in crime dramas. And, when they are, many females are co-offenders with another male.

As it pertains to victims, in our data, females are overrepresented as victims of rape and sexual assault in crime dramas. Feminist perspectives argue that females are victims of sexual and domestic violence because of our patriarchal society. Women are viewed as "less than" men and are portrayed as sexual objects. The just world hypothesis argues that people get what they deserve and deserve what they get. Both the feminist perspectives and just world hypothesis contribute to victim blaming. Victim blaming remains a problem in society. Women are likely to be blamed for rape, for reasons related to their clothing, lack of resistance, not voicing consent, and so on.

NOTES

1. "Crime in the United States 2013." Federal Bureau of Investigation (FBI), 2013, https://ucr.fbi.gov/crime-in-the-u.s/2013/crime-in-the-u.s.-2013/violent-crime/rape.

2. "Rape and Sexual Assault." Bureau of Justice Statistics (BJS), n.d., https://www.bjs.gov/index.cfm?ty=tp&tid=317.

3. MacLin, M. Kimberly, and Vivian Herrera. "The Criminal Stereotype." *North American Journal of Psychology*, vol. 8, no. 2, Jun/Jul 2006, pp. 197–207; Esther I. Madriz, "Images of Criminals and Victims: A Study on Women's Fear and Social Control," *Gender & Society*, vol. 11, no. 3, 1997, pp. 342–356.

4. Reed, John P., and Robin S. Reed. "Status, images, and consequence: Once a criminal always a criminal." *Sociology & Social Research*, vol. 57, no. 4, 1973, pp. 460–472; MacLin and Herrera, "The Criminal Stereotype," p. 200; Madriz, "Images of Criminals and Victims: A Study on Women's Fear and Social Control," p. 342.

5. Howard, Judith A. "The 'Normal' Victim: The Effects of Gender Stereotypes on Reactions to Victims." *Social Psychology Quarterly*, vol. 47, no. 3, 1984, pp. 270–281; Madriz, "Images of Criminals and Victims: A Study on Women's Fear and Social Control," p. 342.

6. Madriz, "Images of Criminals and Victims," p. 342.

7. Rudman, Laurie A., Anthony G. Greenwald, and Debbie E. McGhee. "Implicit Self-Concept and Evaluative Implicit Gender Stereotypes: Self and Ingroup Share Desirable Traits." *Personality and Social Psychology Bulletin*, vol. 27, no. 9, 2001, pp. 1164–1178.

8. Archer, John. "Sex Differences in Aggression in Real-World Settings: A Meta-Analytic Review." *Review of General Psychology*, vol. 8, no. 4, 2004, pp. 291–322; Alice H. Eagly and Valerie J. Steffen. "Gender and Aggressive Behavior: A Meta-Analytic Review of the Social Psychological Literature." *Psychological Bulletin*, vol. 100, no. 3, 1986, pp. 309–330.

9. Simpson, Sally S. "Feminist Theory, Crime, and Justice." *Criminology*, vol. 27, no. 4, 1989, pp. 605–631.

10. Ibid, pp. 611–612.
11. Ibid, p. 612.
12. Ibid, p. 613.
13. Sink, Alexander, and Dana Mastro. "Depictions of Gender on Primetime Television: A Quantitative Content Analysis." *Mass Communication and Society*, 2016, 1–33; Lisa Cuklanz, "Feminist Theory in Communication," *The International Encyclopedia of Communication Theory and Philosophy*. John Wiley & Sons, Inc., 2016.
14. Ibid, p. 5.
15. Ibid, p. 3.
16. Ibid.
17. Ibid, p. 4.
18. Ibid, p. 5.
19. Kahlor, LeeAnn, and Matthew S. Eastin. "Television's Role in the Culture of Violence Towards Women: A Study of Television Viewing and the Cultivation of Rape Myth Acceptance in the United States." *Journal of Broadcasting & Electronic Media*, vol. 55, no. 2, 2011, pp. 215–231.
20. Custers, Kathleen, and Jan Van den Bulck. "The Cultivation of Fear of Sexual Violence in Women: Processes and Moderators of the Relationship between Television and Fear." *Communication Research*, vol. 40, no 1., 2013, pp. 96–124.
21. "NCVS Victimization Analysis Tool (NVAT) Report." Bureau of Justice Statistics, 9 March 2021, https://www.bjs.gov/index.cfm?ty=nvat.
22. Ibid.
23. Morgan, Rachel E., and Jennifer L. Truman. "Criminal Victimization, 2019." Bureau of Justice Statistics, September 2020, https://www.bjs.gov/content/pub/pdf/cv19.pdf.
24. Lerner, Melvin J. "The Belief in a Just World." *The Belief in a Just World*. Springer, 1980, pp. 9–30.
25. Dalbert, Claudia. "Belief in a Just World." *Handbook of Individual Differences in Social Behavior*, edited by Mark R. Leary and Rick H. Hoyle, Guilford Publications, 2013, pp. 288–297.
26. Ibid, p. 292.
27. Ibid, p. 291.
28. Ibid.
29. Furnham, Adrian. "Belief in a Just World: Research Progress over the Past Decade." *Personality and Individual Differences*, vol. 34, 2003, pp. 795–817.
30. Ibid, p. 805; Leif A. Strömwall et al., "Blame Attributions and Rape: Effects of Belief in a Just World and Relationship Level," *Legal and Criminological Psychology*, vol. 18, no. 2, September 2013, pp. 254–261; Rebecca L. Vonderhaar and Dianne Cyr Carmody, "There Are No 'Innocent Victims': The Influence of Just World Beliefs and Prior Victimization on Rape Myth Acceptance," *Journal of Interpersonal Violence*, vol. 30, no. 10, 2014, pp. 1615–1632.
31. Kleinke, Chris L., and Cecilia Meyer. "Evaluation of Rape Victim by Men and Women with High and Low Belief in a Just World." *Psychology of Women*

Quarterly, vol. 14, no. 3, 1990, pp. 343–353; Strömwall et al., "Blame Attributions and Rape," p. 254.

32. Hayes, Rebecca M., et al. "Victim Blaming Others: Rape Myth Acceptance and the Just World Belief." *Feminist Criminology*, vol. 8, no. 3, 2013, pp. 202–220.

33. Ibid, p. 214.

34. Kahlor and Eastin, "Television's Role in the Culture of Violence Towards Women: A Study of Television Viewing and the Cultivation of Rape Myth Acceptance in the United States," p. 227.

35. Wolfgang, Marvin E. "Victim Precipitated Criminal Homicide." *The Journal of Criminal Law, Criminology, and Police Science*, vol. 48, no. 1, May–June 1857, pp. 1–11.

36. von Hentig, Hans. *The Criminal and His Victim: Studies in the Sociobiology of Crime*. Yale University Press, 1948.

37. Mendelsohn, Benjamin. "Victimology and Contemporary Society's Trends." *Victimology*, vol. 1, no. 1., 1976, pp. 8–28.

38. "Table 37: Current Year Over Previous Year Arrest Trends." Federal Bureau of Investigation (FBI), 2020, https://ucr.fbi.gov/crime-in-the-u.s/2019/crime-in-the-u.s-2019/topic-pages/tables/table-37

39. Morgan and Truman, "Criminal Victimization, 2019," p. 19.

40. "Incarcerated Women and Girls." The Sentencing Project, November 2020, https://www.sentencingproject.org/wp-content/uploads/2016/02/Incarcerated-Women-and-Girls.pdf.

41. Ibid.

42. "Quick Facts: Women in the Federal Offender Population." United States Sentencing Commission, 2020, https://www.ussc.gov/sites/default/files/pdf/research-and-publications/quick-facts/Female_Offenders_FY19.pdf.

43. Parrott, Scott, and Caroline Titcomb Parrott. "U.S. Television's 'Mean World' for White Women: The Portrayal of Gender and Race on Fictional Crime Dramas." *Sex Roles*, vol. 73, no. 1–2, s2015, pp. 70–82.

44. Ibid, p. 78.

45. Sood, Gaurav, and Daniel Trielli. "The Face of Crime in Prime Time: Evidence from Law and Order." *SSRN Electronic Journal*, 2017, pp. 1–30.

46. Ibid, p. 14.

47. Britto, Sarah, et al. "Does 'Special' Mean Young, White, and Female? Deconstructing the Meaning of 'Special' in Law & Order: Special Victims Unit." *Journal of Criminal Justice and Popular Culture*, vol. 14, no. 1, 2007, pp. 39–56.

48. Ibid, p. 52.

49. Ibid, p. 51.

50. Ibid.

Chapter 9

Missing Pretty White Girls

Mountain Brook, Alabama is a wealthy suburb just outside of the city of Birmingham. Streets filled with stately homes, well-manicured lawns, and lush foliage wind around a little "downtown" section with expensive restaurants, shops, and beauty spas. Natalee Holloway moved to Mountain Brook with her mother in 2000. Natalee was a member of the National Honor Society and the dance team at Mountain Brook High School, among other extracurricular activities. She graduated in 2005, slated to go to University of Alabama with a full scholarship. She planned to study on a pre-med track in college.

Shortly after graduation, 125 seniors from Mountain Brook High School went on an unofficial graduation trip to Aruba. There were seven "adult" chaperones accompanying the students. Natalee, herself, was technically an adult—she was 18 at the time. Bob Plummer, a teacher and chaperone on the trip, spoke with Fox News's Greta Van Susteran in an in-depth interview. He reported that he saw Natalee on Sunday, May 29th, the day before her disappearance. He told Van Susteran he probably saw her that night at the casino. Van Susteran then asked if Natalee had been drinking (a question that possibly leads to victim-blaming, but that is for another discussion) and Plummer replied that he could not say that for sure and never saw her "drinking a lot" during the entire trip. He recalled that the next day, as the students were assembling to go to the airport, some of them told Plummer that Natalee was missing. They also told him they last saw her in a silver car with some guys. Van Susteran asked Plummer a few questions later, if Natalee had been a trouble maker on the trip. He emphatically answered, "No." He further tried to dispel the rumor that these "kids" were wild and out of control.

Natalee's parents were notified that she was missing.

Plummer's story contradicts that of the Aruban Police Commissioner, Gerold Dompig, who headed the investigation from 2005 through 2006. Dompig told Vanity Fair *that Natalee Holloway had been drinking profusely day and night. Meanwhile, when Beth Twitty—Natalee's mother— was informed that her daughter did not show up for the ride to the airport on time, she feared Natalee has been kidnapped, knowing that Natalee had never been late in her life. Her mother, Beth Twitty, was joined by her husband on a private flight to Aruba later that day.*

Three young men from Aruba—Joran van der Sloot and brothers, Deepak and Saltish Kalpoe—were held for this crime, but eventually released because of lack of evidence. While all three admit to having Natalee in a car with them for at least parts of that evening, they all claimed to have left her alive. Joran van der Sloot significantly changed his story three times. In 2008, allegedly under the influence of marijuana, van der Sloot admitted to killing Natalee. He later retracted that and said he had sold her into sex slavery. He also denied this later. In January of 2012, Joran van der Sloot was convicted of the May 30, 2010 murder of Stephany Flores Ramirez in Lima, Peru—the same day of the year as Natalee Holloway disappeared. As of this writing, Natalee's remains have still not been found.[1]

To illustrate the enormous media frenzy following Holloway's disappearance, a search on imdb.com[2] *shows two full-length movies were made about this incident and at least twenty-two episodes of various television programs, the most recent airing in 2019. According to a 2006 article in* Vanity Fair, *the entire Natalee Holloway story was "very, very good for cable television." Cable news anchor Greta Van Susteran moved to Aruba for the summer and her ratings jumped 60 percent. Holloway's case enabled Rita Cosby to rocket to #1 at MSNBC. Further, "At CNN Headline News, Holloway served to introduce viewers to the frightening former prosecutor Nancy Grace. Not to mention the endless hours of programming by Bill O'Reilly of Fox, and Dan Abrams and Joe Scarborough of MSNBC." Anyone old enough to have gone to a grocery store in the United States could remember seeing pictures of Holloway on countless magazine covers. Finally, there are 38 books on Amazon about Natalee Holloway.*[3]

On December 26, 1996, the body of JonBenét Ramsey was found in the basement of her Boulder, Colorado home. Her death was ruled a homicide by strangulation. She was a former beauty contest winner and she was six years old.

To say this case was a celebrated case is an extreme understatement. While it is true that the death of a "beauty queen" would garner much media attention, this case captured the attention of national and international media for much longer than any "normal" news-cycle. To begin with, people were both enthralled and repelled by the idea of a six-year-old being dressed up and paraded around by her mother. Pictures of the child with highly styled hair and pageant-worthy makeup graced the covers of magazines and newspapers for months. On imdb.com (the Internet Movie Database,[4] which comprehensively lists movie and television credits), JonBenét Ramsey has nineteen credits, but those nineteen include, for example, four individual episodes of the *Dr. Phil* show, but only list that as one credit. She "appeared" on *Entertainment Tonight* six times, *Dateline NBC* twice, *20/20* twice, and there are at least seven documentaries and a TV movie about her. On Amazon, you can find at least 21 books about the death of JonBenét.[5]

MISSING AND WHITE

The syndrome has various names—"missing pretty White girl syndrome" or "missing White woman syndrome"—but the meaning is the same: it refers to the mainstream media's fascination with missing or endangered White woman, while virtually ignoring the cases of missing women of color. PBS news anchor Gwen Ifill is said to have coined the phrase. Social scientists, media scholars, and members of the media themselves use this term to denote extensive media coverage of missing persons which continues the disproportionate focus on White women as violent crime victims.

Researcher Sarah Stillman says that the mainstream media play a vital role in constructing certain endangered young women as "valuable front-page victims," while dismissing others as disposable.[6] Stillman contends that these media messages are powerful and position certain subgroups of women as deserving our collective resources while marginalizing others. She further divides these groups into women who are often "wealthy, white, and conventionally attractive" and "those who may be low-income women of color."[7]

In his article "Missing White Woman Syndrome," Zach Sommers includes the idea that missing men are completely ignored, while women of color are largely ignored. A conference paper called "Missing Pretty Girl Syndrome" calls attention to the "alarming number of people who missing each year . . . who may be Black, Hispanic, and Asian or old, fat, and unattractive," but few of these people will "make it to CNN."[8] The authors of this conference paper contend that White people will not connect to the story, if they do not see themselves as possible victims.

A sharp comparison in coverage occurred in 2004, when a 24-year-old Black woman named Tamika Huston vanished from Spartanburg, South Carolina, one month before the disappearance of Lori Hacking, a 27-year-old White woman from Salt Lake City, Utah. Huston's story received no national news, as opposed to Hacking's story which produced a picture of her within hours of being officially missing.[9] Hacking's disappearance made it to the news show *20/20, E! Investigates,* and spawned a documentary about her husband, who was convicted of her murder. Meanwhile, Huston's aunt, Rebkah Howard, made numerous phone calls to various news outlets, to no avail. One year after Tamika Huston went missing, the story appeared on Fox News's *America's Most Wanted.* After the release of that episode, the national discussion included how "disappeared" Black women did not receive the same media attention as missing White women.

GATEKEEPING AND FRAMING THEORIES

Historically, there have been checkpoints along the process of releasing crime news; the term for the person controlling this was coined the gatekeeper. This concept of the gatekeeper is a key theory in the field of mass communication.[10] All the way back in 1985, John Bittner laid out variables that influence why the gatekeeper chooses certain stories over others.[11] We have listed a few pertinent ones here:

- Economics: now, more than ever, there is usually a profit motive in mass communication outlets.
- Deadlines: in a world of continuously breaking news.
- Ethics: both personal and professional.
- Competition among media: breaking news at breakneck speed.
- News value: the intensity of an item compared to all others available.
- Reaction to feedback: weighing media goals versus public opinion.

Today's number of possible stories appear limitless, as news gatherers' access to them increases, as does the growing number of outlets for dissemination. Social media platforms change the way many people get their news. This makes the function of the gatekeeper more and more complicated[12] and adds to the number of gatekeepers themselves. With social media, however, the gatekeepers are often not professional journalists. All of this adds to the mix.

> Gatekeeping models have become increasingly sophisticated as theorists consider wider ranges of the external pressures on [individual] gatekeepers . . . and the system that employs them. . . . And the theory has gained new interestor at least an upswing in the use of the word "gatekeeping"as the Internet has made it easier for anyone to publish on nearly any topic without the traditional gatekeeping of traditional mass media.[13]

When we consider how the focus of the mainstream media has obviously been centered on young, White, and predominately well-to-do girls or women, we have to consider that the gatekeepers are basing their choices on some combination of the aforementioned list and pressure from their "bosses"—producers, news directors, executive producers.

Frames

Because media and crime are inextricably linked, theories that operate in these fields may also be linked, but viewed through a different prism. Framing theory in media studies suggests that certain aspects of a story are covered, while other aspects are excluded; additionally, they propose an evaluative perspective to readers. What this means is that reporters will focus on certain events, thereby granting those events to be relevant. Media professionals create frames in the context of complex organizations—they pick and choose—but stories never make the air on just a reporter's say-so. All stories must be approved by the producers, news directors, and executive producers who oversee each and every newscast. While the audience at home may believe that reporters are the final gatekeepers, they are indeed, not.

When criminologists speak of frames, they include a bit more of a sociological slant—namely social construction.[14] Criminologist Ray Surette says that in the crime-and-justice arena, frames include factual and interpretive claims and associated policies. Surette further states that frames simplify one's dealing with the world by organizing experiences and events into groups and guiding what are seen as the appropriate policies and actions. So how does this work for the viewer of news? If a crime can quickly be placed into a pre-established frame, the viewer sees it as another example of a certain crime that requires a certain response.

In the "missing White woman syndrome," there is already an established frame. The consumer of news does not need to spend much time trying to understand this crime, because the frame is so familiar. Another criminologist who studies media and crime, Theodore Sasson, contends that there are five long-standing crime-and-justice frames with deep historical roots that still compete today in the United States.[15]

Sasson's Five Crime-and-Justice Frames include:

- Faulty system—crime stems from criminal justice leniency and inefficiency
- Blocked opportunities—crime stems from poverty and inequality
- Social breakdown—crime stems from family and community breakdown
- Racist system—the criminal justice system operates in a racist fashion
- Violent media—crime stems from violence in the mass media

Looking at these five frames carefully, it is hard to see how the "missing White woman syndrome" readily fits into any one of them. It seems that the more logical structure for this syndrome exists in the idea of crime-and-justice narratives. These narratives—also known as scripts—are pre-established, social constructions. Narratives are already accepted by the public. The idea of the female victim is certainly a narrative that existed long before there were radios, televisions, computers, and podcasts.

An aspect of framing theory is the natural corollary that these frames influence crime-and-justice policy. It is, perhaps, in this case that we see the missing pretty girl syndrome having some effect on policy—as witnessed by the names of the laws honoring victims of crime, for example, Megan's Law and Amber Alert. Both of these policies were named after young, murdered White girls. These are called memorial criminal justice policies.[16]

- Megan's Law—Named for Megan Kanka, a 7-year-old New Jersey girl who was raped and murdered by a neighbor. The law requires registration and community notification of sex offenders.
- AMBER Alert—Nine-year-old Amber Hagerman was abducted while riding her bike in Arlington, Texas. A system was made into law in 1999 that created America's Missing Broadcast Emergency Response.
- Laci and Connor's Law—The Unborn Victims of Violence Act of 2004 is nicknamed after a pregnant Laci Peterson was murdered by her husband.

OVERREPRESENTATION OF WHITE PEOPLE

As we noted before, sociologist Zach Sommers published an extensive study in 2016 that provides additional insight into the matter. Whites' disproportionate representation in news coverage cannot be explained by differences in real-world victimization rates.[17] There is evidence that suggests news stories featuring White victims with Black perpetrators receive even more media attention. This goes beyond the category of victim, as discussed in chapter 7, studies show that people of color are far more likely to be shown on the news as the nameless perpetrators of crime. Sommers, however, says that this concept does not necessarily relate to missing people cases. He explains that when someone is missing, there is usually no alleged perpetrator at the outset, therefore, the focus must remain on the victim.

INTERSECTIONALITY OF GENDER AND RACE

It is not news that females have been left out of a substantial amount of criminological research—as both perpetrators and victims. Although predictions that the women's movement and the influx of women into the workforce would lead to women's criminality increasing did not pan out—women reliably commit far less crime than men—they are victimized at almost the same rate.

An obvious reason for a lack of focus on female victimization in criminological research is that the crimes most commonly committed against females are those that so often go unreported—sexual assault and domestic violence. This, however, is where criminological research and media diverge—recent work on crime, media, and gender indicate that women are overrepresented as victims in news coverage.[18]

Sommers states that Missing White Woman Syndrome is by definition an intersectional theory—meaning that it combines two elements of race and gender but also includes class and age. Sommers points out that very little empirical research has focused on this intersectionality and instead, focused on the aspect of race. A compelling theory is the concept of "racial grammar."[19] Bonilla-Silva posits that this racial grammar reinforces White supremacy. This grammar normalizes the standards of White supremacy as the standards for all sort of social events and transactions; this in turn, he suggests, makes it easier for people to identify with White people and therefore, care more about missing White people than people of color.

Let's take this concept into the realm of gender. Not only is Whiteness normalized in society, so is maleness. We call athletes "female basketball players" "or "female tennis players." We call it the "women's soccer team." We differentiate between sports and women's sports. If we continue the premise of Bonilla-Silva that there is a racial grammar, can we not also propose that there is a gendered grammar? If we add that to the equation, we can perhaps understand why missing males are overlooked. Females are considered weaker, more vulnerable, and certainly sexual beings. Researcher Sarah Stillman points to the media taking advantage of this "damsel in distress" trope.[20] The concept of the damsel in distress is so normalized in Western civilization that an audience has little difficulty accepting this idea in a news story. This, of course, reinforces the damsel as victim. Stillman finds this phenomenon especially troubling because of its exploitative nature: "news corporations use the stories of abduction, which are often associated with fears of rape and sexual abuse, to cash in on the victims' bodies."[21]

TROUBLING BREW

Stillman proposes that only a small segment of the population is "qualified" to be declared a damsel in distress. The damsels are usually White, attractive, and wealthy. Her suppositions are, therefore, in agreement with Bonilla-Silva in that "the neglect of other stories about missing persons makes clear that there is a hierarchy in the value of abductees' lives." Sommers says we must go back to the idea of intersectionality to truly understand MWWS. Black women are members of both a marginalized race group and a marginalized gender group. So, White women are subject to sexism but for Black women that is compounded by the effects of racial discrimination. Likewise, Black men are subject to racism but Black women must also face racism with the added burden of sexism. Some researchers insist that the intersection of this marginalization must be considered in the context of media coverage.

Some competing theories on this marginalization:

- The tone of media coverage of Black female victims differs in that these women are more likely to be blamed for purportedly putting themselves in harm's way, either knowingly or unknowingly.[22] Victim blaming in this context suggests that the victims are not only less innocent, but less worthy of rescue. Victim blaming in this case is not limited to Black women, as there was clearly evidence of this with Natalee Holloway, but it would appear that even victim-blaming is part of the intersectional bias.[23]
- Some observers decry the lack of publicity given to Black female victims of police brutality, attributing the silence to a tradition of sexism and patriarchy in both the Black tradition and American society. A prime example of this is the Breonna Taylor case discussed in chapter 3—it took months for protesters in the Black Lives Matter movement to fully embrace the issue of Taylor's death. Acknowledgment of this biased delay led to the concept and then movement, "Say Her Name."[24]
- Researches Bonilla-Silva, Yewkes, and Gilchrist (although not working together) hypothesize that coverage disparities are the result of what—or who—is or is not newsworthy.[25]

SAY HER NAME

In 2020, a year that saw social unrest and a contentious presidential race garner much more media attention than usual because of a global pandemic that kept everyone indoors and glued to television sets, a social movement came to light—#SayHerName. While this movement began in 2015, it never received the kind of attention it desired or deserved. The African American Policy Forum released a report titled "Say Her Name: Resisting Police Brutality against Black Women," which outlined the goals and objectives of the #SayHerName movement.[26] The report provides an analytical framework for understanding Black women's susceptibility to police brutality and state-sanctioned violence, as well as offers some suggestions on how to effectively mobilize various communities and empower them to advocate for racial justice. The #SayHerName movement strives to address the "invisibilization" of Black women within mainstream media and, more specifically, the #BlackLivesMatter movement.[27] Of the movement's many agendas, one includes commemorating the women who have lost their lives due to police brutality and anti-Black violence. To advance this agenda, the AAPF, along with twenty local sponsors and the Center for Intersectionality and Social Policy Studies at Columbia Law School, organized a vigil on May 20, 2015, in New York City, where dozens gathered to demand that the public no longer ignore Black women's struggles against gendered, racialized violence.[28] The #SayHerName movement does not specifically address MWWS, although it can be deduced that if gendered, racialized violence is no longer ignored, this would include missing persons.

This brings us to three more issues: (1) The nature of missing person stories, (2) other women of color, and (3) socio-economic class. We will begin with other missing persons. Most of the empirical research does not include an exhaustive reckoning of ethnic groups. Sommers's study is perhaps the most extensive and quantitatively includes White, Black, Hispanic, and other; although there is a mention of a Canadian study that shows Canadian Aboriginal populations "missing" from their mainstream media.

A QUICK LOOK AT THE MEDIA BREAKDOWN OF SOMMERS'S CATEGORIES—AS COMPARED TO FBI DATA—LOOKS LIKE THIS:[29]

- Black female: 14.32 percent (53)
- Black male: 8.65 percent (32)
- Hispanic female: 5.95 percent (22)
- Hispanic male: 6.49 percent (24)
- Other female: 2.97 percent (11)
- Other male: 1.08 percent (4)
- White female: 32.97 percent (122)
- White male: 27.57 percent (102)

Sommers cautions that FBI data are not broken down into gender and race proportions, so this only indirectly links media overrepresentation to white women. Sommers included four sources in this study—CNN, the *Chicago Tribune*, the *Minnesota Star*, and the *Atlanta Journal-Constitution*. If we parse this study further, we have the findings in table 9.1.

Sommers finds Blacks to be disproportionately underrepresented by a statistically significant margin. He also warns that White women may not be as proportionately overrepresented as these numbers would indicate, because the FBI does not distinguish between Hispanics and Whites in this data set.

MEDIA WHITE OUT

What can we conclude about media coverage of missing White females? It is obviously real. A blog called *Code Switch* on NPR (National Public Radio) ran an article on the syndrome in 2017.[30] What prompted this posting was a recent spate of stories on social media about missing Black and Latina girls that appeared to be ignored by local news in the Washington, D.C. area. The uproar that his instigated on Facebook and Twitter galvanized Black members of Congress to do more to investigate cases of missing Black girls. The author of the blog, Gene Demby, states that his NPR colleague, Ian Stewart, reported no actual spike in missing Black girls, but that with police publicizing missing young women on social media, it gave the impression that there had been an increase.[31]

Although there was no sudden rise in the number of cases, just the idea of media ignoring missing Black girls produced rallies and protests in the D.C. and all the way to southern Virginia, where Old Dominion University students gathered with signs and chants. The memory of extensive coverage of all those missing White women fanned the flames of a group already weary of being marginalized by the media.

Demby looked to the study by Zack Sommers for some answers to the problem. As shown in the boxes above, there is an issue of overrepresentation

Table 9.1. Sommers Findings on Race in the Media

Race	Media	FBI
Black	22.97 percent (85)	35.25 percent (27,797)
Hispanic	12.43 percent (46)	-------------
Other	4.05 percent (15)	4.43 percent (3,489)
White	60.54 percent (224)	60.32 percent (47,560)

Source: Sommers, Zach. "Missing White Woman Syndrome: An Empirical Analysis of Race and Gender Disparities in Online News Coverage of Missing Persons." The *Journal of Criminal Law and Criminology*, vol. 106, no. 2, Spring 2016, pp. 275–314.

of white women who are missing.[32] What Demby does not bring forth from Sommers's 40-page academic article is just how much age and wealth play into this biased coverage. There is no way to tackle this much information in a blog, but Demby interviewed Sommers and made the situation clear.

White women are more likely to be mentioned in the media and women overall are more likely to be mentioned than men. Sommers reported that it is not just the numbers of White female missing cases, it is the intensity of the coverage. Writing a blog for a news organization does bring some knowledge of how news decisions are made and Demby states in his blog that many of these decisions are based on the makeup of the people in the newsroom. The majority of decision-making people in a newsroom tend to be White.

NON-STOP COVERAGE OF MWWS

One of the important points that Sommers makes is that the coverage seems greater—not because they are covering so many missing White female cases, but because they keep covering the same case, over and over again. It is not necessarily the magnitude of the numbers but the intensity that weighs on the psyche of the viewer or reader. Now here's a quick break from the conclusion of this chapter for a little insight *From the Field*.

From the Field: "Balls to the Walls"

Here's a little secret about news organizations—they are extremely cautious. They will not let a story drop if the other news organizations are still covering the same story. It is easy to see how this snowballs into non-stop coverage of one story for what seems to be an interminable amount of time.

I could, perhaps, be biased in this next opinion, but I do not think it's because of the reporters. Reporters absolutely do want to cover a huge story, but they do not want to only cover the same story for a prolonged period of time. For one thing, it becomes hard to keep your writing fresh. But when a big story, a sexy story, an extreme tragedy, or a weather event occurs, it becomes "all hands on deck." The news director will call a meeting for the entire news department. News stations will sometimes rent hotel rooms for reporters nearby the station, so the reporters do not have to go all the way home to sleep. "Team coverage" will go into effect. We call this coverage "balls to the walls." (You can see the gendered nature of this expression, but I have heard many a female news director or assistant news director say it.) This laser-beam focus will remain on the story until it truly no longer has "any legs." Here is where the real caution comes in—after a story is no longer "breaking news," local affiliates and local cable news and even national news, obviously, will keep it going instead of finding something new. How? They will "localize it" or find other aspects to the story. They will "blow it out." This often causes dread in the reporter who is given this assignment. If there is no local connection to the story, how do you localize it? When your boss says localize it or "find another angle," you do it.

So, if for example, there is a young, White, wealthy girl missing in Arizona and you are reporting in New Jersey, you find some connection to New Jersey. Perhaps her aunt lives in Paramus? Perhaps her father, who may be a suspect, spent a summer as a lifeguard at the Jersey Shore? Reporters will climb into the news vehicle with the videographer and get on the phone, doggedly trying to find someone who knows that aunt or worked with that father as a lifeguard.

> The issue here is not when the news organizations will stop covering a story, it is when the viewers will stop watching.
>
> —Beth Adubato

This kind of incessant coverage has two results. One desired result would be that covering the story day after day, on every station and in every newspaper would lead to the safe recovery of the missing person. There is no data that suggests media exposure helps to solve these cases.[33] The second result is not desired and that is the message that White girls' lives matter more than Black girls' lives. Sommers explains "equitable coverage matters even if it's of as-yet-unproven investigative value—media attention shapes how and to whom people extend their sympathies."

Many of the theories reflect and reinforce social hierarchies. Researchers can discuss this and study it and apply learned theories and advanced understanding of human behavior, but the traditions of the newsroom play a large part in decision-making on what is newsworthy. Additionally, the prurient nature of female bodies as a source of news allure is problematic. It is indeed reflective of society, but society also needs to stop tuning in or buying the magazines with the pictures of the young, missing White girls in order for there to be a change.

CHAPTER SUMMARY

Missing and White, missing and young, missing and wealthy—whatever name you choose for this concept, coverage of White females who are missing and believed to be abducted far exceeds coverage of missing Black women or any missing males. This brings us to the next point, who chooses what is considered newsworthy? To answer this, we introduced the concepts of gatekeeping and framing.

Memorial criminal justice policies (for example, Megan's Law) did not necessarily originate as a media construction; in the case of Megan's Law, it originated with grieving parents and grassroots policy changes. When laws are named for crime victims, it makes it easier for the media to deliver the message, by giving the crime a face. Seldom, however, is the face a face of color.

NOTES

1. On the Record with Greta. "Holloway Chaperone Speaks Out." Fox News. 24 February 2006, https://web.archive.org/web/20080423140126/http://www.foxnews.com/story/0,2933,186017,00.html.

2. https://www.imdb.com/find?q=Natalee%20Holloway&s=tt&ref_=fn_al_tt_mr.

3. https://www.amazon.com/s?k=natalee+holloway&i=stripbooks&crid=1GQIFSA17L1G8&sprefix=natalee%2Caps%2C149&ref=nb_sb_ss_ts-doa-p_4_7.

4. Imdb—Jon Benet Ramsey https://www.imdb.com/name/nm2338600/?ref_=fn_al_nm_1 https://smile.amazon.com/s?k=jonbenet+ramsey&i=stripbooks&page=2&qid=1616432054&ref=sr_pg_2.

5. https://smile.amazon.com/s?k=jonbenet+ramsey&i=stripbooks&page=2&qid=1616432054&ref=sr_pg_2.

6. Stillman, Sarah. "'The Missing White Woman Syndrome': Disappeared Women and Media Activism." *Gender and Development*, vol. 15, no. 3, Taylor & Francis, Ltd., pp. 491–502.

7. Ibid.

8. Sommers, Zach. "Missing White Woman Syndrome: An Empirical Analysis of Race and Gender Disparities in Online News Coverage of Missing Persons." *The Journal of Criminal Law and Criminology*, vol. 106, no. 2, Spring 2016, pp. 275–314. https://www.jstor.org/stable/45163263.

9. Burrough, Bryan. "Missing White Female." *Vanity Fair*, November 2006. https://www.vanityfair.com/news/2006/01/natalee200601.

10. Beth Adubato, Nicole M. Sachs, and Donald F. Fizzinoglia (2020). Gatekeepers: Controlling Communication in a Time of Crisis," *Atlantic Journal of Communication*, DOI: 10.1080/15456870.2020.1779724.

11. Tubbs, Stewart and Moss, Sylvia. *Human Communication: Principles and Concepts*, Tenth Edition, McGraw-Hill, New York, 2006.

12. Op cit. Adubato, Sachs, and Fizzinoglia.

13. Roberts, Chris. "Gatekeeping Theory: An Evolution," Communication Theory and Methodology Division, Association for Education and Journalism and Mass Communication, San Antonio, Texas, 2005.

14. Op cit. Surette.

15. Sasson, Theodore. "Crime Talk." Aldine de Gruyter, ed. Hawthorne, NY, 1995.

16. Op cit., Surette, p. 185.

17. Op cit., Sommers, p. 283.

18. Belknap, Joanne. *The Invisible Woman: Gender, Crime, & Justice*, fourth ed. Stamford, CT, Cengage Learning, 2015.

19. Bonilla-Silva, Eduardo. "Feeling Race: Theorizing the Racial Economy of Emotions." *American Sociological Review*, vol. 84, 1, February 2019, pp. 1–25.

20. Op cit., Stillman.

21. Ibid.

22. Op cit., Sommers, p. 23.

23. Bonilla-Silva, Eduaro. "The Invisible Weight of Whiteness: The Racial Grammar of Everyday Life in Contemporary America." *Ethnic and Racial Studies*, 35:2, 173–194, DOI: 10.1080/01419870.2011.613997.

24. "#SayHerName: Black Women And Girls Matter, Too." *The Huffington Post*. Retrieved 2015-10-11.

25. Op cit., Sommers., p. 28.

26. African American Policy Forum. "#SayHerName. Black Women are Killed by Police Too." Retrieved from: https://www.aapf.org/sayhername.

27. Ibid.

28. Ibid.

29. Op cit., Sommers, p. 29.

30. Demby, Gene. "What We Know (and We Don't Know) About Missing White Syndrome." NPR, Code Switch, 13 April 2017, https://www.npr.org/sections/codeswitch/2017/04/13/523769303/what-we-know-and-dont-know-about-missing-white-women-syndrome.

31. Ibid.

32. Ibid.

33. Ibid.

Chapter 10

It's Hard Being a Girl ... Even Harder Being a Girl of Color

OVERSEXUALIZATION OF GIRLS IN THE MEDIA

When six-year-old JonBenét Ramsey was learned to be missing and then found dead within 24 hours, pictures of the little girl began their takeover of American media. One could write an entire treatise on the exploitation of this child (as many have), but it is easy to assess the coverage because it was there for all to see—cover after cover of magazines and newspapers and news programs and eventually books and documentaries and made-for-TV movies. Were the pictures of a little girl playing outside or on a swing or hugging her grandmother? No, they were pictures from professional photoshoots with JonBenét wearing eye makeup and lipstick with quaffed hair and often in suggestive poses. One could argue that this is the parent's fault for oversexualizing this child in the first place, but this is a book about the media. If the desire (at least in the first 24 hours) was to find the missing child, why not post "regular" pictures, pictures that would represent more accurately what the little girl would look like on a normal day? The answer is abundantly clear—sex sells. As abhorrent as the idea of sexualizing a six-year-old is, it is also apparent that this was a major part of the overwhelming media appeal of this story.

Sexualization of young girls in the media is "an ongoing problem in America that's leading to a myriad of problems, from exposing girls to societal pressures to perpetuating sexualized violence."[1] While it is perpetuated, even in our more "enlightened society," it is not, however, a new problem.

HISTORY OF STEREOTYPED BLACK FEMALES

Culturally, Black women and girls took the brunt of this oversexualization in the United States. Initially, the stereotype of the oversexualized African female stemmed from the "lack of clothing" in which they appeared in America.[2] The idea that they were captured and stolen and stowed on slave ships from a hot climate did nothing to stop this belief system that by nature these women were oversexed. An advocacy group in Pennsylvania, known as the Blackburn Center, posits that this history of equating African clothing to a "voracious sexual appetite" was used by slaveowners as part of their justification for rape. Another "proof" that Black women were highly sexualized was that slave women were often pregnant. Considering that raping a slave was not a punishable crime, it is unsurprising that these women were often pregnant. Finally, another sharp contrast between how Black women and White women were perceived is that slaves on the "trading block," both female and male, were often naked or partially naked. In contrast to the "buttoned-up" clothing of white women, this added to the impression of the African nature being inherently sexual. One may wonder how people could have come to these conclusions, but we are talking about a country that endorsed the enslavement of other human beings.[3]

Sociologist K. Sue Jewell says that through the 1980s, there were four categories of which African American women were portrayed—mammy, Aunt Jemima, Sapphire, and Jezebel or the bag girl.[4] Jewell further says that after the 1980s, two practices were introduced: (1) more positive, representative images of Black women alongside an old stereotype and (2) introduce an image that reinforces strength and positive images of a Black woman and then, seek to invalidate these positive images. Jewell's book, *From Mammy to Miss America and Beyond*, was written in 1993 with a second edition published in 2002.[5] Nearly two decades later, the only Black woman serving in the United States Senate was chosen as the running mate for the presumptive Democratic candidate for president. A former attorney general of the state of California—the most populated state in the U.S. by far with 40 million residents—Kamala Harris is of African American and Asian American descent. Obviously accomplished enough to become the A.G. of the largest state and then a member of the U.S. Senate, once she took the national spotlight, the latest in the series of stereotypes of Black women quickly appeared in the media—the trope of the "angry Black woman." [6,7]

IT'S NOT EASY BEING A GIRL AND EVEN HARDER BEING A GIRL OF COLOR

As discussed in chapter 9, there is intersectionality of gender bias and race bias. Added to the mix are class and ethnicity. What it means to be a "good girl" varies within the "intersections" one finds oneself in, but the Venn diagram of cultural influences presents a confusing mix for young women to face.

How are young men judged? The term "lowlife" could be an unfair moniker faced by some young men, but they would never face the "always pregnant" stereotype. If they are not "virgins," nobody cares. If they are out at night and meet with trouble, nobody asks what they were wearing. In the story of Natalee Holloway, you had many people coming out and saying she had been drinking for days, that she was not the "virgin" that her mother claimed her to be. What is the implication of that? Her unvirginal behavior got he abducted and probably murdered. Young Black women face the long-held stereotype of the oversexualized and uncontrollable temptress. As the good, innocent, virginal girl continues to be an idealized image of womanhood associated with white females, it remains largely unattainable for young women of color, who are often characterized as hypersexual, manipulative, violent, and sexually dangerous.

LATINXS IN THE MEDIA

Latinos have historically been cast following stereotypes such as the criminal, the law enforcer, the Latin lover, the Harlot, and the comic/buffoon.[8] Vera Lopez and Meda Chesney-Lind conducted a study in which they asked nineteen "high-risk" Latina girls how they viewed themselves and how "others" perceived them. The girls saw themselves positively, but they believed they were seen as "lowlifes," "cholas," and "always pregnant."[9] The authors point out that young women must often navigate a complicated terrain replete with gendered messages about how they think, feel, and act. Further, they say that stereotypes have real-world implications for Latinas because assumptions about cultural/racial groups often serve as the linchpin for institutional racism.[10]

MEDIA PORTRAYALS

Latinos have been historically underrepresented on television, making up 17 percent of the population but only being cast in 3 percent of primetime television roles.[11] Some of the questions this leads to are:[12]

1. How are they perceived by others in society? Does the stereotype stack the odds against young Latinx job seekers and their career goals?
2. How does it affect the self-esteem of Latinx youth?
3. How are they perceived by law enforcement?

As long as there has been television, Latina women have largely been cast in secondary or nonrecurring roles and what little roles they do have rely heavily on stereotypes.[13] Although this has been the rule, the recent exception has been an increase in Netflix original series which focus on Latina women, such as *Orange Is the New Black* and *Brujas*.

A BRIEF HISTORY OF LATINO PORTRAYALS IN TELEVISION

Much of early television in the 1950s was populated by white actors. As previously mentioned, researchers Dana Mastro and Elizabeth Behm-Morawitz describe in *Latino Representation on Primetime Television* that Latinos are historically cast to follow stereotypes.[14]

- The criminal is a youthful male who is aggressive, dishonest, and unkempt. We can see the criminal cast in various crime dramas as a nonrecurring character, maybe a gang member or a drug dealer. Many shows have highlighted gangs and the involvement of Latinos in them. For example, the portrayal of the Mexican Mafia in Jenji Kohan's *Weeds*, or the cartel of *Breaking Bad*.
- The law enforcer is described as articulate, well-groomed, and respected. We can see police officers and police chiefs cast in this role, particularly David Zayas's role as Angel Batista on the crime drama *Dexter*. Zayas's character is usually seen in a fedora, printed shirt, and slacks; emphasizing his attention to his appearance. Many Latino television police chiefs or others who work at a higher administrative level are portrayed to be very "White," speaking without an accent.
- The Latin lover is similar to the law enforcer in that he is well-kept, but he has an obvious accent, hot temper, and sexual aggression. We see him

in *Weeds* when lead character Nancy marries the head of the Mexican drug cartel, a man who is well-spoken but with an accent, has a fiery temper, and often shows that he is just as aggressive during coitus in the way he handles her.
- The female counterpart to the Latin lover is the Harlot. She is hot-tempered and sexually aggressive as well, but she is dressed provocatively. Sophia Vergara's character in *Modern Family* is a loud and sultry housewife. Vergara is typically dressed in high heels and a low-cut dress or some other provocative outfit. This conveys a very different message compared to Julie Bowen's character, a housewife as well, who is typically dressed modestly in button-up shirts, jeans, and sneakers.
- The comic or buffoon is a comic relief character who lacks intelligence, is lazy, and has a heavy accent. Many shows from the 90s have used this stereotype to characterize maids and other blue and pink collar work, naming Rosario on *Will & Grace*. One of the best examples of this is Esteban, the bellhop from *The Suite Life of Zack and Cody*. On this children's show, a bellhop is characterized by his thick accent and apparent lack of intelligence, constantly made the butt of jokes.

There have been few Latino sitcoms which shed a positive light on the Latino family. The most notable of which is George Lopez's eponymous show, where Lopez plays a factory manager. Lopez himself does not really fit the stereotypes mentioned, as he is portrayed to be a man just trying to make a living. His wife is a stay-at-home mother to their two children and wedding planner who works from home. She is not characterized by what kind of provocative clothing she wears. The series, likely because it was created by a Latino man to be a portrayal of the modern Latino family, has characters whose depth offsets stereotypical traits they exhibit; for example, Lopez's friend Ernesto is child-like and could fit the buffoon stereotype, but his character's development does show growth. Unfortunately, despite its refreshing take on the modern Latino family, *George Lopez* was not afforded the same run as the similarly groundbreaking *Cosby Show*. It was cancelled after airing 120 episodes over five years from 2002 to 2007.[15]

ORANGE IS THE NEW BLACK AND MAYBE THE NEW PARADIGM

Latinas have widely been portrayed as either cops, maids, housewives, or prostitutes on television, seldom being seen in white collar positions. As a whole, Latinos make up 5 percent of television characters and 17 percent of the United States population.[16] This is an increase from the previous to 3 percent and can be evidenced by various shows such as *Brujas*, *Jane the Virgin*, *Queen of the South*, *Cristela*, and *Devious Maids* which have particularly centered around Latina women. *Orange Is the New Black* also has a high representation of Latinas.

Since finishing *Weeds*, Jenji Kohan moved on to produce *Orange Is the New Black* with Netflix in 2013, a show centered around a minimum-security women's prison. While the characters on this series may not be professionals or even proper role models (given that they are offenders and there may be a high possibility of the characters having been guilty at the time of sentencing), the characters have depth. They are not cardboard characters or simply stereotypes.

Though the show's main character is supposed to be Piper Chapman, a white woman, Kohan used her as a kind of Trojan Horse to sell her show to a network. We soon realize it is really more about the other women in the prison than just Chapman.[17] Chapman enters prison with a fiancé who will be eagerly awaiting her release, but over time they fall out of touch, as she ends up pursuing her previous girlfriend who happens to be serving time in the same prison. The upshot of this storyline is that almost all of Piper's family, who figured prominently in the first season, have abandoned her for the most part. This change in the narrative leads to Piper losing much of her significance. Because of this, we get a good look into the lives of many other inmates around Chapman, many of them Black and Latina.

Kohan's characterizations of these women go far beyond stereotypes, giving depth and meaning to their stories. Instead of writing these women off as simply being unintelligent and/or choosing the wrong paths in life, we see them as people, we experience their humanity. We are privy to their backstories. These stories give context and illuminate the social ills that may explain *why* they have committed such crimes. Underlying social ills seldom make it to episodic television. When we meet one of the minor characters, Maria Ruiz, for example, she is far along in her pregnancy. After the birth of her child, we witness Maria's struggle to maintain good behavior and persuade the parole board of her worthiness. The audience feels her dismay every time her parole is postponed or denied. This character's arc represents a storyline that is clearly an advance in Latina portrayal.

THE IMPACT OF TELEVISION ON LATINA ADOLESCENTS

The consumption of television from a young age can leave a lasting impact, positive or negative. Children who grow up seeing heroes and role models on television who don't look like them can internalize this as discouraging them from becoming like these role models. A renegade children's program which breaks the mold, *Dora the Explorer,* portrays a Latina protagonist who empowers her young female audience.

Erin Ryan, professor of communications at Kennesaw State University, posits that children are a unique audience who are vulnerable in the media environment and thus "may fail to understand or process a media message completely."[18] They "often have difficulty putting mediated messages into context, but at the same time display an eagerness to learn that is not seen in adults."[19] *Dora the Explorer* panders to this young audience who function in the preoperational stage of cognitive development by utilizing overt descriptions of physical setting and repetition in dialogue.

Dora was intended to be a show that "broke new ground with a Latina heroine" and "was created within an initiative at Nickelodeon to expand the presence of Latino creators and actors on television."[20] Race and gender in children's programming, according to polls of children, majorly impact them and the message they receive. Children of all races "agreed on three reasons why it was important to see people of their own race on television: it told them that people of their race were important, it made children of that race feel included, and it provided role models."[21] Ryan explains that "due to the lack of diversity on television, children of color who watch a lot of television may have low self-concepts, feel alienated, and become uninterested in participating in activities outside of their communities."

Ryan's compilation of research furthers the theory that children are heavily influenced by media. Thus, underrepresentation of Latinas in children's television alone can have a detrimental impact on their social and emotional development. Just as Black women face the problem of intersectional bias, so, obviously, do other women of color. "Parents are loyal to the program because they see it as being educational for their children," Erynn Masi de Casanova told the *New York Times*.[22] A sociology professor at the University of Cincinnati, Ms. Masi de Casanova has studied how "Dora" and other children's shows depict Latinos. "There are not many girls at the center of a television show. Dora has been a pathbreaker," she said. Dora is not identified as being from a specific country, but as a character who could be from anywhere. "And that means no one is excluded culturally," said Ms. Masi de Casanova.

Television programs targeted toward preteens and young adults are just as impactful and formative. Recent times have seen a diversification of television actors and actresses. However, Latina-led shows remain few and far between, with one of the only notable examples being Disney's *Wizards of Waverly Place*, a show which centers around a Latino family. However, these programs are few and far between. Preteen and teenage Latina-oriented content thus remains underrepresented.

Rita Marie Herron conducted a project that studies the negative influence media can have on Latina adolescents. "Young Latinas may desire to achieve unattainably high standards of beauty if comparing themselves to idealistic portrayals of attractiveness in magazines, movies, on television, and on the internet."[23] She discusses the perception of female beauty as "characterized by young, tall, extremely thin women who have Euro-American features" and explains that this "may cause teen girls in the Latino community to attempt to achieve an unobtainable standard."[24] The pressure to conform to this standard "could lead to body dissatisfaction, depression, anxiety, and eating disorders." While this research applies to beauty standards that affect the mental health of Latina adolescents, it can be used to infer the implications of lacking Latina representation in television on young Latinas' aspirations.

WOKE ADVERTISING AND THE LATINX COMMUNITY

Unlike *Dora*, much of the aforementioned adult-oriented programming does not take initiative to fill the niche of creating positive Latina role models. The past few years, though, have seen a rise in "woke" advertising. These campaigns seek to "commodify the politically correct" in an effort to stand out in the current media landscape.[25] Anomaly, a self-proclaimed change-agent in advertising, is a champion of "woke" advertising that capitalizes on "challenging societal stereotypes and biases."

Rubio looks at the practices of Anomaly through their "Keep Walking" campaign created for Johnnie Walker. By selecting celebrated Latinx spokespeople, and reinterpreting Woody Guthrie's "This Land Is Your Land" into an anthem used to "mobilize Latinx identity and politics tied to immigration," the campaign's messaging is "said to convey the idea of what 'America has been and what America should be,' and that rewards are for people of all colors and creeds."[26]

Woke advertising, while attempting to combat stereotypes, utilizes long-held Latinx tropes and confirms that "these identity configurations are deeply rooted in our media systems even when the pendulum swings in the other direction." Rubio found "metaphors and symbols that relate back to the long-held belief that Latinx immigrants are unable or unwilling to assimilate, as well as the constant grouping of all Latinx into one homogenous group."[27] Imagery mostly contained aspects of Mexican culture, failing to represent other Latinx heritage "and new cultural artifacts of an assimilated men." Further, grouping all immigrants into one group of Mexican men "silences the immigrant experience of other groups such as women, the queer, or those of Caribbean backgrounds who also migrate."[28] While this is a step toward the direction of inclusivity, the failure to truly deviate from long-held media tropes and stereotypes has not made it successful in doing so.

In sum, Latina representation in television has definitely increased and continues to increase. Television shows, however, perpetually fall short in establishing positive role models for young Latinas to look up to and aspire to be like. Woke advertising, while noble in its intentions, attempts to capitalize on political correctness as opposed to attempting to create content that addresses underrepresentation and the dearth of role models.

STUDY

We conducted an anonymous, online survey and asked respondents in what careers they saw Latina women portrayed on television, how common they believed representation to be, and their opinions on how representation impacts Latina youth. Our sample of 179 participants included 61 males, 114 females, and 3 non-identifying. The majority of our respondents were between the ages of 18 and 24 (N=115). We are not going to show all of the responses from our survey, but here are two tables of interest to Latina representation in media.

For table 10.1, we asked: Of the television and movies you've watched, do you recall seeing Latina women in any of the following careers? (select all that apply) We provided participants with the possible careers, and they checked the box if they recalled a Latina woman in one or more of the careers. We then summed the number of participants who checked each career box; frequencies are listed next to the careers in table 10.1.

As can be seen above, participants recalled seeing Latina women in the following top five careers on television or in movies: criminal, celebrity, housewife, maid, dancer. In table 10.2, we compare these top five careers in movies and TV to *actual* careers of Latina women, as reported in the 2014 American Community Survey, in order from the top career (1) to the fifth most frequent career (5).

The obvious problem from these two particular tables is that the most prominent portrayal of Latina women, at least in the experience of our respondents, was that of criminal.

Table 10.1 Portrayals of Latina Women in the Media and Their Impact on Latina Youths

Career	
Celebrity	97
Criminal	101
Dancer	78
Doctor	39
Firefighter	21
Housewife	85
Lawyer	58
Law Enforcement Officer (Police, Detective, FBI, Etc.)	74
Maid/Housekeeper	80
Model	73
Musician	46
News Anchor/Weather Reporter	28
Nurse	54
Politician (Governor, Senator, Mayor, etc.)	33
Aprostitute	60
Secretary	44
School Teacher	55
Other	11
Total:	1037

Source: Study by Leanna Hernandez

POWER OF THE PURSE

Legislating equality seems to be a slow process in this country—change is incremental and not everyone agrees on what is right. While criminal justice reform may look different in different states and different regions of the country, the movement itself must have a public policy dimension for it to be legal, for it to work. When (and if, because not all media is created equal) various forms of media continue to stereotype or misrepresent in the form of gender bias or racial and ethnic bias or sexual orientation bias or class bias, we can make a difference. We can boycott the offending shows or news programs.

Table 10.2 Comparison of Top 5 Portrayed Occupations to Actual American Community Survey Statistics

	Portrayed Occupation	American Community Survey, 2014
(1)	Criminal	Maids and Housekeeping Cleaners
(2)	Celebrity	Cashiers
(3)	Housewife	Secretaries and Administrative Assistants
(4)	Maid	Retail Salespersons
(5)	Dancer	Janitors and Building Cleaners

Source: CEPR analysis of American Community Survey, 2014. Retrieved from: https://www.census.gov/acs/www/data/data-tables-and-tools/data-profiles/2014/

Television shows feature mostly males working in positions of power in the criminal justice system, which does, in fact, reflect reality. More programming that inspires young girls—especially little girls of color—can only be a positive for society.

As far as news coverage, when White women are stereotyped simply as vulnerable victims, Black women are angry, and Hispanic, Asian American Pacific Islanders, and Native American women are not even on the radar, we may see real demand for equal coverage. The crossroad where media and the criminal justice meet is garnering new attention and the time may be here for meaningful change. The complexion and gender of the United States Congress has changed considerably in just one generation, giving many possible paths to this change. While real policy change is often slow, corporations often react quickly when their bottom lines are affected. Women may not earn as much as men in the United States, but they certainly earn far more than when television first entered our living rooms.

CHAPTER SUMMARY

Following our chapter about "missing, pretty White girl syndrome," we delve into the issue of oversexualization of women and girls in the media. In the case of oversexualizing females, the focus is not merely on White women; indeed, the focus takes a different turn and we examine the degradation of women and girls of color. Again, the storytelling or media reporting often falls back on demeaning stereotypes of Black and Latina women. New research includes a study on the impact of portrayals of Latinas in film and television.

What can be done to change this oversexualization of women? While legislating behavior of large media conglomerates may prove difficult and time-consuming, another way for women—and their forward-thinking brethren—to take a stand against this is "hitting them where it hurts," their bottom lines. The power of the purse is so much sweeter when it is a literal purse.

NOTES

1. Sheppard, S. (n.d.). "How Sexualizing Young Girls May Lead to Mental Health Problems." Retrieved November 02, 2020, from https://www.verywellmind.com/damaging-effects-of-sexualizing-girls-4778062.

2. Center, B. (2019, February 20). The Historical Roots of the Sexualization of Black Women and Girls. Retrieved November 02, 2020, from https://www.blackburncenter.org/post/2019/02/20/the-historical-roots-of-the-sexualization-of-black-women-and-girls.

3. Jewell, K. Sue. *From Mammy to Miss America and Beyond: Cultural Images and the Shaping of U.S. Social Policy.* Taylor & Francis, 1992. https://ebookcentral-proquest-com.proxy.libraries.rutgers.edu/lib/rutgers-ebooks/detail.action?docID=179834.

4. Ibid., p. 36.

5. Angry Black Women—MSNBC. Retrieved from: https://www.msnbc.com/the-sunday-show/watch/michelle-obama-meghan-markle-vice-president-kamala-harris-wrongly-called-angry-black-women-102238789563.

6. Clifton, Derrick. "Trump Deploys Angry Black Woman Trope Against Kamala Harris." NBC News, 17 August 2020, https://www.nbcnews.com/news/nbcblk/trump-deploys-angry-black-woman-trope-against-kamala-harris-n1236975.

7. Mastro, Dana and Elizabeth Behm-Morawitz, E. "Latino Representation on Primetime Television." *Journalism & Mass Communication Quarterly*, 82(1), 110–130. 2005 doi:10.1177/107769900508200108.

8. Lopez, Vera and Meda Chesney-Lind. "Latina Girls Speak Out: Stereotypes, Gender and Relationship Dynamics." *Latino Studies* Vol. 12, 4, 527–549 Retrieved from: https://www.researchgate.net/profile/Vera-Lopez/publication/269285914_Latina_Girls_Speak_Out_Stereotypes_Gender_and_Relationship_Dynamics/links/5bfee73792851c63caafb2cb/Latina-Girls-Speak-Out-Stereotypes-Gender-and-Relationship-Dynamics.pdf.

9. Ibid.

10. Ibid.

11. Ibid.

12. Op cit., Lopez and Chesney-Lind.

13. Ibid.

14. Ibid.

15. Ibid.

16. Haynes, Michael, "Latino Stereotypes in Television." 2018 Symposium. 31. https://dc.ewu.edu/scrw_2018/31.

17. O'Sullivan, S. "Who Is Always Already Criminalized? An Intersectional Analysis of Criminality on Orange Is the New Black." *The Journal of American Culture*, 39(4), 2016, 401–412. doi:10.1111/jacc.12637.

18. Ryan, Erin. "Dora the Explorer: Empowering Preschoolers, Girls, and Latinas." *Journal of Broadcasting & Electronic Media*, 54(1), 2010, pp. 54–68.

19. Ibid.

20. Ibid.

21. Ibid.

22. Olsen, Elizabeth. "'Dora' Special Explores Influence on Children." *The New York Times*, 8 August 2010, Retrieved from: https://www.nytimes.com/2010/08/09/business/media/09dora.html?searchResultPosition=1.

23. Herron, R. M. (2013). Media impact on the mental health of Latina adolescents in America (Order No. 1545168). Available from ProQuest Dissertations & Theses Global. (1442593002).

24. Ibid.

25. Ibid.

26. Rubio, Solange. "This Land: A Media Analysis of Latinx Representation in 'Woke' Advertising. Media and Communication Studies: Culture Collaborative Media, and the Creative Industries, 2018.
27. Ibid.
28. Ibid.

Chapter 11

Good Cops, Bad Cops, Dirty Cops, and Mad Cops

Five Hollywood Films

"The Movies" have formed a powerful force with respect to public opinion, and films about law enforcement are no different. What is different has perhaps been the changing nature of the industry's attitude about the police, which first took shape over a hundred years ago, when slapstick humor by Mack Sennett's Keystone Cops and Charlie Chaplin riled the police enough to get it censored. Later, the self-censorship of the Hollywood Production Code of the Studio System forced it to respect the heroes of law enforcement until all this changed when the "New Hollywood" era of the 1960s and 1970s allowed film makers to count on few restrictions in an (almost) anything goes mentality.

There's a jagged line that points from the early films about the police to today, where attitudes about real life policing are being challenged by the Black Lives Matter Movement, stemming from the high-profile police killing of George Floyd and other incidents that came before.

The Michael Brown (Ferguson, Missouri), John Crawford (Beavercreek, Ohio), Walter Scott (North Charleston, South Carolina), Tamir Rice (Cleveland, Ohio), and Freddie Gray (Baltimore, Maryland) incidents, as well as many others, provoke discussion about police response and when deadly force is appropriate, given the demands on law enforcement. A quieter but no less important element of that discussion is related to the nation's preconceived notions of cops—who often are the most common public administrator with whom citizens interact—and where those perceptions might originate.[1]

Protests and calls for radical changes in policing and an acknowledgment of institutional racism have become the subject of the ultimate populist film making: footage of police action from smart phone cameras and police body cams, the flipside of the Hollywood productions we will be discussing here.

COPS AND MOVIES

In 1910, the International Association of Chiefs of Police adopted a resolution condemning the movie business because, as the organization's president put it, "the police are sometimes made to appear ridiculous."[2]

Early comedy creator Mack Sennett and his Keystone Studios were popular for their slapstick comedies that made fun of the police with pie-throwing, cross-eyed, clumsy, inept chases, with the Keystone Cops falling all over themselves to gales of laughter from the lower-class audiences at the nickelodeons, makeshift storefront theaters that cost 5 or 10 cents admission.

In the early days, movies were considered an industry that needed to be at least contained, and the PR problems they might create needed to be completely controlled by those parties most interested in public appearances, such as the police or politicians.

In 1908, New York Mayor George McClellan Jr. used police power to close every movie theater in the city. To prove they could manage themselves, theater owners and movie distributors founded what eventually became known as the National Board of Review of Motion Pictures, which examined movies for objectionable content and suggested cuts that directors should make before films reached the public.[3]

Chicago was first to enact a film censorship ordinance, authorizing its police chief to screen all films to determine whether they should be permitted on screens. Detroit and other cities followed and Pennsylvania became the first to enact state-wide censorship of movies followed by Ohio (1914), Kansas (1915), Maryland (1916), New York (1921), and Virginia (1922). Eventually, at least one hundred cities across the nation empowered local censorship boards.[4]

Statistics at the time show that the number of nickelodeons in the United States doubled between 1907 and 1908 to around 8,000, and it was estimated that by 1910 as many as 26 million Americans visited these theaters weekly.[5]

Movies were obviously making an impression on the lower-class men and women who attended these silent films, whether they were working class citizens or immigrants who didn't need to speak the language to laugh at the Keystone Cops.

Five years later, the Supreme Court ruled in *Mutual Film Corporation v. Industrial Commission of Ohio* that a 1913 state censorship statute did not infringe on either free speech or interstate commerce. Movies weren't independent arguments worthy of First Amendment protection, Associate Justice Joseph McKenna wrote in the court's decision, but rather "mere representations of events, of ideas and sentiments ... vivid, useful, and entertaining, no doubt, but . . . capable of evil." It would take 37 years for the Supreme Court to reverse itself.⁶

Outside of issues of censorship by the police, Hollywood in the 1920s began to realize that the police could be viewed as an ally, if not a necessary partner. Seen as a proverbial den of iniquity by religious groups, politicians and the press of the period, Hollywood needed to keep stories of its stars' parties and peccadillos from being publicized, and the Los Angeles Police Department could be counted on for a cover-up of crimes and embarrassing episodes of decadence.

Starting with a spate of celebrated trials of the popular star, Roscoe "Fatty" Arbuckle, accused of rape and manslaughter, followed by other high-profile scandals of sex, drugs, and tax evasion, the accelerating financial and popular success of the movie industry of the time was in danger of being derailed by public criticism and potential boycotts. Montana senator Henry Myers excoriated Hollywood's "debauchery, riotous living, drunkenness, ribaldry." The *Baltimore Sun* decried the "orgies of [the] film colony." "LAPD historian Joe Domanick wrote [that] cooperation between the movie business and police ensured discretion for 'carousing wild men like Errol Flynn and homosexual stars.'"⁷ These factors, along with the ability of the police to smooth over potential logistical problems of production, made it likely that the two entities—the motion picture industry and the police—would find a common ground of cooperation for their common good.

CLEAN-UP TIME: ENTER THE HAYS CODE, THE PRE-CODE ERA, AND THE MPA PRODUCTION CODE

In 1922, the film industry formed the Motion Picture Producers and Distributors of America (MPPDA) with former Postmaster General Will Hayes as its first president. This was a trade organization with the purpose of creating good public relations so as to maintain interest from Wall Street investors and not inflame the public. Hays was hired to suggest voluntary "Dos and Don'ts" to avoid the industry being seen as immoral and to forestall the threat of outside censorship. By 1930, it became clear that this wasn't working and the MPPDA came up with the Production Code, also known as the Hayes Code, consisting of moral guidelines about what could and could not be portrayed on film. Because these restrictions were not binding, producers, anxious to stay ahead of the Depression, often broke the rules, giving rise to this paradoxically being known as the "Pre-Code Era," from 1930 to 1934.

In 1933 and 1934, the Catholic Legion of Decency, along with a number of Protestant and women's groups, launched plans to boycott films that they deemed immoral.⁸

In order to avert boycotts which might further harm the profitability of the film industry, the MPPDA created a new department, the Production Code Administration (PCA), with Joseph Breen as its head. Unlike previous attempts at self-censorship, PCA decisions were binding—no film could be exhibited in an American theater without a stamp of approval from the PCA, and any producer attempting to do so faced a fine of $25,000. After ten years of unsuccessful voluntary codes and expanding local censorship boards, the studio approved and agreed to enforce the codes, and the nationwide "Production Code" was enforced starting on July 1, 1934.[9]

This was now an institutionalized act of self-censorship. Virtually all of the Hollywood studios adhered to this code until the Studio System itself was weakened by anti-trust decisions of the Supreme Court and the Code was repeatedly challenged by film makers in the 1950s and early 1960s. By 1968, the ratings system, with which we're familiar today, came into being to replace it.

Besides the strictures involving sex, nudity or illicit behavior, crime, criminal behavior, and by association, police action was also relevant. Thus, movies would put the police in the enviable position of always being on the right side of the law, heroes in the fight against crime. Most of the movies were in black and white, and so were the unambiguous views by the public of who was good (the police) and who was evil (the criminals).

"There are eight million stories in the Naked City. This has been one of them."

While the gangster genre dominated 1930s crime dramas (where in the end, the bad guys necessarily ended up lying dead in the gutter, usually in the rain, their spats splattered with mud—the code wouldn't allow anything gory as blood), they were followed by films of crime-fighting federal agents or the wisecracking private detectives of 1940s *film noir*. It was not until the late 1940s that competent municipal officers began to take center stage in a sub-genre of *film noir*-style crime dramas known as the police procedural.

A hero too, albeit more complex, is the short Irish detective of the Naked City, who believes in God and consecrates his nights to the triumph of justice. An edifying film, the American police documentary is, in fact, a documentary to the glory of the police.[10]

Considered the first of these police procedurals was Jules Dassin's *Naked City* (1948), in which a competent and professional police officer appeared in the lead role. He and his neophyte partner are depicted using "realistic" police procedures to solve a murder case. This began a new genre of films based on investigative procedure and which was lauded by many real-life cops across the country.[11]

In the middle of the night, while the majority of New York City sleeps, ex-model Jean Dexter dies in her apartment and is found the next morning by her housekeeper. Homicide detective Lt. Dean Muldoon (Barry Fitzgerald) and his partner, Detective Jimmy Halloran (Don Taylor), are called in to solve the case. In searching every inch of her apartment, interviewing suspects, and walking the streets of New York, a simple suicide by drowning is quickly revealed to be the tip of a larger series of crimes, a series of crimes that could happen to anyone, anywhere, at almost any time.[12]

This isn't Hollywood glamour or stunning heroism on display, but two policemen doing their jobs in the city—the REAL city—where an old hand of an Irish cop is at work, step by step, using the grisly murder of an ex-model to show a young, future old hand how to walk every street, talk to every face, "ask a thousand questions to get one answer," and follow every lead, everywhere in New York City. Unlike the vast majority of Hollywood movies of that era, this one wasn't shot on a sound stage or back lot in Hollywood—it actually uses the real city as the "set"—so much so that the city and its denizens almost become one of the characters.

In order to make it feel so intimate, Dassin embraces the style of contemporary Italian neorealists like Roberto Rossellini and Vittorio De Sica, resulting in a film which feels less like a staged film and more like a documentary by using real locations and real citizens of New York City amid the actors' performances. With the city entirely as the backdrop, the Naked City transforms from traditional crime drama into something more alive and unpredictable.[13]

Naked City became the blueprint for not only a slew of police procedurals in the movie world but also spawned all manner of TV police shows from *Hawaii Five-0* to *Blue Bloods* to *Hill Street Blues* to *The Mod Squad*, and many others—but first and foremost Jack Webb's *Dragnet* (1951), which, like *Naked City*, relied heavily on the cooperation of the real police, which is noted in the ending credits of *Naked City*, thanking the NYPD.

1967

It is no secret that movies and TV shows have historically presented American policing in a broadly positive light, by accident or design. Hollywood has done much to promote the good deeds of law enforcement, but in failing to critically assess its failings, they could find themselves complicit in a whitewash.

By the civil rights era, Hollywood was at least going through the motions of acknowledging police racism.[14] In 1967, when Hollywood was palpably shifting away from the past and into what was termed "New Hollywood," the country was aflame with riots and unrest, much of it the byproduct of calls for action to correct the racism that was born of slavery and continued to live on as Jim Crow policies of discrimination and violence against Blacks.

During the summer of 1967, the United States continued to burn. Streets stewed with riots, protests, and violence. That July in Detroit and Newark, police beat, tortured, and murdered black bodies in the hundreds.

The promises of the Civil Rights Act of 1964 were repeatedly frustrated. Institutionalized racism persisted, as it continues to do today. In the South, and especially in Mississippi, change was met with vicious hostility. Stained with the blood of countless lynchings—including the 1955 murder of Emmett Till, the assassination of Medgar Evers in 1963, and the murder of three civil rights workers in the so-called Freedom Summer of 1964—Mississippi was the site of ongoing racial terrorism. *In the Heat of the Night* rises from this horror, and the ghosts of the dead follow Tibbs around town.[15]

Here was a film that framed the two lead characters as policemen representing the two sides of the conflict: Rod Steiger, winning the Best Actor Oscar that year, as the police chief filled with racial bigotry and Sidney Poitier, the first Black man to play a police detective in a Hollywood picture, as Virgil Tibbs, at first caught up as a suspect in the murder of a white man when he's found waiting for a connecting train—while Black—after visiting his mother. When the dignified Tibbs's skills as a homicide investigator are forced on the two of them by superiors to help solve the crime, neither is happy.

The mechanics of the thriller are less important than the attempt to confront the reality of a divided nation and an acknowledgment that the two policemen, Poitier's Detective Tibbs and Steiger's Chief Gillespie could represent movement in the right direction, as difficult as that might be to pull off.

In the Heat of the Night is not a "historical fiction" so much as an urgent product of its time. Producer Walter Mirisch has recounted United Artists' concerns about whether the film would lead to riots.[16] When production moved from Illinois to Tennessee for just a few days, the cast and crew were regularly harassed; Poitier was so unnerved he slept with a gun under his pillow.[17]

In the end, with the two opposing policemen solving the murder together, and the bigoted police chief perhaps learning something about race, liberal audiences could feel better about themselves and the situation on the streets, even if temporarily. The film won the Academy Award for Best Picture, over New Hollywood icons, *Bonnie and Clyde*, *The Graduate*, and *Guess Who's Coming to Dinner.*

PEOPLE NEED HEROES

By the 1950s, the romanticized version of the cowboy rode into the sunset as western mythology gave way to east-coast reality. Naked City replaced Cheyenne, and the street cop was the new cultural hero. The myth of the incorruptible lawman persisted until policing scandals started multiplying. The age of innocence was over with the Kennedy and King assassinations and the Vietnam War, so that after Watergate in 1972, people would believe anything about corruption in all walks of life. The 70s brought a seismic change to the way American films were made, and the sensibilities of the film-makers ushered in the era of the antihero.[18] (William Friedkin, Director, The French Connection)

After the all the painful "revolutions" that took place in the 1960s were replaced by scandals and moral ambiguity, film makers like William Friedkin (*The French Connection,* 1971) and Don Siegal (*Dirty Harry,* 1971), recognized that the old order in Hollywood—and the country—had changed, and that a Production Code, whether instituted for cynical or moral purposes, was no more. The days when police were portrayed simply as heroes were over, perhaps replaced by a knowing wink to the truth behind the moral ambiguity.

Those of us who made films in the 70s were not following the zeitgeist: we shaped it. We no longer believed in a man on a white horse. We knew he was flawed because we were flawed. Dirty Harry would shoot a suspect in cold blood and audiences would applaud. When Popeye Doyle shot the French hitman in the back in my film The French Connection, audiences around America stood and cheered. When Doyle used the "N" word, African-American audiences laughed because they recognized it as a true portrayal of police attitudes.[19] (William Friedkin, Director, The French Connection.)

Both 1971 films were big box office hits, and both have been seen as the reaction to the Miranda Rights–loving, "societal, political and racial rebellion of the 1960s, as course correctors to a fractured, permissive liberal society. They reassured white audiences by embodying what critic and film historian J. Hoberman called the "Legal Vigilante" archetype, in his excellent books *The Dream Life* and *Make My Day*, exploring 1960s, 1970s, and 1980s filmmaking and politics.

Dirty Harry, Hoberman wrote, arrived as "the antidote to the permissive Sixties and Lyndon Johnson's Great Society. Harry embodied (Nixon's) promise to restore Law and Order . . . his enemies were the black militants, hippie crazies, loose women and bleeding-heart liberals." [20]

WAIT . . . WHAT?!

Training Day is an equal-opportunity police brutality picture, depicting a modern Los Angeles in which the black cop is slimier and more corrupt than anybody ever thought the white cops were. Alonzo Harris, played by Denzel Washington, makes Popeye Doyle look like Officer Friendly. So extreme is his mad dog behavior, indeed, that it shades over into humor: Washington seems to enjoy a performance that's over the top and down the other side.[21]

What to make of *Training Day* (2001), which finds the great actor Denzel Washington playing "the meanest, baddest narcotics cop in the city" of LA, tasked with showing his white rookie sidekick (played by Ethan Hawke) just how to be properly corrupt, violent, and perhaps effective on South Central's mean streets? "His pose is that the job must be done this way: If you don't intimidate the street, it will kill you" (Ebert). Is this an extreme subversion of the white cop antihero trope which allows that "the end justifies the means" excessively because his superiors or the politicians or the courts or society writ large will only be in his way, blocking him from defeating evil, and the only way to do right is to do wrong? Or perhaps it's a send-up, a parody of the antihero cop trope, using today's most talented and beloved Black actor, Denzel Washington, as Sidney Poitier's twisted doppelganger to create a Black Dirty Harry/Popeye Doyle character?

Still, trashy and opportunistic as some of it is, *Training Day* is the most vital police drama since *The French Connection* or *Serpico*.

The Sidney Lumet movies about the police—*Serpico*, *Prince of the City*, and *Q & A*—dealt with corrupt white cops. Ayer and Fuqua, in making their rogue cop a brilliant African American, exploit the speed, verve, and knowingness of the black street idiom while pushing past liberal pieties about race. Alonzo is a powerfully ambiguous figure emerging from a chaotic ghetto culture; he's so relaxed on the streets that he's a hero of sorts, even to the people he frightens. The young white guy is doubly out of it, not just because of his race but because he expects the world to make sense morally, and his moral instructor turns out to be Dirty Harry (though much more conscious and treacherous than Harry ever was).[22]

This film's opening was delayed two weeks because of the terrorist attacks of 9/11. Roger Ebert, in a footnote of his review, asked, "Will audiences accept this movie in the current climate, when cops and firemen are hailed as heroes? I think maybe so; I think by delaying the movie's opening two weeks, Warner Bros. sidestepped a potential backlash. And Denzel's performance is sure to generate strong word-of-mouth. Second question: It's been asked if violent movies will become rare in these sad days after the terrorism. The box-office performance of 'Training Day' may provide the answer."[23]

Answers: The film's box office of $76 million domestically and $104 million worldwide after a budget of $45 million is a success.[24]

Violence in movies rare after this? No.

In conclusion, the treatment of police in film has, since the beginnings of cinema, fluctuated with cycles of positive and negative representation.

Early on, the slapstick comedies featuring the Keystone Kops or Charlie Chaplin presented incompetent policemen as objects of ridicule.

During the period of the Production Code (1934–68), movies censored themselves, never presenting authority, especially the police, in a negative light. The police procedural, like *Naked City* (1948), which presented the most realistic attempt to entertain by showing competent police at work, spawned numerous films and a seemingly endless supply of television series.

When the Production Code constraints were over, followed by the election of the "law and order" President Nixon in 1968, movies seemed to rebound from the liberalism of the 1960s, and a bevy of hard right 1970s films saw antihero cops personify both the horrific and the heroic, sometimes at the same time. We got both the trigger-happy "Dirty Harry" and the violent and plainly racist antihero of *The French Connection*, in 1971.

What's come later is a generation of movies where an antihero rogue cop will do whatever he thinks necessary, whether it's his boss or a politician or societal norms of decency that try to apply restraints, he's going to do whatever he has to, mayhem be damned.

The future, of course, is not here yet. Representations of police on television in series TV and on long-form limited streaming series are plentiful and seem to have no end.

For movies, there will always be a genre that follows the police (although there seems to be a shift toward mostly comic book superhero "cops").

We'll have to see if there's an edge to the movie-going public's view of law enforcement and how current events, particularly regarding race, will shape its attitudes going forward when it comes to police on film.

CHAPTER SUMMARY

In this chapter, we highlight five films to help exemplify shifting public opinion toward the police, focusing on the changes in style and especially restrictions to movie content as they impact the public's attitudes toward law enforcement entities. Starting with the earliest, silent films, often slapstick comedies that made fun of the police, we noted that the police themselves censored them to maintain the public's respect; on to the period of Hollywood's self-censorship (1934–1968), where the Production Code restricted depicting the police in a negative light and framed law enforcement characters as spotless "heroes." A sub-genre of *film noir*, the "police procedural" was highlighted next, where in the late 1940s, a more "realistic" depiction included the detailed and thorough day-to-day activities of police at work solving crimes and resulting in a rash of movies and especially television shows representing this feeling of watching "real" law enforcement members doing their jobs. In the 1960s, racial issues and police actions became a topic of interest for Hollywood, as the civil rights movement and the end of the Production Code could bring into focus the clashes between traditional police action and the systemic racism many feel still exist. The film we chose to highlight was produced in 1967, a turning point year for Hollywood, racial unrest and society writ large. *In the Heat of the Night* grasped both the racism inherent in some law enforcement communities as well as an optimism that individual connections could bring positive changes to problems of police and race. Finally, we highlight the rise of vigilantism and the anti-hero cop that takes this optimism of the late 1960s, coupled with an almost restriction-free Hollywood, and turns it on its head.

NOTES

1. Pautz, Michelle C., doi:10.1017/S1049096516000159 © American Political Science Association, 2016.
2. Rosenberg, Alyssa, "How Police Censorship Shaped Hollywood." https://www.washingtonpost.com/sf/opinions/2016/10/24/how-police-censorship-shaped-hollywood/).
3. Ibid.
4. Wittern-Keller, Laura. *Freedom of the Screen: Legal Challenges to State Film Censorship*, University Press of Kentucky, 2008.
5. Bowser, Eileen. *The Transformation of Cinema, 1907–1915*. Berkeley: University of California Press. pp. 4–6.
6. Op cit., Rosenberg,
7. Ibid.
8. Bernstein, Matthew. *Controlling Hollywood: Censorship and Regulation in the Studio Era*, Continuum International Publishing Group. ISBN 0813527074.
9. Bernstein, Matthew. *Controlling Hollywood: Censorship and Regulation in the Studio Era*, Continuum International Publishing Group. ISBN 0813527074.
10. Black, Gregory D. *Hollywood Censored: Morality Codes, Catholics and the Movies*. Cambridge University Press. ISBN 0521565928.
11. Borde and Chaumeton. *A Panorama of American Film Noir (1941–1953)*, p. 7.
12. Reiner, R. "The New Blue Films." *New Society*, 43 p.708 (March).
13. Douglas Davidson, https://elementsofmadness.com/2020/09/07/the-naked-city/.
14. Ibid.
15. Rose, Steve, "How Hollywood Has Tried, and Mostly Failed, to Tackle Police Racism." https://www.theguardian.com/culture/2020/jun/08/how-hollywood-has-tried-and-mostly-failed-to-tackle-police-racism.
16. Di Mattia, Joanna, https://www.sensesofcinema.com/2017/1967/in-the-heat-of-the-night/.
17. Hoad, Phil, "How We Made In the Heat of the Night," *The Guardian* (November 22, 2016). https://www.theguardian.com/film/2016/nov/22/how-we-made-in-the-heat-of-the-night-norman-jewison.
18. Harris, Mark. *Pictures at a Revolution: Five Movies and the Birth of the New Hollywood* (New York, Penguin Press, 2008), p. 225.

19. Friedkin, William. "We're All Popeye Doyle Now." https://www.theguardian.com/film/2008/nov/28/william-friedkin-french-connection.

20. Ibid.

21. Phillips, Michael. "Commentary: Out of 60s Chaos, Dirty Harry band Popeye Doyle Ruled the Streets, and We've Been Paying for it Ever Since." https://www.chicagotribune.com/entertainment/movies/michael-phillips/ct-ent-movie-cops-commentary-0607-20200603-442gvirklvcpvdowsibbmnl4tu-story.html.

22. Ebert, Roger. https://www.rogerebert.com/reviews/training-day-2001.

23. Denby, David. https://www.newyorker.com/magazine/2001/10/15/on-the-beat.

24. Ebert, Roger. https://www.rogerebert.com/reviews/training-day-200125.24. https://www.boxofficemojo.com/release/rl1165460993/weekend/.

Chapter 12

From the TV Screen to the Ballot Box

The press secretary is asked about the president being sued by journalists. The press secretary does not know how to respond and ends the conference. The team discusses the president being sued. This rumor winds up being true and is related to a statement made months ago about seatbelts. The president walks by and discusses issues with his press team. He is told not to discuss seatbelts. Then, the team moves on to an arms deal struck with another country.

In another office, the deputy chief of staff is at his desk when the first lady enters, wanting to discuss the language in a United Nations treaty regarding prostitution. The wording in the treaty was "forced prostitution," and women's action groups wanted the word "forced" removed, to include all types of prostitution. The deputy chief of staff is advised to meet with political lobbyist.

Next, a roundtable discussion is held about Mad Cow disease. There is concern, but the scene cuts to other policies and issues facing the president's cabinet. The conversation returns to seatbelts. To combat the lawsuit, it is suggested a national seatbelt law be proposed. No decision is made, but in further conversations all staff members shoot down the proposed legislation.

The team returns to Mad Cow. The question is whether to declare a national emergency and inform the public. The president decides to wait to make an announcement on the presumptive positive Mad Cow results, as the release of information will affect the stock market, agricultural, restaurant, and fast-food industries (among others).

A new issue is then presented. A woman in Qumar was executed for adultery on only the word of her husband. The press secretary raises concern—how is she supposed to announce an arms deal?

Now we return to the prostitution issue at hand. The deputy chief of staff meets with the political lobbyist, who advises him of the horrors of prostitution and human trafficking, noting that women and children are often tricked into prostitution by initially agreeing to work overseas as babysitters or au pairs. The two go back and forth on the removal of the word "forced." No resolution occurs. But the chief of staff of the first lady asks whether including the word forced implies that the U.S. condones consensual prostitution . . . it's all about appearances.

In other discussions, the press secretary continues to grapple with the arms deal being made between the U.S. and Qumar. Is $1.5 billion worth looking the other way when women continue to be beaten by their husbands and sons for acts they may not have even committed?

Back to Mad Cow. The president's team again discusses when to release the information to the public. The press secretary makes the argument that public trust and confidence is gained via transparency, so a decision is made to release the information.

The deputy chief of staff and political lobbyist meet again. It seems the language around the word "forced" is going to be reviewed. The two have a conversation about the difference between burglary for need of money and prostitution. The lobbyist points out that the difference is that women may enter prostitution out of need to survive, but that in and of itself is coercion.

The decision ends with the arms deal. The press secretary is making the case that the U.S. should not make deals with countries who allow the suppression of and violence against women. But it seems a refueling site for U.S. aircrafts is more important than women's rights. Angry and upset, the press secretary quickly composes herself to enter the press room, where she quickly announces the refueling location. She is poised one the outside while fighting a fierce moral battle inside. The long day of decision-making ends.

You may recall this plot from an episode of *The West Wing*, titled "The Women of Qumar."[1] This episode exemplifies the many issues faced by politicians daily, and how decisions they make about policies related to illegal behavior (like prostitution) can affect citizens. For those of you who may not be familiar with *The West Wing*, it is a political drama that won many Emmy awards over its seven-season run. We begin this chapter, then, discussing politics, political news, and TV networks' influence on crime policies. As usual, we also discuss how crime dramas can affect support for crime policies and can affect public perception of crime overall.

The two major political parties in the United States are Republicans (or conservatives) and Democrats (or liberals). People who identify as conservative tend to have different views on crime, criminals, and crime policies compared to people who identify as liberal. For example, those with more conservative views tend to support Second Amendment rights (gun ownership), harsh crime control policies (like three-strikes), and harsher sentences (like the death penalty). Those with more liberal views tend to support rehabilitation, stricter requirements for gun ownership, reduced sentences for drug offenders (or legalization/decriminalization of one or more drugs), and abolishment of the death penalty.

Some television networks cater to a specific political party. Fox News, One America News, and Max News provide a conservative perspective, while CNN, CNBC, and MSNBC provide a liberal perspective. And these networks will advocate for policies supported by politicians and policy makers of their respective ideology. For example, Fox News will discuss the benefits of passing legislation to construct a border wall that spans the U.S. Mexico border, while CNN may discuss the benefits of policies allowing additional immigrants to settle in the U.S. That said, people are likely to gravitate to whatever networks support their beliefs and values. Thinks of the news channels you personally watch. Why do you watch these channels? Do you notice that the messages being relayed align with your own opinions and beliefs?

When it comes to crime, television networks, depending on how they are politically aligned, may emphasize certain aspects of a story or focus on certain players in the case. And some networks may highlight certain crimes over others. The same goes for crime policy.

For example, networks that provide a more conservative perspective may focus on crimes by illegal immigrants, as a way to paint people in these groups as violent and urge viewers to vote against pro-immigration policies. Networks that provide a more liberal perspective may instead focus on the terrible outcomes of crimes where a gun was involved, to argue for legislation that calls for stricter gun policies. We call all of this media bias.

HOW MEDIA BIAS AFFECTS VOTING AND PUBLIC PERCEPTION

Morris finds that people who watch news on cable TV channels are polarized along party lines.[2] As we have seen in the examples above, this can affect the stories people are exposed to and the content of the stories. For people who identify politically as Independents, the channel they watch is important in influencing their votes. Independents who watched CNN during the Bush-Kerry presidential election were more likely to vote for Kerry, while independents who watched Fox News were more likely to vote for Bush (721).[3] Similarly, DellaVigna and Kaplan found that, upon the introduction of Fox News in cable markets, the channel persuaded between 3 and 28 percent of viewers to vote Republican.[4] As you can imagine, depending on each candidate's stance on crime and crime policy, this can greatly affect the criminal justice system.

Aside from voting, news can also affect how we perceive crime. Those who watch general or local news (and crime dramas) are more likely to believe that crime is rising (which it has not; crime has generally been declining since the early 1990s).[5] This is especially true for White viewers who live near a greater number of Black residents. Viewing local crime news also affects how people perceive crime both locally and across the U.S. And local news influences people's support for the death penalty (more on that below) and more money being directed toward law enforcement; this holds true regardless of political party.[6] If we think that crime, particularly violent or other sensationalized criminal acts, near our home is rising, we are more likely to support measures to combat crime both locally and nationally. Do you agree with this? Are you likely to see crime as a major problem based on what you see on the news? And if so, would you vote for policies that are intended to reduce crime? Continue reading below to see how crime dramas influence support for criminal justice policies, namely capital punishment (the death penalty).

FROM TV TO THE BALLOT BOX: TV CRIME DRAMAS AND CRIME POLICY

Viewing crime dramas seems to be related to people's fear of crime and support of more punitive criminal justice policies. Eschholz et al. suggest the relationship between crime dramas and fear of crime may be due to the violence included in crime dramas.[7] We have already discussed how crime dramas tend to depict more serious crimes like homicides, rape, and aggravated assault. To provide further confirmation, we return to the data we collected from 280 hours (episodes) of crime dramas. Of the 922 total crimes identified across these episodes, the most frequent crimes were homicide (31.7 percent), kidnapping (12.2 percent), aggravated assault (7.8 percent), and rape or sexual assault (6.1 percent).

Much research regarding the impact of TV dramas, and crime dramas specifically, on crime policies focuses on support (or not) of the death penalty and handguns. Holbert et al. examined the impact of viewing news, reality police shows, and crime dramas on both capital punishment and handgun acceptance and ownership. Those who watch police reality shows and/or crime dramas are more likely to support the death penalty.[8] And those who watch police reality shows are more likely to support handgun use and are more likely to own a handgun.[9] The authors also explored fear of crime in their analyses, finding that news and reality police show viewing led to respondents' heightened fear of crime.[10] Similarly, Kort-Butler and Hartshorn found that people who view crime dramas more frequently were more likely to support the death penalty.[11]

Mutz and Nir compared two different *Law & Order* episodes—one that painted the criminal justice system in a positive light, and another that painted the criminal justice system in a negative light. Perhaps unsurprisingly, participants who viewed the positive episode had more positive views about the criminal justice system; participants who viewed the negative episode viewed the criminal justice system and unfair.[12] And participants who viewed the negative episode (which featured a person who was wrongfully convicted) were less likely to support the death penalty. Other policies explored that were supported by those viewing the negative episode were greater funding for defense lawyers and higher taxes for better prison conditions; these same participants also agreed that prison sentences are too punitive.[13]

Slater et al. also examined the effect of watching an episode of *Law & Order* on people's support for the death penalty. The authors found that watching the episode did in fact increase support for the death penalty among participants, even those who identified as liberal.[14] Because the *Law & Order* episode focused on the violent murder of a woman, a topic which receives much liberal attention and support (support to reduce violence against women), the authors suggest it was the possible framing of the issue—death penalty as a way to protect women—that led to the increased support from liberals.[15]

Based on Slater et al.'s study, then, if crime dramas shape issues in such a way that appeals to the ideologies of liberals and/or conservatives, can this change public perception of a criminal justice policy? And does the change in support only last in the minutes and hours after watching an episode, or can it be longer lasting?

POLITICS AND CRIME DRAMAS

In an explorative study, we looked at people's political affiliations and their crime drama viewership. We asked people specifically about their political affiliation, favorite genre of television, number of crime shows watched each week, number of hours of crime shows watched each week, and whether they think crime dramas accurately portray the criminal justice system. Of the 229 people who completed the survey, 224 identified their political affiliation: 30 (13.4 percent) were Republicans, 133 (59.4 percent) were Democrats, and 61 (27.2 percent) were Independents. Most people did not report crime dramas as their favorite genre of television (153 of 227, or 67.4 percent); however, a majority of respondents did watch at least one crime show each week (181 of 224 participants, or 80.8 percent). Most people watched between one and four hours of crime dramas weekly (63.8).

We conducted a number of chi-square tests to see whether there was a relation between political affiliation and crime dramas as favorite genre, political affiliation and number of crime shows watched per week, and political affiliation and number of hours of crime dramas watched each week. In short, there was no significant relation found between political affiliation and crime dramas as favorite genre ($X2(2, N = 224) = 1.31, p = .520$), number of crime shows watched ($X2(4, N = 215) = .50, p = .973$), or hours of crime dramas watched per week ($X2(10, N = 222) = 9.23, p = .510$).

VIEWERS' FAVORITE CRIME DRAMAS AND THEIR INFLUENCE ON PERCEPTIONS OF CRIME AND THE CRIMINAL JUSTICE SYSTEM

In the same study discussed above, we also asked people to report their favorite crime drama, to explain why they chose that drama, and to write about how crime on TV has influenced how they view crimes in real life. Of those who reported their favorite crime dramas, *Criminal Minds and Law & Order* (any series, but mostly SVU) were the clear favorites, liked by 30 and 37 people (out of 173), respectively. *NCIS* and *Blue Bloods* were also reported as favorites by eight participants each. Reasons as to why certain shows were people's favorites varied, but common responses included liking a particular actor in the show (or the entire cast), understanding how the criminal mind functions, because viewers like trying to solve the crimes, and because different episodes featured different crimes.

Interestingly, a couple of respondents reported liking crime dramas for their accuracy in portraying police or the criminal justice system more generally. For example, one participant said they liked *Brooklyn Nine-Nine* because "My father, who is a police officer, says that it is actually more accurate than most shows." Another two participants liked *Law & Order: SVU* because, "I think it represents the current justice system and it actually showcases real-life cases that happened or are currently happening, like immigration (ICE) or injustice for minorities" and "because it captures the realities of rape and sexual assault victims who struggle to adapt with their traumas while the show also gives a real life depiction of other crimes that are intertwined with rape such as murder, domestic violence, etc." Quantico was noted as, "Very realistic, [a] really good view of the CJ system." Similarly, *The Wire* as recognized by a respondent as, "actually portray[ing] some real life scenarios."

Whether people watch crime dramas for their interesting storylines or their accurate portrayals of crime and police, there is no doubt that these shows leave an impression on viewers. Box 12.1 includes selected written responses from participants explaining how crime on TV has influenced how they view crimes in real life.

CHAPTER SUMMARY

Our country is divided by political party. The two main political parties in the U.S. are Republicans and Democrats. Independents represent a third party. Each political party differs in its stance on crime and criminal justice policy. TV news channels tend to lean toward one political party, and may highlight some stories, or content of stories, over others. This is media bias. Media bias can affect people's voting decisions, and decisions on criminal justice policies.

Local news and crime dramas affect people's perceptions of crime, people's support of increased funding for police, and the death penalty. We find in our own research that viewing TV crime dramas leads people to perceive crime in different ways. For example, people report being more cautious, report that African Americans commit more crime, that crime solving is easy, and the crime is high.

NOTES

1. "The Women of Qumar." *The West Wing*, created by Aaron Sorkin, season 3, episode 9, John Wells Productions, 2001.
2. Morris, Jonathan S. "Slanted Objectivity? Perceived Media Bias, Cable News Exposure, and Political Attitudes." *Social Science Quarterly*, vol. 88, no. 3, September 2007, pp. 707–728.
3. Ibid, p. 721.
4. DellaVigna, Stefano, and Ethan Kaplan. "The Fox News Affect: Media Bias and Voting." *The Quarterly Journal of Economics*, 2007, pp. 1188–1234.
5. Baranauskas, Andrew J., and Kevin M. Drakulich. "Media Construction of Crime Revisited: Media Types, Consumer Contexts, and Frames of Crime and Justice." *Criminology*, vol. 56, no. 4, 2018, pp. 679–714.
6. Ibid, p. 693.
7. Eschholz, Sarah et al. "Television and Fear of Crime: Program Types, Audience Traits, and the Mediating Effect of Perceived Neighborhood Racial Composition." *Social Problems*, vol. 50, no. 3, August 2003, pp. 395–415.
8. Holbert et al. "Fear, Authority, and Justice: Crime-Related TV Viewing and Endorsements of Capital Punishment and Gun Ownership." *J&MC Quarterly*, vol. 81, no. 2, Summer 2004, pp. 343–363.
9. Ibid, p. 353.

10. Ibid, p. 351.

11. Kort-Butler, Lisa A., and Kelley J. Sittner Hartshorn. "Watching the Detectives: Crime Programming, Fear of Crime, and Attitudes about the Criminal Justice System." *The Sociological Quarterly*, vol. 52, no. 1, Winter 2011, pp. 36–55.

12. Mutz, Diana C., and Lilach Nir. "Not Necessarily the News: Does Fictional Television Influence Real-World Policy Preferences?" *Mass Communication and Society*, vol. 13, no. 2, pp. 196–217.

13. Ibid, pp. 209–210.

14. Slater, Michael D. et al. "Television Dramas and Support for Controversial Public Policies: Effects and Mechanisms." *Journal of Communication*, vol. 56, 2006, pp. 235–252.

15. Ibid, p. 249.

Conclusion

On a March 2021 episode of Saturday Night Live, *the iconic sketch comedy show that has been commenting and lampooning culture for more than forty years, the cast performed a skit that encapsulated America's love of crime entertainment.*

The pre-produced video titled "Murder Show," begins with a young woman telling her male partner that she was going to spend the evening "relaxing." Four other women are featured in their individual homes, getting ready for a night of "self-care," that one character says is "the only way I know how."

Then, the song begins, "I'm gonna watch a murder show, a murder show, a murder show." Another lyric states, "got killed in the Bahamas, I'm gonna watch while I fold my pajamas." "A body builder is chopped up by an old lady—I watch it while I text my sister 'bout her baby." "As soon as I'm done I listen to a podcast about the same guy as the show I just watched."[1]

Cosmopolitan's online magazine immediately posted an article with the video from SNL. The writer is excited because "It pokes fun at everyone's weekend activity."[2]

Crime . . . it is the mainstay of media. Crime . . . it is fun to go to the movies and be scared when a madman in a hockey mask terrorizes a bunch of teenagers in a lake house. Crime . . . it is what politicians often use to frighten the voting populace and persuade the voters that only THEY can keep your children safe. Crime . . . it is the reason we have law enforcement officers and prosecutors and defense attorneys and judges. Crime . . . it is the reason we have prisons and all of the employment that goes along with incarceration and its aftermath. Crime . . . it sells gates and padlocks and home security systems. Crime . . . it sells newspapers and has you glued to your television screens and your phone! Imagine . . . if there was no crime.

Well, there is crime. Not every act that is a crime in one state is a crime in another—the same goes with countries. Almost everyone has committed a crime at one time. Students will bristle when you say that in a juvenile delinquency class, but as you mention a few "crimes," they have to admit that they have partaken. (Some of these crimes are status crimes, in other words, a person's status as a minor makes the act a crime but if committed by someone over a certain age, it is not illegal.)

- Did you ever drive over the speed limit?
- Did you ever speak on your cell phone while driving? (Not illegal in every state!)
- Did you ever skip school?
- Did you ever deface public property?
- Did you ever stay out past your town's curfew?
- Did you ever steal anything?
- Did you ever take anything from your job? If you say, "Of course not!" just be sure. Did you ever eat some French fries from the bin? Did you ever eat food that customers didn't touch, a.k.a. "garbage mouthing"? Did you ever give a free donut to a friend who came into to see you at work? Did you ever take paper or a stapler or scotch tape or paper clips? You get the idea.
- Did you ever have a drink of alcohol when you weren't old enough to legally do so?
- Did you ever text while driving?
- Did you ever smoke weed?
- Did you ever sneak into the movies without paying?
- Did you ever go into a club with a fake ID?
- Did you ever work a job "under the table"?

Now, here's the next question . . . when you read through this list and you thought about your complicities, did your heart race a bit? It is sort of exciting, right? If it is exciting, it is because you have not been arrested for your transgression. You have not been confronted by police officers. You have not been taken away in handcuffs in front of your neighbors. Crime is much more exciting when you are not the victim and you are not being accused. It is this glimpse into danger, into trouble, into the dark side that we find appealing about crime dramas. It is a different feeling from learning about crime on the news—that is actually scary, because you have to consider you could be a victim. You must keep yourself and your loved ones safe. All of this is apparently part and parcel of the human psyche.

It is not just Americans who enjoy crime drama, although news in other countries does not focus on crime nearly as much as ours. The American movie *Traffic* is based on a British television series *Traffik*.[3] The movie won four Academy Awards (including Best Actor in a Supporting Role, Benicio Del Toro, to be cognizant of Latino representation in media) and was nominated for Best Picture.[4] The movie is an intriguing combination of the illegal drug trade, politics, and yes, personal drama and violence. The television series had all of the same intrigue, but a good portion of it set in Germany and later the United Kingdom. The BBC has many crime shows on its airwaves, including *Wire in the Blood* and *Luther*.[5] One of the most popular television programs from 2020 (a year during which networks, cable, and streaming videos were the main option for entertainment) was a television show called *Money Heist*. It takes place in Spain and has all the qualities that Americans enjoy so much in their entertainment. According to imdb.com, the most popular crime drama—at this moment—comes from France, *Lupin,* about a gentleman thief, who sets out to avenge the death of his father at the hands of a wealthy family. The number three show presently is *Peaky Blinders* from the U.K.[6] Why do we love it so? This is not a psychology book, but we do need to discuss voyeurism. Here is an exhaustive definition, courtesy of Merriam-Webster:[7]

> the desires or behavior of a voyeur: such as a: the practice of obtaining sexual gratification from observing others. Psychiatrists generally divide paraphilias into two groups: those focused on objects, like a foot fetish, and those focused on behaviors, like exhibitionism, voyeurism or frottage.
>
> —Benedict Carey Ward, if he was guilty of anything at all, was guilty of observation.

> Looking, or (if you will) leering and ogling are not normally considered indictable offenses in British courts of law, but they do shade over into voyeurism.
>
> —Paul Thomas

> also: the criminal act of surreptitiously viewing a person without their consent in a place where the person has a reasonable expectation of privacy (such as a home or public bathroom) or of using a device (such as a camera) for the purpose of such viewing. A 21-year-old man has been charged with voyeurism for allegedly using his phone's camera to view the person using the restroom in the stall next to him in a dorm on the Notre Dame campus, according to court records.
>
> —Melissa Hudson

b: the practice of taking pleasure in observing something private, sordid, or scandalous. Now there's a volume for those who are . . . bored by the salacious voyeurism of tell-alls.

—Steven M. Zeitchik

Voyeurism allows us to experience all the excitement of disaster, catastrophe, and pain, to witness the most horrible human events, without any danger of feeling real pain.

—Gerald Mast

But the voice of the diarist . . . will always exert a fascination close to voyeurism.

—Rosellen Brown

Zhanna Bagdasarov and colleagues published a study in the *Journal of Broadcasting and Electronic Media*, titled "I Am What I Watch: Voyeurism, Sensation Seeking, and Television Viewing Patterns."[8] In this article, they discuss the appeal of reality television. They investigated the idea that the appeal of reality TV is its access to pure voyeuristic desires. They also wanted to know if reality TV and fictional drama provide the same quality of content; in other words, do they satisfy the same curiosity?

YOU CALL IT VOYEURISM, I CALL IT SENSATION-SEEKING

Is it possible that the sensationalism, excitement, and novelty of reality TV programs that result in increase of psychological arousal, may play a significant role in satisfying the need for both sensation-seeking and voyeurism? And in the end, does that really matter? People are viewing. At the beginning of the chapter, when we went through the list of (non-violent) crimes, admit it—there is something sensational about the idea of getting away with something!

Bagdasarov et al. found that college students' (this was their target study group) viewing choices were, indeed, relevant to voyeurism and sensation-seeking, but varied according to overall watching habits and gender. The differences they found between gender choices is that men preferred more action and women preferred more situational presentations. Females also scored lower on animated action shows and higher on the voyeurism scale.[9] (Remember the *SNL* skit that started this chapter?)

IT'S NOT YOUR GRANDMOTHER'S NEWS, OR IS IT?

According to Ray Surette, contemporary news is essentially voyeurism.[10] We are not calling your grandmother a voyeur, but in crime-and-justice news, we are usually informed about real events and real people, but these events are rare and distant. They display the lives of people caught up in extreme circumstances, involving bizarre crimes, spectacular trials, and extraordinary situations. News provides filtered, molded snippets of the abnormal crime events in the world.[11] As discussed in chapter 5, a fender-bender is not going to lead a news broadcast, but a 20-car pile-up with an overturned tractor trailer could be a lead story—unless there is something *worse*.

DEFINITELY NOT YOUR GRANDMOTHER'S NEWS—SOCIAL MEDIA

This is not to say that there are no grandparents who are social media savvy, but this is definitely not how news was disseminated in the past. As all four of the authors of this book teach college courses in both criminal justice and communications, we can give you anecdotal evidence that many students do not get their news in what would be considered traditional ways. Students and other young people regularly get their news from social media.

For our media analysis study that is referenced in both chapters 3 and 7, we also analyzed news found on social media. Using the same time frame during which we observed international cable news, national cable news, network nightly news, and local news—January 2018 through 2019—we periodically compared Snapchat, Twitter, Facebook, and Buzzfeed. The methodology differed slightly for this part of the study, because we compared three of the four, all in the same hour, on different times of the day. We also considered the "top ten" stories on each of the sites, because social media news does not function the same way traditional news programming does. The idea was to see if the differences were drastic. Table 13.1 displays different social media platforms, the percentage of violent crime as a top story in each platform, and an example of one or more actual headlines describing a violent crime that earned a top story spotlight, in a sample of social media headlines between January 2018 and November 2019.

As you can see, Facebook led the way with more than half of its top stories with violent crime as the topic and Snapchat showed the least. During one particular hour, Twitter had "Black teenager shot at after knocking on door to ask for directions," BuzzFeed had "Eight-year-old Muslim girl drugged, kidnapped, chained-up, raped, and murdered," and Snapchat had "Incest couple

Table 13.1 Social Media News Analysis, January 2018 through November 2019

Social Media Platform	Percentage Of Violent Top Story	Sample Headlines
Facebook	55 percent	"20-year-old allows her 2-year-old child to smoke meth"
		"Horrified tourists find bullet-riddled body on Mexican beach'
		"Trump again calls Comey a slimeball"
Twitter	47.6 percent	"Toronto restaurant asks Black customers to prepay their meals"
		"Body of a 2-year-old flushed down a toilet"
		"Seven dead after fights at max security prison in South Carolina"
Buzzfeed	42.1 percent	"Muslim woman was banned from wearing religious attire to testify in court"
		"Cardi B Flawlessly Performed on Stage at Coachella and People Are in Awe"
Snapchat	31.8 percent	"Brooke Skylar, 18, has been arrested and charged with murder in Ohio"
		"Beyoncé dances her top off"
		"Black men arrested for 'trespassing' at Starbucks"
		"Man robs a bank to impress Taylor Swift"

Source: Facebook, Twitter, Buzzfeed, Snapchat

murder-suicide." If we refer back to chapter 5 and think about "news you can use," how many of these stories really fit into the category? Obviously, stories that deal with racism have meaning for more than just one region, as do stories about politics, but do we really need to know about a woman who let her baby smoke meth? Apparently, editorial decisions were made and the answer was "Yes!" Just as with the national and local headlines we gave you in previous chapters, there is not enough space to include all of them, but some of the social media headlines do seem to be rather trivial.

A November 2020 article from the Pew Research Center bears the title (and the bad news), "Americans Who Get News Mainly on Social Media Are Less Knowledgeable and Less Engaged: And Social Media Is Now among the Most Common Ways People—Particularly Young Adults—Get Their Political News."[12] This report comes at the close of a year that saw America divided by many factors, but the fight over what is "fake news" and what is not is a sort of circular argument that appears to have no winner. Pew found:[13]

> A Pew Research Center report published in July shows that Americans who rely primarily on social media for news—which describes about 18 percent of adults in the U.S.—tend to know less about the 2020 election, less about the coronavirus pandemic, and less about political news in general than people who

rely on news websites, cable or network TV, radio, and print. Those who depend on social media are also more likely than other news consumers to be exposed to made-up news, such as the conspiracy theory that powerful people planned the pandemic and invented the coronavirus in a lab, and to give credence to falsehoods.[14]

"Coming Up Next . . . We'll Tell You Why This All Matters!"

Why does it matter how crime is portrayed on television? Why does it matter if Americans devoted hours to a story about a man who exhibited some shady behavior toward tigers and perhaps tried to have his rival killed? According to "Bingeclock.com"[15] (yes, there is such a thing), if you watched the entire *Tiger King* series, you spent 5 hours and 17 minutes of your life doing so. And what is so bad about that?

The Tiger King's story may not influence a person to commit a crime or even to change the way they see the criminal justice system. It is possible that the series could lead a person to become a more active animal rights' activist, but it is a specific story with specific characters who do not represent a large swath of the American population. *Tiger King* will probably not give rise to misrepresentation of the workings of the criminal justice system—the problems occur when media influence an audience

UPDATED PERCEPTION OF THE POLICE

As discussed in chapter 4, in this one particular about "gatekeepers" consumers of news trust the police over the media. While the study by Adubato, Sachs, and Fizzinoglia is a recently published study, we wondered if clashes between protesters and the police over the summer of 2020 changed the public's view of law enforcement. The death of George Floyd galvanized many young people and many not-so-young to take to the streets and decry what they saw as police brutality. The calls for defunding the police came from a small number of protesters and from some political actors, but the policy initiative to defund the police was not embraced as widely as perhaps portrayed on social media. Many misconceptions and false claims were leveled at opposing political sides and as mentioned in the preface of this book, with so many Americans in varying degrees of quarantine and/or lockdown throughout this volatile news year, tensions were running high.

It may take years to sort out the results of false social media reports, but somehow a false equivalency arose in the ethos that if a person was against police brutality that person was anti-police. The research from Pew alluded to conspiracy theories and falsehoods and the call for "defunding the police" as a policy plan was one of those conspiracies. It is under these circumstances that we conducted one final survey for this book. We asked 12 substantive questions and four demographic questions. We had a sample size of 180 respondents. Table 13.2 shows all substantive questions, and then in each of the following columns displays the top three most frequent response categories selected by participants (as percentages).

The answers we found did not startle us, although 43 percent of our respondents indicated indifference at the idea of defunding the police. That seems interesting because of what a political hot-button issue that was during the long, hot summer of 2020. Our sample was not large and did mostly consist of respondents from the New York metropolitan area, but that was an area where many clashes between protesters and police took place within just months of this survey being given. Also, this is a sample with a high percentage of

Table 13.2 Perceptions of Police Survey

Question	Highest Percentage Response	Second Highest Percentage Response	Third Highest Percentage Response
Q1: Do you know what #DefundThePolice is?	Definitely yes=56.2 percent	Probably yes=24.4 percent	Might or might not=12.5 percent
Q3: How do you feel about it?	Indifferent=43.0 percent	Support it, defund the police=31.4 percent	Do not support it, leave the funds alone=25.5 percent
Q5: Do you feel that the criminal justice system needs to be reevaluated for social equality?	Definitely yes=68.9 percent	Probably yes=22.4 percent	Might or might not=7.4 percent
Q7: Do you feel that the media may stretch the truth for some police encounters?	Definitely yes=38.8 percent	Probably yes=26.8 percent	Might or might not=23.4 percent
Q8: Do you have friends or family in law enforcement?	Yes=56.9 percent	No=43.1 percent	
Q10: Do you support the idea of social workers taking over mental illness-related situations?	Definitely yes=32.1 percent	Might or might not=29.8 percent	Probably yes=25.2 percent
Q11: Have you ever been racially profiled?	Yes=28.0 percent	No=52.5 percent	Probably not=19.4 percent

N=180

Source: Table created by authors based on author study.

both young people, people of color, and people with family members working in the criminal justice system. This combination could definitely conjure mixed feelings.

The racial/ethnic makeup of the group was evenly split between white and Hispanic at 32.5 percent each and 28 percent Black. For gender, the breakdown was 63.5 percent female with just over 1 percent who preferred not to say. Sixty percent of the respondents associated with the Democratic party and 25.8 percent consider themselves Independent. Eight-two.eight% of the respondents were between 18 and 24 years old. This is not only the age of most of the protesters and most college students, but it is also a particularly dangerous age for criminality—as both offenders and victims.

If we had time, we could conduct a larger study and perhaps evaluate how much social media played a role in forming their opinions. As a snapshot of mostly young people in the country's largest metropolitan area, it does seem that cooler heads prevailed and no one side was overwhelmingly influential.

INFORMATION MATTERS

Why does matter coverage matter? For one thing, news shows are the vehicle by which important, accurate, and breaking information is imparted to the public. We do not have town criers on corners and we do not have loudspeakers in our streets. We have news on our televisions and news in our cars and now we have news in the palms of our hands. For many reasons and certainly in times of emergencies or crises, we need direction and stability. It is crucial that news produce the highest level of those entities during those times when life or death is at stake.

Why does truth in reality TV or "infotainment" matter? It does not actually matter as much as from a news source, but viewers must be aware of the non-reality of reality TV. Maybe disclaimers are necessary? Or maybe media literacy should be taught on the high school level? The subject is somewhat mysterious and exceptionally clever at "fake" and "deep fake" constructions. Why not teach media as a required course in our schools? After all, we are exposed to media every day. It may be time to revamp some of the subjects that have comprised the traditional curriculum.

Does violence on TV matter? That is the subject for many other books. Does portrayal of police matter? Perhaps that is something else we can examine for our K–12 curricula; after all, how much do we learn about the police after the grammar school trip to the local police station? Maybe better education about law enforcement could lead to better understanding on both sides.

Does portrayal of race and ethnicity in the media matter? Indeed, it does. The dual issue of role models—positive and negative—can have a serious impact on the self-confidence and aspirations of young children.

Finally, does portrayal of gender in the media matter? Here is a test: watch a television show from the 1970s and see how women are portrayed and you may cringe. Sadly, even an award-winning show from only two decades ago may surprise you. *The West Wing*, an award-winning, intelligent show that regularly hits on criminal justice decisions within the context of the presidency and the executive branch, will surprise you with its engendered language, its assumptions about women's roles in the government, and lack of women at the proverbial table. As of this writing, there is a Black, Asian American woman who is vice president of the United States and that is not a media construction.

The following truncated events of January 6, 2021, are taken from an article in the *Washington Post* that pieces together a timeline. While the article is extensive, this is just a snippet.

On January 6, 2021, Americans and the world watched in horror as an angry, armed, and dangerous crowd stormed the United States Capitol. Earlier that day, supporters of then-President Donald Trump, gathered on the Ellipse, for a rally with the theme, "Save America." During this rally, Trump spoke for more than an hour, exciting the crowd (some would say "inciting") with the idea that the must protest the result of the 2020 presidential election, by which he, Donald Trump, lost the presidency to Joseph R. Biden. He told the group that they must fight and they must march to the Capitol and he would be there with them.

- By 1:00 p.m., an "initial wave of protesters" broke through the outer barricade west of the Capitol Building, just as Vice President Mike Pence and senators walked into the House chamber. As the mob grew, it forced its way into the building, breaking down doors and shattering windows.
- The crowd overtook Capitol Police, while members of Congress were led out to safety or hid in various places around the building. People sheltered in the House gallery as rioters tried to break into the House chamber.
- After more than four hours, the mob was cleared. They had not managed to stop the certification of the electoral vote tally and Joe Biden was affirmed as the winner and president-elect.
- Five people died as a result of the Capitol breach, including Capitol Police Officer Brian Sicknick.[16]

This attack on the Capitol building, the seat of American democracy, will be written about and analyzed for years and hopefully, nothing like this will ever happen again. A new report released on March 26, 2021, suggests that disinformation in our society has produced "A Contagion of Institutional Distrust."[17] This is precisely the opposite of what this book is meant to encourage. Rutgers University's Miller Center for Community Protection and Resilience published a joint report with the Network Contagion Research Institute. The report, by faculty and student researchers, "chronicles the growth of a conspiracy theory about a coming 'New World Order' through a totalitarian world government."[18] Proponents of this new theory use social media as a mechanism to join this belief system with other existing conspiracy theories in an effort to "virally spread disinformation to the masses."[19]

> "The research undertaken by Rutgers faculty and students, in cooperation with the Network Contagion Research Institute, has established that in the wake of the January attack and the subsequent deplatforming of QAnon and other extremist groups, extremists have migrated to a broader umbrella conspiracy," said John J. Farmer, Jr., director of both the Miller Center and the Eagleton Institute of Politics at Rutgers University-New Brunswick. "Although their agenda to undermine institutional trust remains the same, the focus has shifted from election disinformation to disinformation about the COVID-19 vaccines and to hate speech directed at Asians, Jews, and other vulnerable populations."[20]

Joel Finkelstein, director of the NCRI and senior research fellow at the Miller Center, who is directing the joint project, further says, "If we don't restore trust to our democracy and one another, the road to public health and political reconciliation alike are in jeopardy."[21]

FIVE KEY FINDINGS[22]

- In the wake of the election and events of Jan. 6, articles and memes containing the term "New World Order" and other anti-government and anti-"globalist" symbols not only exploded on fringe web communities and fake news platforms but also surged across mainstream platforms, making them more available to the general public.
- "New World Order" and other anti-government and anti-"globalist" online content spiked in tandem with vaccine distribution disruption during an anti-vaccine protest at Dodger Stadium.
- Anti-government and anti-"globalist" content on social media increasingly includes anti-restriction and anti-vaccine content.

- NCRI analysis indicates three indicators of anti-restriction and anti-vaccine protests at the county level. They include a county's history of intimidating counterprotest activity running concurrent with Black Lives Matter protests, the severity of covid restrictions (such as enforced lockdowns) and searches for "New World Order" on Google.
- NCRI aggregates data sets both in the real world and online to perform a geographically weighted regression which provides a spatial model for anti-restriction and anti-vaccine protests for counties across the U.S.

WHAT CAN YOU DO?

Become better consumers of news. Become better informed members of law enforcement. Be more vocal in student government or local government. Obtain your news from more than one source, but understand the difference between news and opinion. Demand that news gives you a full picture and demand that your government gives you transparency. Make sure you vote and that you are fully informed before you do. Help others to do the same.

Politics matter. Laws matter. Law enforcement matters. Media presentations matter. Without the careful construction and guardianship over those entities, our democracy may no longer matter. A strong and mutually respectful relationship between media and the criminal justice system will shore-up our democracy and give it room to breathe . . . and hopefully, thrive.

NOTES

1. Saturday Night Live. "Murder Show." NBC, https://youtu.be/J4RdcE6H4Gs.
2. Stein, Megan. "This 'SNL' Skit About 'Murder Shows' Will Make Any True Crime Fan Laugh: It Pokes Fun at Everyone's Favorite Weekend Activity." *Cosmopolitan Online*, 4 March 2021, https://www.cosmopolitan.com/entertainment/tv/a35730648/saturday-night-live-murder-show-skit/?source=nl&utm_source=nl_cos&utm_medium=email&date=030521&utm_campaign=nl23115867.
3. https://www.imdb.com/title/tt0181865/awards?ref_=tt_awd.
4. www.imdb.com/search/title/?genres=crime&explore=title_type,genres&title_type=tvSeries.
5. Ibid.
6. Ibid.
7. https://www.merriam-webster.com/dictionary/voyeurism.
8. Zhanna Bagdasarov, Kathryn Greene, Smita C. Banerjee, Marina Krcmar, Itzhak Yanovitzky, and Dovile Ruginyte. (2010). I Am What I Watch: Voyeurism, Sensation Seeking, and Television Viewing Patterns, *Journal of Broadcasting & Electronic Media*, 54:2, 299–315, DOI: 10.1080/08838151003734995.

9. Ibid.

10. Surette, Ray. *Media, Crime and Criminal Justice: Images, Realities, and Policies*. Belmont, CA, Cengage Learning, 2011.

11. Ibid.

12. Infield, Tom. "Americans Who Get News Mainly on Social Media Are Less Knowledgeable and Less Engaged: And Social Media Is Now among the Most Common Ways People—Particularly Young Adults—Get Their Political News." Pew Trust, 16 November 2020, Retrieved from: https://www.pewtrusts.org/en/trust/archive/fall-2020/americans-who-get-news-mainly-on-social-media-are-less-knowledgeable-and-less-engaged.

13. Ibid.

14. Ibid.

15. https://www.bingeclock.com/s/tiger-king/.

16. Tan, Shelly, Youjin Shin, and Danielle Rindler. "How one of America's Ugliest Days Unraveled Inside and Out the Capitol." *The Washington Post*, 9 January 2021, https://www.washingtonpost.com/nation/interactive/2021/capitol-insurrection-visual-timeline/.

17. Rutgers Today. "A Contagion of Institutional Mistrust: New Report Analyzes New and Dangerous Trends of Disinformation in Wake of U.S. Capitol Attack." 26 March 2021,: https://www.rutgers.edu/news/contagion-institutional-distrust?utm_source=newsletter&utm_medium=email&utm_campaign=rutgerstoday&utm_content=Research%20%26amp%3B%20Innovation.

18. Ibid.

19. Ibid.

20. Ibid.

21. Ibid.

22. Ibid.

Bibliography

Adler, Freda, Gerhard Mueller and William Laufer. *Criminal Justice: An Introduction.* New York, McGraw Hill, 2000.
Adubato, Beth, Nicole M. Sachs and Donald F. Fizzinoglia. "Gatekeepers: Controlling Communication in a Time of Crisis." *Atlantic Journal of Communication,* (2021). DOI: 10.1080/15456870.2020.1779724.
Anderson, D. C. *Crime & the Politics of Hysteria.* New York: Random House, 1995.
Andersen, Robin. *Consumer Culture and TV Programming (Critical Studies in Communication and in the Cultural Industries).* Boulder: Westview Press, 1995.
Andreeva, Nellie. "COPS Back In Production On New Episodes Following Cancellation." *Deadline* online. Last modified October 1, 2020. https://deadline.com/2020/10/cops-back-in-production-new-episodes-following-cancellation-1234590025/.
Angry Black Women. MSNBC. https://www.msnbc.com/the-sunday-show/watch/michelle-obama-meghan-markle-vice-president-kamala-harris-wrongly-called-angry-black-women-102238789563.
Archer, John. "Sex Differences in Aggression in RealWworld Settings: A Meta Aanalytic Review." *Review of General Psychology,* 8, no. 4, (2004): 291–322.
Aspinwall, Cary, and Sachi McClendon. "Did Live PD Let Police Censor Footage ?" The Marshall Project online. Last modified July 1, 2020. https://www.themarshallproject.org/2020/07/01/did-live-pd-let-police-censor-footage.
"ATF's NIBIN Program." Bureau of Alcohol, Tobacco, Firearms and Explosives (ATF) online. 2011. https://www.atf.gov/file/3826/download.
"Automated Firearms Ballistic Technology." Bureau of Alcohol, Tobacco, Firearms and Explosives (ATF) online. 2016. https://www.atf.gov/firearms/automated-firearms-ballistics technology.
Bagdasarov, Zhanna, Kathryn Greene, Smita C. Banerjee, Marina Krcmar, Itzhak Yanovitzky, and& Dovile Ruginyte. "I Am What I Watch: Voyeurism, Sensation Seeking, and Television Viewing Patterns." *Journal of Broadcasting & Electronic Media,* 54:2, 299–315, DOI: 10.1080/08838151003734995.
Baranauskas, Andrew J., and Kevin M. Drakulich. "Media Construction of Crime Revisited: Media Types, Consumer Contexts, and Frames of Crime and Justice." *Criminology,* 56, no. 4, 2018, 679–714.

Baskin, Deborah R., and Ira B. Sommers. "Crime-Show-Viewing Habits and Public Attitudes Toward Forensic Evidence: The 'CSI Effect' Revisited." *The Justice System Journal* 31, no. 1 (2010): 97–113.

Belknap, Joanne. *The Invisible Woman: Gender, Crime, & Justice*, fourth ed. Stamford, CT: Cengage Learning, 2015.

Bernstein, Matthew. *Controlling Hollywood: Censorship and Regulation in the Studio Era*, Continuum International Publishing Group.

Black, Gregory D. *Hollywood Censored: Morality Codes, Catholics and the Movies*. Cambridge University Press.

Blake, Meredith."Tina Fey, Amy Poehler Lampoon HFPA, Life in Lockdown in Golden Globes Monologue." *Los Angeles Times*, February 28, 2021, https://www.latimes.com/entertainment-arts/tv/story/2021-02-28/golden-globes-2021-tina-fey-amy-poehler-monologue#:~:text=%E2%80%9CTV%20is%20the%20one%20that,five%20times%2C%E2%80%9D%20said%20Poehler.

Bonilla-Silva, Eduardo. "Feeling Race: Theorizing the Racial Economy of Emotions." *American Sociological Review*, 84, 1, (February 2019): 1–25.

Borde and Chaumeton. *A Panorama of American Film Noir (1941–1953)*, City Lights Publishers; 1st US edition (November 1, 2002).

Bose, Palash Kumar, and Mohammad Jubaidul Kabir. "Fingerprint: A Unique and Reliable Method for Identification." *Journal of Enam Medical College* 7, no. 1, (2017): 29–34.

Bowser, Eileen. *The Transformation of Cinema, 1907–1915*. Berkeley: University of California Press.

Box Office Mojo by IMDbPro. "Training Day," https://www.boxofficemojo.com/release/rl1165460993/weekend/.

Braga, Anthony A., and Glenn L. Pierce. "Reconsidering the Ballistic Imaging of Crime Bullets in Gun Law Enforcement Operations." *Forensic Science Policy & Management* 2, (2011): 105–117.

Braga, Anthony A., and Glenn L. Pierce. "Linking Crime Guns: The Impact of Ballistics Imaging Technology on the Productivity of the Boston Police Department's Ballistics Unit." *Journal of Forensic Science* 49, no. 4 (2004): 1–6.

Brenner, Emily. "Justifying Force: Police Procedurals and the Normalization of Violence." Empirical Research Capstone thesis, Arcadia University, 2020.

Britto, Sarah et al. "Does 'Special' Mean Young, White, and Female? Deconstructing the Meaning of 'Special' in Law & Order: Special Victims Unit." *Journal of Criminal Justice and Popular Culture* 14, no. 1 (2007): 39–56.

Brown, Chris. "Twin Town Crier Help Keeps the Beer Flowing." Windsor and Maidenhead Town Crier, April 19, 2013.

Browne, Malcolm W. "The 20th Century Makes Final Run; Economics Force Central to End Luxury Service." The *New York Times*, December 3, 1967. Retrieved from: https://timesmachine.nytimes.com/timesmachine/1967/12/03/84990019.html?pageNumber.

Bureau of Justice Statistics. "NCVS Victimization Analysis Tool (NVAT) Report." March 9, 2021, https://www.bjs.gov/index.cfm?ty=nvat.

Bureau of Justice Statistics. "Rape and Sexual Assault." n.d., https://www.bjs.gov/index.cfm?ty=tp&tid=317.

Burrough, Bryan. "Missing White Female." *Vanity Fair*, November 2006. https://www.vanityfair.com/news/2006/01/natalee200601.

Butler, John M. "The Future of Forensic DNA Analysis." *Philosophical Transactions* 370, (2015): 1–10.

Campbell, Rebecca, et al. "The National Problem of Untested Sexual Assault Kits (SAKs): Scope, Causes, Future Directions for Research, Policy, and Practice." *Trauma, Violence, & Abuse* 18, no. 4 (2017): 363–376.

Campbell, Rebecca, and Giannina Fehler-Cabral. "Why Police 'Couldn't or Wouldn't' Submit Sexual Assault Kits for DNA Testing: A Focal Concerns Theory Analysis of Untested Rape Kits." *Law & Society Review* 52, no. 1 (2018): 73–105.

Canemaker, John. "The Kid from Hogan's Alley." The *New York Times*, December 17, 1995. Retrieved from: https://www.nytimes.com/1995/12/17/books/the-kid-from-hogan-s-alley.html.

Carson, E. Ann. "Prisoners in 2019." Bureau of Justice Statistics (BJS) online. October 2020. https://www.bjs.gov/content/pub/pdf/p19.pdf.

Cather, Karin H. "The CSI Effect: Fake TV and its Impact on Jurors in Criminal Cases." *The Prosecutor* 34, (2004): 9–16.

Center, B. "The Historical Roots of the Sexualization of Black Women and Girls." February 20, 2019. https://www.blackburncenter.org/post/2019/02/20/the-historical-roots-of-the-sexualization-of-black-women-and-girls.

Chavez, Nicole. "Lori Loughlin and Felicity Huffman Are Two Contrasting Faces in the College Admissions Scam." CNN, October 23, 2019. https://www.cnn.com/2019/10/22/us/lori-loughlin-felicity-huffman-fallout.

Chiricos, Ted, and Sarah Eschholz. "The Racial and Ethnic Typification of Crime and the Criminal Typification of Race and Ethnicity in Local Television News." *Journal of Research in Crime and Delinquency* 39, no. 4 (2002): 400–420.

Ciulla Lipkin, Michelle. "4 Essential Skills for Media Literacy." https://www.renaissance.com/2018/07/26/blog-4-essential-skills-media-literacy/.

Clifton, Derrick. "Trump Deploys Angry Black Woman Trope Against Kamala Harris." NBC News. August 17, 2020, https://www.nbcnews.com/news/nbcblk/trump-deploys-angry-black-woman-trope-against-kamala-harris-n1236975.

Çobanoğlu, Özkul. "Cultural Interrelationships between Turkish Minstrel Tradition and Egyptian Folk Culture in the Socio-Cultural Context of Coffeehouses in Alexandria and Cairo." *International Journal of Modern Anthropology*, vol. 2 (2009).

Cole, Simon, and Rachel Dioso. "Law and the Lab." The *Wall Street Journal* online. Last modified May 13, 2005. https://www.wsj.com/articles/SB111594466027532447.

"Crime Dramas." Public Broadcasting Service online. 2014. https://www.pbs.org/wnet/pioneers-of-television/pioneering-programs/crime-dramas/.

Criss, Doug. "25 Years Ago Today, America Stopped to Watch the Cops Chase O.J. in a White Ford Bronco." CNN, June 17, 2019. https://www.cnn.com/2019/06/17/us/oj-simpson-car-chase-anniversary-trnd.

"CSI: Maricopa County: The CSI Effect and Its Real-Life Impact on Justice." Maricopa County Attorney's Office online. 2005. http://www.ce9.uscourts.gov/jc2008/references/csi/CSI_Effect_report.pdf.

Cuklanz, Lisa. "Feminist Theory in Communication." *The International Encyclopedia of Communication Theory and Philosophy*. John Wiley & Sons, Inc., 2016.

Curry, Kathleen. "Mediating COPS: An Analysis of Viewer Reaction to Reality TV." *Journal of Criminal Justice and Popular Culture* 8, no. 3 (2001): 169–185.

Custers, Kathleen, and Jan Van den Bulck. "The Cultivation of Fear of Sexual Violence in Women: Processes and Moderators of the Relationship between Television and Fear." *Communication Research*, 40, no 1., (2013): 96–124.

Dalbert, Claudia. "Belief in a Just World." *Handbook of Individual Differences in Social Behavior,* edited by Mark R. Leary and Rick H. Hoyle, Guilford Publications, 2013, 288–297.

Davidson, Douglas. "Observe the Birth of the Modern Police Procedural in Jules Dassin's 'The Naked City,' Restored via the Criterion Collection." https://elementsofmadness.com/2020/09/07/the-naked-city/.

Davis, Jeff, writer. *Criminal Minds*. Season 1, episode 1, "Extreme Aggressor." Directed by Richard Shepard, featuring Mandy Patinkin, Thomas Gibson, Lola Glaudini, Shemar Moore, Matthew Gray Gubler, and A. J. Cook. Aired September 22, 2005, in broadcast syndication.

DellaVigna, Stefano, and Ethan Kaplan. "The Fox News Affect: Media Bias and Voting." *The Quarterly Journal of Economics*, (2007): 1188–1234.

Denby, David. "On the Beat." *The New Yorker*. https://www.newyorker.com/magazine/2001/10/15/on-the-beat.

Demby, Gene. "What We Know (and We Don't Know) About Missing White Syndrome." NPR, Code Switch, April 13, 2017. https://www.npr.org/sections/codeswitch/2017/04/13/523769303/what-we-know-and-dont-know-about-missing-white-women-syndrome.

Di Mattia, Joanna. "In the Heat of the Night (Norman Jewison, 1967)" https://www.sensesofcinema.com/2017/1967/in-the-heat-of-the-night/.

Dixon et al. "The Portrayal of Race and Crime on Television Network News." *Journal of Broadcasting & Electronic Media* 47, no. 4 (2003): 498–523.

Dixon, Travis L., and Daniel Linz. "Race and the Misrepresentation of Victimization on Local Television News." *Communication Research* 27, no 5 (2000): 547–573.

Dixon, Travis L., and Keith B. Maddox. "Skin Tone, Crime News, and Social Reality Judgments: Priming the Stereotype of the Dark and Dangerous Black Criminal." *Journal of Applied Social Psychology* 35, no. 8 (2005): 1555–1570.

Dixon, Travis L., and Charlotte L. Williams. "The Changing Misrepresentation of Race and Crime on Network and Cable News." *Journal of Communication* 65, (2015): 24–39.

Donovan, Kathleen M., and Charles F. Klahm IV. "The Role of Entertainment Media in Perceptions of Police Use of Force." *Criminal Justice and Behavior* 42, no. 12 (2015): 1261–1281.

Dowler, Kenneth. "Media Influence on Citizen Attitudes Toward Police Effectiveness." *Policing and Society* 12, no. 3 (2002): 227–238.

Dowler, Kenneth, and Valerie Zawilski. "Public Perceptions of Police Misconduct and Discrimination: Examining the Impact of Media Consumption." *Journal of Criminal Justice* 35, (2007): 193–203.

Doyle, Aaron. "'Cops': Television Policing as Policing Reality." In *Entertaining Crime: Television Reality Programs*, 95–116. Oxforshire: Routledge, 1998.

Eagly, Alice H., and Valerie J. Steffen. "Gender and Aggressive Behavior: A Meta-Analytic Review of the Social Psychological Literature." *Psychological Bulletin*, 100, no. 3, (1986): 309–330.

Ebert, Roger. "Training Day." October 05, 2001, https://www.rogerebert.com/reviews/training-day-2001.

Edelstein, Arnon. "Cooling-off Periods among Serial Killers." *Journal of Psychology & Behavior Research* 2, no. 1 (2020): 1–15.

Encyclopedia of Race and Crime, ninth ed. (2009), s.v. "Beltway sniper attacks."

"End the Backlog." Joyful Heart Foundation online. 2021. https://www.endthebacklog.org/.

Entman, Robert M. "Modern Racism and the Images of Blacks in Local Television News." *Critical Studies in Mass Communication* 7, (1990): 332–345.

Entman, Robert M. "Representation and Reality in the Portrayal of Blacks on Network Television News." *Journalism Quarterly* 71, no. 3 (1994): 509–520.

Eschholz, Sarah et al. "Race and Attitudes towards the Police: Assessing the Effects of Watching 'Reality' Police Programs." *Journal of Criminal Justice* 30, (2002): 327–341.

Eschholz, Sarah et al. "Television and Fear of Crime: Program Types, Audience Traits, and the Mediating Effect of Perceived Neighborhood Racial Composition." *Social Problems*, 50, no 3, (August 2003): 395–415.

Estep, Rhoda, and Patrick T. Macdonald. "How Prime Time Crime Evolved on TV, 1976–1981." *Journalism Quarterly* 60, no. 2 (1983): 293–300.

"Expanded Homicide Data Table 1." Federal Bureau of Investigation (FBI) online. Fall 2020. https://ucr.fbi.gov/crime-in-the-u.s/2019/crime-in-the-u.s.-2019/tables/expanded-homicide-data-table-1.xls.

"Expanded Homicide Data Table 2." Federal Bureau of Investigation (FBI) online. Fall 2020. https://ucr.fbi.gov/crime-in-the-u.s/2019/crime-in-the-u.s.-2019/tables/expanded-homicide-data-table-2.xls.

"Expanded Homicide Data Table 3." Federal Bureau of Investigation (FBI) online. Fall 2020. https://ucr.fbi.gov/crime-in-the-u.s/2019/crime-in-the-u.s.-2019/tables/expanded-homicide-data-table-3.xls.

"Expanded Homicide Data Table 4." Federal Bureau of Investigation (FBI) online. Fall 2020. https://ucr.fbi.gov/crime-in-the-u.s/2019/crime-in-the-u.s.-2019/tables/expanded-homicide-data-table-4.xls.

"Expanded Homicide Data Table 6." Federal Bureau of Investigation (FBI) online. Fall 2020. https://ucr.fbi.gov/crime-in-the-u.s/2019/crime-in-the-u.s.-2019/tables/expanded-homicide-data-table-6.xls.

Federal Bureau of Investigation. "Crime in the United States 2013." 2013, https://ucr.fbi.gov/crime-in-the-u.s/2013/crime-in-the-u.s.-2013/violent-crime/rape.

Federal Bureau of Investigation. "Oklahoma City" Famous Cases and Criminal, History Page. Retrieved from: https://www.fbi.gov/history/famous-cases/oklahoma-city-bombing.

Fellow, R. Anthony. *America Media History*. Ed. Rebeckah Matthews and Megan Garvey. Fullerton: California State University, 2005.

Fox, James Alan et al. *Extreme Killing: Understanding Serial and Mass Murder*. Thousand Oaks: Sage Publications, 2018.

Fox, James Alan, and Jack Levin. "Multiple Homicide: Patterns of Serial and Mass Murder." *Crime and Justice* 23 (1998): 407–455.

Franklin, Benjamin. Apology for Printers. Retrieved from: https://www.pbs.org/benfranklin/pop_apology.html.

"Frequently Asked Questions on CODIS and NDIS." Federal Bureau of Investigation (FBI) online. 2021. https://www.fbi.gov/services/laboratory/biometric-analysis/codis/codis-and-ndis-factsheet#:~:text=CODIS%20is%20the%20acronym%20for,used%20to%20run%20these%20databases.

Friedkin, William. "We're All Popeye Doyle Now," https://www.theguardian.com/film/2008/nov/28/william-friedkin-french-connection.

Friedland, Barbara. "The Penny Press: Origins of the Modern News Media, 1833–1861." *Journalism History* 31, no.1 (2005): ProQuest.

Furnham, Adrian. "Belief in a Just World: Research Progress over the Past Decade." *Personality and Individual* Differences, 34, (2003): 795–817.

Garland, David. *The Culture of Control*. The University of Chicago Press, Chicago, 2000.

Gerbner, George. "Cultivation Analysis: An Overview." *Mass Communication & Society* 1, no. ¾ (1998): 175–194.

Gerbner et al. "Cultural Indicators: Violence Profile No. 9." *Journal of Communication* 28, no. 3 (1978): 176–207.

Gerbner, George et al. "TV Violence Profile No. 8: The Highlights." *Journal of Communication* 27, no. 2 (1977): 171–180.

Gerbner, George, and Larry Gross. "Living with Television: The Violence Profile." *Journal of Communication* 2, (1976): 171–80.

Gibb, Jane, and Roger Sabin. "Who Loves Ya, David Simon? Notes towards Placing The Wire's Depiction of African Americans in the Context of American TC Crime Drama." *Darkmatter*, (2009): 1–14.

Gilliam Jr., Franklin D., et al. "Crime in Black and White: The Violent, Scary World of Local News." *Press/Politics* 1, no. 3 (1996): 6–23.

Gilliam Jr., Franklin D., and Shanto Iyengar. "Prime Suspects: The Influence of Local Television News on the Viewing Public." *American Journal of Political Science* 44, no. 3 (2000): 560–573.

Grabe, Maria Elizabeth and Dan G. Drew. "Crime Cultivation: Comparisons across Media Genres and Channels." *Journal of Broadcasting and Electronic Media*, vol.51, 1, (2007).

Graziano, Lisa M. "News Media and Perceptions of Police: A State-of-the-Art Review." *Policing: An International Journal* 42, no. 2 (2019): 209–225.

Guerrasio, Jason. "Joe Berlinger Has Now Made Two Movies about Ted Bundy for Netflix, But Yhinks the Public's 'Insatiable Appetite for True Crime' Has Been Overstated." *Insider*. May 3, 2019. https://www.businessinsider.com/inside-2-ted-bundy-netflix-movies-by-joe-berlinger-extremely-wicked-2019-5

Harr, J. Scott, Kären M. Hess, Christine H. Orthmann, and Jonathon Kingsbury. *Constitutional Law and the Criminal Justice System*. Cengage Learning, Boston, 2018.

Harris, Mark. *Pictures at a Revolution: Five Movies and the Birth of the New Hollywood*, Penguin Press, New York, 2008.

Hayes, Rebecca M., et al. "Victim Blaming Others: Rape Myth Acceptance and the Just World Belief." *Feminist Criminology* 8, no. 3 (2013): 202–220.

Haynes, Michael, "Latino Stereotypes in Television." 2018 Symposium. 31. https://dc.ewu.edu/scrw_2018/31

Hays, Kristen. "Edinboro Teen Killer Sentenced." *Pittsburgh Post-Gazette*. September 10, 1999

Hazarika, Pompi, and David A. Russell. "Advances in Fingerprint Analysis." *Angewandte Chemie International Edition* 51, no. 15 (2012): 3524–3531.

Herron, R. M. (2013). Media Impact on the Mental Health of Latina Adolescents in America (Order No. 1545168). Available from ProQuest Dissertations & Theses Global. (1442593002)

Hersko, Tyler. "'Tiger King' Had 34 Million Viewers Within 10 Days of Launch, Fox to Air Special." *Indie Wire*. April 8, 2020. https://www.indiewire.com/2020/04/tiger-king-netflix-viewership-fox-special-1202223808/

History Channel. This Day in History September 15, 1963. https://www.history.com/this-day-in-history/four-black-schoolgirls-killed-in-birmingham.

History.com. "The Printing Press." https://www.history.com/topics/inventions/mankind-the-story-of-all-of-us-videos-the-printing-press-video.

History.com. "This Day in History, September 6, 2005." This Day in History, September 5, 2006, https://www.history.com/this-day-in-history/katie-couric-makes-network-anchor-debut#:~:text=Barbara%20Walters%20was%20the%20first,University%20of%20Virginia%20in%201979.

Hoad, Phil. "How We Made In the Heat of the Night," *The Guardian* (November 22, 2016) https://www.theguardian.com/film/2016/nov/22/how-we-made-in-the-heat-of-the-night-norman-jewison.

Holbert et al. "Fear, Authority, and Justice: Crime-Related TV Viewing and Endorsements of Capital Punishment and Gun Ownership." *J&MC Quarterly*, 81, no. 2 (Summer 2004): 343–363.

Howard, Judith A. "The 'Normal' Victim: The Effects of Gender Stereotypes on Reactions to Victims." *Social Psychology Quarterly*, 47, no. 3, (1984): 270–281.

"H.R. 1620 – Violence Against Women Act Reauthorization Act of 2021." Library of Congress online. 2021. https://www.congress.gov/bill/117th-congress/house-bill/1620/text.

Hughes, Michael. "The Fruits of Cultivation Analysis: A Reexamination of Some Effects of Television Watching." *The Public Opinion Quarterly* 44, no. 3 (1980): 287–302.

IMDB. "Jon-Benet Ramsey." https://www.imdb.com/name/nm2338600/?ref_=fn_al_nm_1

IMDB. "Natalie Holloway." https://www.imdb.com/find?q=Natalee%20Holloway&s=tt&ref_=fn_al_tt_mr

"Incarcerated Women and Girls." The Sentencing Project online. November 2020. https://www.sentencingproject.org/wp-content/uploads/2016/02/Incarcerated-Women-and-Girls.pdf.

Infield, Tom. "Americans Who Get News Mainly on Social Media Are Less Knowledgeable and Less Engaged: And Social Media Is Now among the Most Common Ways People—Particularly Young Adults—Get Their Political News." Pew Trust, November 16, 2020. https://www.pewtrusts.org/en/trust/archive/fall-2020/americans-who-get-news-mainly-on-social-media-are-less-knowledgeable-and-less-engaged

"Inmate Race." Federal Bureau of Prisons online. March 2021. https://www.bop.gov/about/statistics/statistics_inmate_race.jsp.

Intravia, Jonathan, and Justin T. Pickett. "Stereotyping Online? Internet News, Social Media, and the Racial Typification of Crime." *Sociological Forum* 34, no. 3 (2019): 616–642.

Iyengar, Shanto, and Donald R. Kinder. *News that Matters: Television and American Opinion*. Chicago: University of Chicago Press, 2010.

Jamieson, Patrick E., and Daniel Romer. "Violence in Popular U.S. Prime Time TV Dramas and the Cultivation of Fear: A Time Series Analysis." *Media and Communication* 2, no. 2 (2014): 31–41.

Jewell, K. Sue. "From Mammy to Miss America and Beyond: Cultural Images and the Shaping of U.S. Social Policy." Taylor & Francis, 1992. https://ebookcentral-proquest-com.proxy.libraries.rutgers.edu/lib/rutgers-ebooks/detail.action?docID=179834.

Jones, Tom. "America Is Watching the Evening News Again. TV Numbers Are Up. Way Up." The Poynter Report. April 16, 2020. https://www.poynter.org/newsletters/2020/america-is-watching-the-evening-news-again-tv-news-numbers-are-up-way-up/.

"Justification for Non-Competitive Procurement." City of Chicago online. 2012. https://www.chicago.gov/content/dam/city/depts/dps/SoleSource/NCRB2012/ForensicTechnologyApproved.pdf.

Kahlor, LeeAnn, and Matthew S. Eastin. "Television's Role in the Culture of Violence Towards Women: A Study of Television Viewing and the Cultivation of Rape Myth Acceptance in the United States." *Journal of Broadcasting & Electronic Media*, 55, no. 2, (2011): 215–231.

Kaiser, Jocelyn. "A Judge Said Police Can Search the DNA Database of 1 Million Americans without Their Consent. What's Next?" *Science* online. Last modified November 7, 2019. https://www.sciencemag.org/news/2019/11/judge-said-police-can-search-dna-millions-americans-without-their-consent-what-s-next.

Kampfe, Karson. "Police-Worn Body Cameras: Balancing Privacy and Accountability Through State and Police Department Action." *Ohio State Law Journal* 76, no. 5 (2015): 1153–1200.

Kaplan, Richard. "Yellow Journalism." *International Encyclopedia of Communication*, edited by Wolfgang Donsbach, Volume XI, 2000.

Keeney, Belea T., and Kathleen M. Heide. "Serial Murder: A More Accurate and Inclusive Definition." *International Journal of Offender Therapy and Comparative Criminology* 39, no. 4 (1995): 299–306.

Kelling, George. "The Development of Broken Windows Theory." *Foundations of Criminological Theory* 27:202:511. Class lecture: Rutgers School of Criminal Justice, Newark, NJ, November 2000.

Kleinke, Chris L., and Cecilia Meyer. "Evaluation of Rape Victim by Men and Women with High and Low Belief in a Just World." *Psychology of Women Quarterly*, 14, no. 3, (1990): 343–353.

Kim, Young S. et al. "Examining the CSI Effect in the Cases of Circumstantial Evidence and Eyewitness Testimony: Multivariate and Path Analyses." *Journal of Criminal Justice* 37, no. 5 (2009): 452–460.

Kort-Butler, Lisa A., and Kelley J. Sittner Hartshorn. "Watching the Detectives: Crime Programming, Fear of Crime, and Attitudes about the Criminal Justice System." *The Sociological Quarterly*, 52, no. 1 (Winter 2011): 36–55.

Law & Order. https://www.imdb.com/title/tt0098844/.

Lerner, Melvin J. "The Belief in a Just World." *The Belief in a Just World*. Springer, 1980, 9–30.

Levenson, Michael. "Harvey Weinstein Faces Six Additional Sex Charges in Los Angeles." *New York Times*, January 27, 2021.

Levin, Jessica. "Representations of Victims, Suspects and Offenders: A Content Analysis of Four Television Crime Shows." Undergraduate Honors thesis, University of Colorado, Boulder, 2013.

Lipschultz, Jeremy Harris, and Michael L. Hilt. "Race and Local Television News Crime Coverage." *Studies in Media & Information Literacy Education* 3, no. 4 (2003): 1–10.

Lipsitz, Andrew, writer. *CSI: Crime Scene Investigation*. Season 1, episode 5. "Friends and Lovers." Directed by Lou Antonio, featuring William Petersen, Marg Helgenberger, Gary Dourdan, George Eads, Jorja Fox, and Paul Guilfoyle. Aired November 3, 2000, in broadcast syndication.

Lopez, Vera and Meda Chesney-Lind. "Latina Girls Speak Out: Stereotypes, Gender and Relationship Dynamics." *Latino Studies*, 4, vol. 12, (2014): 527–549. https://www.researchgate.net/profile/Vera-Lopez/publication/269285914_Latina _Girls_Speak_Out_Stereotypes_Gender_and_Relationship_Dynamics/links /5bfee73792851c63caafb2cb/Latina-Girls-Speak-Out-Stereotypes-Gender-and -Relationship-Dynamics.pdf.

MacLin, M. Kimberly, and Vivian Herrera. "The Criminal Stereotype." *North American Journal of Psychology*, 8, no. 2, (Jun/Jul 2006): 197–207.

Madriz, Esther I. "Images of Criminals and Victims: A Study on Women's Fear and Social Control." *Gender & Society*, 11, no. 3, (1997): 342–356.

Mastro, Dana and Elizabeth Behm-Morawitz, E. "Latino Representation on Primetime Television." *Journalism & Mass Communication Quarterly*, 82 no.1, (2005) 110–130. doi:10.1177/107769900508200108.

Mastro, Dana E., and Amanda L. Robinson. "Cops and crooks: images of minorities on primetime television." *Journal of Criminal Justice* 28, no. 5 (2000): 385–396.

Mendelsohn, Benjamin. "Victimology and Contemporary Society's Trends." *Victimology* 1, no. 1 (1976): 8–28.

Mitovich, Matt Webb. "TV Ratings: Prodigal Son Slips with Tuesday Move, This Is Us Tops Night." *TV Line* online. Last modified January 13, 2021. https://tvline.com/2021/01/13/tv-ratings-prodigal-son-season-2-premiere/.

Morgan, Anthony, and Penny Jorna. "Impact of Ballistic Evidence on Criminal Investigations." *Trends and Issues in Crime and Criminal Justice* 28, (2018): 1–16.

Morgan, Rachel E., and Jennifer L. Truman. "Criminal Victimization, 2019." *Bureau of Justice Statistics*, September 2020, https://www.bjs.gov/content/pub/pdf/cv19.pdf.

Morris, Jonathan S. "Slanted Objectivity? Perceived Media Bias, Cable News Exposure, and Political Attitudes." *Social Science Quarterly*, 88, no. 3 (September 2007): 707–728.

Morton, Robert J., and Mark A. Hilts. "Serial Murder." Hilts, FBI online. Last modified May 21, 2010. www.fbi.gov/stats-services/publications/serial-murder.

Moses, Kenneth R., et al. "Automated Fingerprint Identification System (AFIS)." In *SWGFAST-The Fingerprint Sourcebook*, edited by the Scientific Working Group on Friction Ridge Analysis Study and Technology and National institute of Justice, 1–33. Washington, DC: U.S. Department of Justice, 2011.

Moy, Patricia et al. "Agenda-Setting, Priming, and Framing." In *The International Encyclopedia of Communication Theory and Philosophy*, 1–13. Hoboken: John Wiley & Sons, Inc., 2016.

Mulford, Carla. "Figuring Benjamin Franklin in American Cultural Memory." *The New England Quarterly*, vol. 72, no. 3 (Sep., 1999): 415–443. https://www.jstor.org/stable/366890

Murphey, Murray G. and Perry Miller. "American Studies." *American Studies*, vol. 42, no. 2, 2001.

Mutz, Diana C., and Lilach Nir. "Not Necessarily the News: Does Fictional Television Influence Real-World Policy Preferences?" *Mass Communication and Society*, 13, no. 2, 196–217.

National Park Service. "Birmingham Civil Rights Monument." https://www.nps.gov/bicr/learn/historyculture.htm

"NCVS Victimization Analysis Tool (NVAT) Report." Bureau of Justice Statistics online. Last modified March 9, 2021. https://www.bjs.gov/index.cfm?ty=nvat.

Nerone, John C. "The Mythology of the Penny Press." *Critical Studies in Mass Communication* 4, no. 4, (2009): 376–404. DOI: 10.1080/15295038709360146.

New York Times. "What to Know About the Death of George Floyd in Minneapolis." March 10, 2021. https://www.nytimes.com/article/george-floyd.html?name=styln-floyd-trial&region=TOP_BANNER&block=storyline_menu_recirc&action=click&pgtype=Article&impression_id=&variant=show.

"NIBIN." Bureau of Alcohol, Tobacco, Firearms and Explosives (ATF) online. June 2020. https://www.atf.gov/resource-center/docs/undefined/nibin-fact-sheet-june-2020/download.

"Normalizing Injustice." Color of Change and The University of Southern California Annenberg Norman Lear Center. Accessed April 21, 2020. https://hollywood.colorofchange.org//wp-content/uploads/ 2020/02/Normalizing-Injustice_Abridged-1.pdf.

Novak, Kenneth and Gary Cordner, Bradley Smith, and Roy Roberg. *Police & Society*. New York, Oxford University Press, 2017.

Oliver, Mary Beth. "Portrayals of Crime, Race, and Aggression in 'Reality Based' Police Shows: A Content Analysis." *Journal of Broadcasting & Electronic Media* 28, no. 2 (1994): 179–192.

Oliver, Mary Beth, and G. Blake Armstrong. "Predictors of Viewing and Enjoyment of Reality-Based and Fictional Crime Shows." *Journalism and Mass Communication Quarterly* 72, no. 3 (1995): 559–570.

Olsen, Elizabeth. "'Dora' Special Explores Influence on Children." The *New York Times*, August 8, 2010. https://www.nytimes.com/2010/08/09/business/media/09dora.html?searchResultPosition=1.

O'Sullivan, Shannon. "Who is always already criminalized? an intersectional analysis of criminality on orange is the new black." *The Journal of American Culture*, 39(4), (2016): 401–412. doi:10.1111/jacc.12637

Oxford Research Encyclopedia of Criminology and Criminal Justice (2016), s.v. "Police Dramas on Television."

Parrott, Scott, and Caroline Titcomb Parrott. "U.S. Television's 'Mean World' for White Women: The Portrayal of Gender and Race on Fictional Crime Dramas." *Sex Roles* 73, no. 1–2 (2015): 70–82.

Pautz, Michelle C. doi:10.1017/S1049096516000159. American Political Science Association, 2016.

Pelecanos, George, writer. *The Wire*. Season 4, episode 12, "That's Got His Own." Directed by Joe Chappelle, featuring Wendell Pierce, Dominic West, Lance Reddick, Michael K. Williams, and Felicia Pearson. Aired on December 3, 2006, in broadcast syndication.

Petski, Denise. "Live PD Hits Series Ratings High in Live+Same Day." *Deadline* online. Last modified June 25, 2019. https://deadline.com/2019/06/live-pd-series-ratings-highs-livesame-day-ae-dan-abrams-1202637653/.

Phillips, Michael. "Commentary: Out of 60s Chaos, Dirty Harry and Popeye Doyle Ruled the Streets, and we've been paying for it ever since." https://www.chicagotribune.com/entertainment/movies/michael-phillips/ct-ent-movie-cops-commentary-0607-20200603-442gvirklvcpvdowsibbmnl4tu-story.html.

Podlas, Kimberlianne. "The CSI Effect and Other Forensic Fictions." *Loyola of Los Angeles Entertainment Law Review*, vol. 27 (2006): 87–125.

Pogrebin, Robin. "Amy Sherald Directs Her Breonna Taylor Painting Toward Justice." *New York Times*, March 7, 2021. https://www.nytimes.com/2021/03/07/arts/design/amy-sherald-breonna-taylor-painting.html?searchResultPosition=1.

"Police Get Help from TV Show to Test Unprocessed Rape Kits." The *Press of Atlantic City* online. Last modified April 6, 2015. https://pressofatlanticcity.com/life/police-get-help-from-tv-show-to-test-unprocessed-rape-kits/article_cafe760c-8a95-5462-9e3b-3ca93a946cba.html.

Porter, Rick. "TV Long View: How Much Network TV Depends on Cop Shows." The *Hollywood Reporter* online. Last modified June 20, 2020. https://www.hollywoodreporter.com/live-feed/heres-how-network-tv-depends-cop-shows-1299504.

Puff Daddy and The Family."It's All About the Benjamins." EMI Music, 1997.

"Quick Facts: Women in the Federal Offender Population." United States Sentencing Commission online. 2020. https://www.ussc.gov/sites/default/files/pdf/research-and-publications/quick-facts/Female_Offenders_FY19.pdf.

Reed, John P., and Robin S. Reed. "Status, Images, and Consequence: Once a Criminal Always a Criminal." *Sociology & Social Research*, 57, no. 4, (1973): 460–472.

Reider, Rem. "O.J. Simpson's Huge Impact on the News Media." *USA Today*, June 16, 2014. https://www.usatoday.com/story/money/columnist/rieder/2014/06/16/oj-saga-ushered-in-new-media-era/10574759/

Reiner, R. "The New Blue Films." *New Society*, 43 (March).

Reiner, Robert. "Policing and the Media." *Handbook of Policing* (2008): 313–335.

Rhineberger-dunn et al. "Clearing Crime in Prime-Time: The Disjuncture Between Fiction and Reality." *American Journal of Criminal Justice* 41, no. 2 (2016): 255–278.

Rich, Paul. "Poor Richard in 2011." *Policy Studies Journal*. https://onlinelibrary-wiley-com.proxy.libraries.rutgers.edu/doi/pdfdirect/10.1111/j.1541-0072.2010.00387.x.

Roberts, Chris. "Gatekeeping Theory: An Evolution," Communication Theory and Methodology Division, Association for Education and Journalism and Mass Communication, San Antonio, Texas (2005).

Rosenberg, Alyssa. "How Police Censorship Shaped Hollywood" https://www.washingtonpost.com/sf/opinions/2016/10/24/how-police-censorship-shaped-hollywood/.

Rose, Steve. "How Hollywood Has Tried, and Mostly Failed, to Tackle Police Racism." https://www.theguardian.com/culture/2020/jun/08/how-hollywood-has-tried-and-mostly-failed-to-tackle-police-racism.

Rubio, Solange. "This Land: A Media Analysis of Latinx Representation in 'Woke' Advertising." *Media and Communication Studies: Culture Collaborative Media, and the Creative Industries* (2018).

Rudman, Laurie A., Anthony G. Greenwald, and Debbie E. McGhee. "Implicit Self-Concept and Evaluative Implicit Gender Stereotypes: Self and Ingroup Share Desirable Traits." *Personality and Social Psychology Bulletin*, 27, no. 9, (2001): 1164–1178.

Rutgers Today. "A Contagion of Institutional Mistrust: New Report Analyzes New and Dangerous Trends of Disinformation in Wake of U.S. Capitol Attack." March 26, 2021. https://www.rutgers.edu/news/contagion-institutional-distrust?utm_source=newsletter&utm_medium=email&utm_campaign=rutgerstoday&utm_content=Research%20%26amp%3B%20Innovation

Ryan, Erin. "Dora the Explorer: Empowering Preschoolers, Girls, and Latinas." *Journal of Broadcasting & Electronic Media*, 54, no.1, (2010): 54–68.

Salam, Maya. "The Unraveling of Jeffrey Epstein: The Story Line Is Moving Quickly. Here's What to Know." *New York Times*, July 16, 2019. https://www.nytimes.com/2019/07/16/us/jeffrey-epstein-what-to-know.html?searchResultPosition=7

Sarapin, Susan H., and Glenn G. Sparks. "Eyewitnesses to TV Versions of Reality: The Relationship between Exposure to TV Crime Dramas and Perceptions of the Criminal Justice System." In *How Television Shapes our Worldview: Media Representations of Social Trends and Change*, 145–170. Lanham, MD: Lexington Books, 2009.

Saturday Night Live. "Murder Show." NBC, 2021. https://youtu.be/J4RdcE6H4Gs.

Scharrer, Erica. "Tough Guys: The Portrayal of Hypermasculinity and Aggression in Televised Police Dramas." *Journal of Broadcasting & Electronic Media* 45, no. 4 (2001): 615–634.

Schroth. "Dime Novels, Pulps, and Thrillers" in *The Social History of Crime and Punishment in America: An Encyclopedia*, ed. Wilbur R. Miller, SAGE Publications, 2012.

Schwartzapfel, Beth. "This Machine Could Prevent Gun Violence—If Only Cops Used It." The Marshall Project online. Last modified October 6, 2016. https://www.themarshallproject.org/2016/10/06/this-machine-could-prevent-gun-violence-if-only-cops-used-it.

Schweitzer, N. J., and Michael J. Saks. "The CSI Effect: Popular Fiction about Forensic Science Affects the Publics Expectations about Real Forensic Science." *Jurimetrics* 47, (2007): 357–364.

Serani, Deborah. "If It Bleeds, It Leads: The Clinical Implications of Fear-Based Programming in News Media." *Psychoanalysis & Psychotherapy*, vol. 238 (Winter 2008). https://www.researchgate.net/profile/Deborah-Serani/publication/247898920_If_It_Bleeds_It_Leads_The_Clinical_Implications_of_Fear-Based_Programming_in_News_Media/links/5a91f67c0f7e9ba4296db443/If-It-Bleeds-It-Leads-The-Clinical-Implications-of-Fear-Based-Programming-in-News-Media.pdf.

Shaw, Gabbi. "The LongestRrunning TV Dramas of All Time." *Insider* online. Last modified March 2, 2020. https://www.insider.com/longest-tv-dramas-2018-10.

Sheley, Joseph F., and Cindy D. Ashkins. "Crime, Crime News, and Crime Views." *The Public Opinion Quarterly* 45, no. 4 (1981): 492–506.

Shelton, Hon. Donald E., et al. "A Study of Juror Expectations and Demands Concerning Scientific Evidence: Does the CSI Effect Exist?" *Vanderbilt Journal of Entertainment and Technology Law* 9, no. 2 (2006): 331–368.

Sheppard, Sarah. "How Sexualizing Young Girls May Lead to Mental Health Problems." https://www.verywellmind.com/damaging-effects-of-sexualizing-girls-4778062.

Shrum, L. J. "The Role of Source Confusion in Cultivation Effects May Depend on Processing Strategy: A Comment on Mares (1996)." *Human Communication Research* 24, no. 2 (1997): 349–358.

Slater, Michael D., et al. "Television Dramas and Support for Controversial Public Policies: Effects and Mechanisms." *Journal of Communication*, 56, (2006), 235–252.

Simpson, Sally S. "Feminist Theory, Crime, and Justice." *Criminology*, 27, no. 4, (1989): 605–631.

Sink, Alexander, and Dana Mastro. "Depictions of Gender on Primetime Television: A Quantitative Content Analysis." *Mass Communication and Society*, (2016): 1–33.

Smith, Erika W. "What Netflix's Unbelievable Gets Right About Rape Kits." Refinery29 online. Last modified September 13, 2019. https://www.refinery29.com/en-us/rape-kit-exam#:~:text=In%20the%20first%20episode%20of,immediately%20after%20reporting%20her%20rape.&text=The%20process%20of%20getting%20a,is%20another%20trauma%20in%20itself.

Sommers, Zach. "Missing White Woman Syndrome: An Empirical Analysis of Race and Gender Disparities in Online News Coverage of Missing Persons." *The Journal of Criminal Law and Criminology*, 106, no. 2, (Spring 2016): 275–314. https://www.jstor.org/stable/45163263.

Sood, Gaurav, and Daniel Trielli. "The Face of Crime in Prime Time: Evidence from Law and Order." *SSRN Electronic Journal*, (2017): 1–30.

Sorkin, Aaron. "The Women of Qumar." *The West Wing*, season 3, episode 9, John Wells Productions, 2001.

"Sort by Popularity—Most Popular Movies and TV Shows tagged with Keyword 'Rape-Kit.'" IMdb online. 2021. https://www.imdb.com/search/keyword/?keywords=rape-kit.

Statista. "Super Bowl Average Costs of a 30-Second TV Advertisement from 2002 to 2021." https://www.statista.com/statistics/217134/total-advertisement-revenue-of-super-bowls/#:~:text=In%202021%2C%20advertisers%20had%20to,the%20Super%20Bowl%20LV%20broadcast.

Stein, Megan. "This 'SNL' Skit About 'Murder Shows' Will Make Any True Crime Fan Laugh: It Pokes Fun at Everyone's Favorite Weekend Activity." *Cosmopolitan Online*, March 4, 2021, https://www.cosmopolitan.com/entertainment/tv/a35730648/saturday-night-live-murder-show-skit/?source=nl&utm_source=nl_cos&utm_medium=email&date=030521&utm_campaign=nl23115867.

Stewart, Daxton R. "Chip." "Freedom's Vanguard: Horace Greeley on Threats to Press Freedom in the Early Years of the Penny Press." *American Journalism*, 29:1, (2013) 60–83, DOI: 10.1080/08821127.2012.10677814, 2012.

Stillman, Sarah. "'The Missing White Woman Syndrome': Disappeared Women and Media Activism." *Gender and Development*, 15, no. 3, Taylor & Francis, Ltd., 491–502.

Strömwall, Leif A. et al. "Blame Attributions and Rape: Effects of Belief in a Just World and Relationship Level." *Legal and Criminological Psychology*, 18, no. 2, (September 2013): 254–261

Surette, Ray. *Media, Crime and Criminal Justice: Images, Realities, and Policies*. Belmont, CA, Cengage Learning, 2011.

"Table 37: Current Year Over Previous Year Arrest Trends." Federal Bureau of Investigation (FBI) online. 2020. https://ucr.fbi.gov/crime-in-the-u.s/2019/crime-in-the-u.s.-2019/topic-pages/tables/table-37.

"Table 43A." Federal Bureau of Investigation (FBI) online. 2019. https://ucr.fbi.gov/crime-in-the-u.s/2019/crime-in-the-u.s.-2019/tables/table-43.

"Table 74." Federal Bureau of Investigation (FBI) online. 2020. https://ucr.fbi.gov/crime-in-the-u.s/2019/crime-in-the-u.s.-2019/tables/table-74/table-74.xls#overview.

Tan, Shelly, Youjin Shin, and Danielle Rindler. "How one of America's Ugliest Days Unraveled Inside and Out the Capitol." The *Washington Post*. January 9, 2021. https://www.washingtonpost.com/nation/interactive/2021/capitol-insurrection-visual-timeline/.

Tankebe, Justice. "Viewing Things Differently: The Dimensions of Public Perceptions of Police Legitimacy. Criminology 51, no. 1 (2013): 103–135.

The Center for Media Literacy. "Media Literacy: A Definition and More." https://www.medialit.org/media-literacy-definition-and-more.

The Specialists LTD. Catalogue.

Tubbs, Stewart and Moss, Sylvia. *Human Communication: Principles and Concepts*, tenth Edition, McGraw-Hill, New York, 2006.

TVJobs.com. "Master Station Index." http://msi.tvjobs.com/.

Tyler, Tom R. "Viewing CSI and the Threshold of Guilt: Managing Truth and Justice in Reality and Fiction." *The Yale Law Journal* 115, no. 5 (2006): 1050–1085.

"Types of Law Enforcement Agencies." International Association of Chiefs of Police online. 2018. https://www.discoverpolicing.org/explore-the-field/types-of-law-enforcement-agencies/.

United States Census Bureau. "Race." https://www.census.gov/topics/population/race.html.

Van Susteren, Greta. On the Record with Greta. "Holloway Chaperone Speaks Out." Fox News. February 24, 2006. https://web.archive.org/web/20080423140126/http://www.foxnews.com/story/0,2933,186017,00.html.

"Violent Crime." Federal Bureau of Investigation (FBI) online. Fall 2020. https://ucr.fbi.gov/crime-in-the-u.s/2019/crime-in-the-u.s.-2019/topic-pages/violent-crime.

von Hentig, Hans. *The Criminal and His Victim: Studies in the Sociobiology of Crime*. New Haven: Yale University Press, 1948.

Vonderhaar, Rebecca L., and Dianne Cyr Carmody. "There Are No 'Innocent Victims': The Influence of Just World Beliefs and Prior Victimization on Rape Myth Acceptance." *Journal of Interpersonal Violence*, 30, no. 10, (2014): 1615–1632.

Walker, Samuel. *Sense and Nonsense about Crime, Drugs, and Communities*, eighth ed., Stamford, CT: Cengage Learning, 2015.

Walther, Joseph B. "Social Media and Intergroup Encounters with 'Cops': Biased Samples, Echo Chambers, and Research Opportunities." In *The Rowman & Littlefield Handbook of Policing, Communication, and Society*, 229–244. Lanham, MD: Rowman & Littlefield, 2021.

Watkins, Michael J. "Forensics in the Media: Have Attorneys Reacted to the Growing Popularity of Forensic Crime Dramas?" Master's thesis, Florida State University, 2004.

Waxman, Olivia B. "How the U.S. Got Its Police Force." *Time* online. Last modified May 18, 2017. https://time.com/4779112/police-history-origins/.

Welch, Kelly. "Black Criminal Stereotypes and Racial Profiling." *Journal of Contemporary Criminal Justice* 23, no. 3 (2007): 276–288.

Williamson, Kevin. "Pilot." *The Following*, Season 1, Episode 1. Fox Searchlight. IMDB. 2013 https://www.imdb.com/search/title/?genres=crime&explore=title_type,genres&title_type=tvSeries.

Wittern-Keller, Laura. *Freedom of the Screen: Legal Challenges to State Film Censorship*, University Press of Kentucky, 2008.

Wolf Harlow, Caroline. "Defense Counsel in Criminal Cases." U.S. Department of Justice, Bureau of Justice Statistics, Special Report, November 2000.

Wolfgang, Marvin E. "Victim Precipitated Criminal Homicide." *The Journal of Criminal Law, Criminology, and Police Science* 48, no. 1 (1857): 1–11.

Worthy, Kym. "What Happened When We Tested Thousands of Abandoned Rape Kits in Detroit." September 26, 2018. Ted Institute, Vancouver, British Columbia, Canada MPEG-4, 18:56. https://www.ted.com/talks/kym_worthy_what_happened_when_we_tested_thousands_of_abandoned_rape_kits_in_detroit/transcript?language=en#t-180943.

Xu, Beina and Eleanor Albert. "Media Censorship in China—Backgrounder."

Council on Foreign Relations. February 17, 2017, https://www.cfr.org/backgrounder/media-censorship-china.

INDEX

Note: Page numbers in *italics* indicate figures and page numbers in **bold** indicate tables in the text

23andMe, 91

ABC (World News Tonight), 77, 78
Abrams, Dan, 65
Acta Diurna, 5
Adams, John, 10, 11
Adubato, Beth, 25, 42, 74, 82, 140, 183
African American Policy Forum, 137
African Americans, 102, 144
"always pregnant" stereotype, 145
AMBER Alert, 134
American Greed (crime show), 63
American Justice (crime show), 63
AncestryDNA, 91
anchors role in news media, 6–7
Arbuckle, Roscoe "Fatty," 159
Armstrong, G. Blake, 65

Bagdasarov, Zhanna, 180
ballistics identification, 90
Baskin, Deborah R., 93
Battling the Backlog (crime drama), 96
BBC, **50**, 52, 179
Behm-Morawitz, Elizabeth, 146
Bellinger, Joe, 2
bias, understanding, 84–85

Blackburn Center, 144
The Blacklist (crime drama), 57, 123
#BlackLivesMatter movement, 81, 104, 105, 137, 157
Black people/women, 102, 136; cultivation theory, 110–11; inequality in media coverage, 153; invisibilization of, 137; media-priming theory, 111–12; media's depiction as criminals, 101–2, 112; as perpetrators and victims in crime dramas, 105–6; portrayal on news, 103–5; stereotyped black females, 144
Black perpetrators: crime drama mirroring official statistics of, 108–10; in crime dramas, 105–6; official statistics, 107–8; from TV crime drama analyses, 106–7
Black victims, 104; crime drama mirroring official statistics of, 108–10; in crime dramas, 105–6; official statistics, 108; from TV crime drama analyses, 107
blocked opportunities, 133

Blue Bloods (crime drama), 57, 124, 125, 161, 174
Bones (crime drama), 124
Bonilla-Silva, Eduardo, 135–36
Bonnie and Clyde (film), 162
Bowen, Julie, 147
Breen, Joseph, 159
Bright, Malcolm, 34
Britto, Sarah, 125
Brooklyn Nine-Nine (crime drama), 57
Brown, Michael, 67, 157
Brown, Rosellen, 180
Brujas (TV series), 146, 148
BTK Killer, 24
BulletTrax-3-D machines, 90
Bundy, Ted (serial killer), 2, 3, 24
Bureau of Justice Statistics, 46, 116
Bush, George H. W., 102
BuzzFeed, 181, **182**

Campbell, Rebecca, 95, 96
CareyWard, Benedict, 179
Castle (crime drama), 123, 124
Cather, Karin H., 93
CBS Evening News, 6, 77, 78
Chaplin, Charlie, 157, 164
Chauvin, Derek, 45
Chesney-Lind, Meda, 145
Chicago PD (crime drama), 57
Chiricos, Ted, 104
"cholas" stereotype, 145
citizen videos on social media, 67–68
Civil Rights Act of 1964, 161
class bias, 152
CNBC, 171
CNN, 6, **50**, 52, 104, 171
Code Switch blog, 138
CODIS. *See* Combined DNA Index System
Cold Case Files (crime show), 63
Cold Justice (crime drama), 96
college admissions scandal, 44
Color of Change, 62
Combined DNA Index System (CODIS), 90–91, 85, 97

Combs, Sean "P. Diddy," 10
comic or buffoon, Latinos portrayed in TV as, 147
competition among news reporters, 79
COPS (crime show), 3, 59, 64–65
cops/policeman portrayal in Hollywood movies, 158–62
Cosby Show (TV series), 147
Couric, Katie, 6
courtroom work group, 47
Court TV, 39
Cracked, Two Sentence Horror Stories (crime drama), 96
Cracker, Born to Kill? (crime drama), 96
Crawford, John, 157
Crime-and Justice Frames, 133–34
crime, 47, 102, 133, 177–78; coverage, 15; fear of, 3–4; growing population causes, 14; in dime novels, 14–15; obsession with, 2; perceptions of police survey, **184**; portrayal on television, 183. *See* cultivation theory; television crime dramas.
Crime Scene Investigation (*CSI*) (crime drama), 92
criminal: criminal-Black association, 110; Latinos portrayed in TV as, 146; stereotypes, 104
criminal justice system, 43, 45, 54, 62, 153; African Americans in, 102; crime statistics in, 29; examples of, 44–45; mischaracterizations of, 2–3; "murder in the first block" syndrome in, 46; work groups, 54
Criminal Justice Wedding Cake Model, 43, 52; dumb criminal story of, 48; felony crimes in, 47–48; full court press in, 46–47; Media Pineapple Upside Down cake news, 52, *53*; top layer of, 44–45
Criminal Minds (drama series), 22, 32, 57, 123–25
Cronkite, Walter, 6
Crow, Jim, 161

INDEX

CSI (crime drama), 2, 96
CSI Effect, 88, 92–94, 97
Cuklanz, Lisa, 118
cultivation theory, 4, 32–34, 49, 110–11, 118
The Culture of Control (Garland), 4

Dahmer, Jeffrey (serial killer), 24
Dassin, Jules, 160
Day, Benjamin, 17
Decision Making in Criminal Justice (Gottfredson and Gottfredson), 43
deep tease, 42–43
DellaVigna, Stefano, 171
Del Toro, Benicio, 179
Demby, Gene, 138–39
deoxyribonucleic acid (DNA) analysis, 90–91
Designated Market Areas (DMAs), 74
Devious Maids (TV show), 148
Dexter, Jean, 160
differential association theory, 101
dime novels, 14–15
Dirty Harry (film), 163–65
Dirty John (crime show), 63
Dixon, Travis L., 103–4, 111
DMAs. *See* Designated Market Areas
Domanick, Joe, 159
domestic violence, 119
Donovan, Kathleen M., 63
Dora the Explorer (animated series), 149
Dowler, Ken, 62, 63
Doyle, Arthur Conan, 14
Dragnet (TV series), 23, 161
Drew, Dan, 4
Dugan, Mickey. *See* Yellow Kid (Cartoon character)
"dumb criminal" story, 40, 48

Ebert, Roger, 164
Edelstein, Arnon, 24
Edison, Thomas, 16
End the Backlog program, 95
Entman, Robert M., 103

Epstein, Jeffrey, 44
Eschholz, Sarah, 104, 172
ethnic bias, 152
Euripides, 4
Evers, Medgar, 162

Facebook, 181, **182**
faulty system, 133
FBI. *See* Federal Bureau of Investigation
federal agents, 61
Federal Bureau of Investigation (FBI), 24, 116
Fehler-Cabral, Giannina, 96
felony murder, 23
female-dominated crimes, 122–23
female-on-female murder, 31
female perpetrators, 122, 135; in crime dramas, 123–24; in crimes of prostitution, 125–26
females: in domestic violence, 119, 125; female-on-male murder, 31; portrayal in crime dramas, 126; portrayal in television 118; in prison, 123; as rape victims, 119, 125; as sexual assault victims, 119. *See also* female victims/victimization
female victims/victimization, 116–17, 120, 125, 135; in crime dramas, 124–25; in criminological research, 135
feminist perspectives, 117–18, 126
feminist theory, 117
film noir, 160, 165
finding source(s) of news, 84
fingerprint analysis, 89–90
first-degree murder, 23, 25–27
The First 48 (crime show), 63
first block, 40, 73; analysis of stories, 49, 52; criminal justice wedding cake model, 43–48; natural disasters in, 48–49; news divisions, 49; news tease in, 42–43; sexy top story in, 40, 41–42; terrible highway accident in, 48–49; top stories from media outlets, **50–51**

Fitzgerald, Barry, 160
Fizzinoglia, Donald F., 82, 183
Floyd, George, 45, 66, 104, 105, 183
forensic investigative technologies, 88–89; ballistics identification, 90; *CSI* Effect, 88, 92–94; DNA analysis and CODIS, 90–91; fingerprint analysis, 89–90; rape kits, 94–96, 97
Forensic Technologies, Inc., 90
Fox News, 6, **50**, 52, 78, 104, 171
framing theory in media studies, 133–34
Franklin, Benjamin, 9–11, 17, 18
Freedom Summer of 1964, 162
The French Connection (film), 163, 165
Friedkin, William, 163
Friedman, Barbara, 12
Friedman, Lawrence, 43
From the Field (Swiderski), 47, 54
full court press, 46–47

Gacy, John Wayne (serial killer), 24
Garland, David, 4
gatekeeping models, 132–33
GEDmatch, 91
gender: bias, 152; intersectionality of, 135; portrayal in media, 186; stereotypes as victims, 116–17
Gerbner, George, 4, 32–33, 49
Gilliam Jr., 103
Good Girls (crime drama), 96
Gottfredson, Don, 43
Gottfredson, Michael, 43
Grade, Maria, 4
The Graduate (film), 162
gratuitous violence, 73–74, 77–78
Gray, Freddie, 157
The Great Train Robbery (film), 16
Greeley, Horace, 12
Grey's Anatomy, 78–79
Guess Who's Coming to Dinner (film), 162
Gutenberg, Johannes, 5
Guthrie, Woody, 150

Hacking, Lori, 131–32

Hagerman, Amber, 134
Hammurabi (King), 89
#HandsUp movement, 104
Hargitay, Mariska, 95
Harris, Alonzo, 163
Harris, Kamala, 144
Hartshorn, Kelley J. Sittner, 172–73
Hawaii Five-0 (TV police shows), 161
Hawke, Ethan, 163
The Hayes Code. *See* The Production Code
Hayes, Will, 159
HBO. *See* Home Box Office
Hearst, Randolph, 15
Hearst, William, 16, 17
heroic cinemas in Hollywood, 162–63
Herrera, Vivian, 102
Herron, Rita Marie, 150
Hill Street Blues (TV police shows), 161
Hilt, Mark A., 111
Hitchcock, Alfred, 2
Hoberman, J., 163
Holder, Eric, 68
Holloway, Natalee (missing case), 129–30, 145
Holt, Lester, 6
Home Box Office (HBO), 35
Howard, Rebkah, 132
How to Get Away with Murder (television show), 123
Huffman, Felicity, 44
Hughes, Michael, 33
Huston, Tamika, 131–32

IAFIS. *See* Integrated Automated Fingerprint Identification System
I Am Evidence (crime drama), 96
IBIS. *See* Integrated Ballistics Identification System
Ifill, Gwen, 131
imdb.com, 2, 131
information, 185
institutional racism, 157

Integrated Automated Fingerprint Identification System (IAFIS), 89–90, 97
Integrated Ballistics Identification System (IBIS), 90
International Association of Chiefs of Police, 158
intersectionality: of gender and race, 135, 145
In the Heat of the Night (film), 162, 165
Intravia, Jonathan, 104
"invisibilization" of Black women, 137

Jack the Ripper (serial killer), 2, 3
Jane the Virgin (TV show), 148
Jefferson, Thomas, 6, 33
Jennings, Peter, 6
Jewell, K. Sue, 144
Joyful Heart Project, 95
#JusticeforGeorgeFloyd movement, 104
Justin T., 104
just world hypothesis, 120–21

Kanka, Megan, 134
Kaplan, Ethan, 171
Kaplan, Richard, 15, 16
'Keep Walking' campaign, 150
Keystone Cops/Kops, 157, 158, 164
Killer Inside: The Mind of Aaron Hernandez (crime show), 63
Kimberly, MacLin, M., 102
King, Martin Luther, 81
KKK. *See* Ku Klux Klan
Klahm IV, Charles F., 63
Kohan, Jenji, 148
Kort-Butler, Lisa A., 172–73
Ku Klux Klan (KKK), 81

Laci and Connor's Law, 134
Larkin, Sean "Sticks," 65
latent fingerprint, 89
Latinas/Latinos/Latinxs: career occupations of, **152**; community, 150–51; inequality in media coverage, 152–53; media portrayals of, 145, 151, **152**; portrayals in television, 146–47, 148, 151; stereotypes of, 145
Latin lover, 146–47
Latino Representation on Primetime Television, 146
Law & Order (crime drama), 2, 43, 57
Law & Order: Criminal Intent, 34, 43, 105
Law & Order: Special Victims Unit (SVU), 34, 35, 43, 96, 105, 116, 123–25
"Legal Vigilante" archetype, 163
Lerner, Melvin J., 120
Lie to Me (crime drama), 124
Lincoln, Abraham, 12
Linz, Daniel, 103
Lipkin, Michelle Ciulla, 83, 85
Lipschultz, Jeremy Harris, 111
LIVE PD (crime show), 59, 65–66
Live Rescue (television series), 66
"local legal culture," 47–48
The Lodger: A Story of the London Fog movie (Hitchcock), 2
Lopez, George, 147
Lopez, Vera, 145
Loughlin, Lori, 44
"lowlife" stereotype, 145
Lumet, Sidney, 164
Lupi (TV show), 179
Luther (crime show), 179

Maddox, Keith B., 111
Madriz, Esther I., 102, 117
"Make My Day" (Hoberman), 163
male-on-male violence, 31
manslaughter, 23–24
Marshall Project report, 66
Masi de Casanova, Erynn, 149
Mast, Gerald, 180
Mastro, Dana, 105, 146
Max News, 171
McClellan Jr., George, 158
McKenna, Joseph, 158
McMillions (crime show), 63

McVeigh, Timothy, 81
media: anchors in, 6–7; bias affecting voting and public perception, 171–72; change in mode of, 9; depiction of Black people as criminals, 101–2; exploring as creator, 84; freedom of press, 5–6; gender portrayal in, 186; history of, 4–5, 9; media-priming theory, 111–12; mischaracterizations of criminal justice system in, 2–3; oversexualization of girls in, 143; race and ethnicity portrayal in, 186; Sommers findings on race in, **138**; as source of information for news, 17; white out, 138–39
Media Literacy, 82–85; essential skills for, 83–85
Media Pineapple Upside Down Cake news, 52, *53*
Megan's Law, 134, 141
memorial criminal justice policies, 134, 141
Mendelsohn, Benjamin, 122
The Mentalist (crime drama), 124
Miami Vice (crime drama), 57, 96
Michigan Militia, 81
Miller, Perry, 10
Milton, John, 5
Mindhunter, 125
Mirisch, Walter, 162
Missing Pretty Girl Syndrome (Sommers), 131
missing pretty white girl syndrome, 131–32, 133; framing theory in media studies, 133–34; gatekeeping models in, 132–33; media breakdown of Sommers's categories, 137–38; media coverage for missing white girls, 139–40; overrepresentation of white people, 134
Missing White Woman Syndrome (Sommers), 131
The Mod Squad (TV police shows), 161
Money Heist (TV show), 179
Monty Python, 5

Morris, Jonathan S., 171
Morris Jr., Tom, 65
Motion Picture Producers and Distributors of America (MPPDA), 159
MPPDA. *See* Motion Picture Producers and Distributors of America
MSNBC, 6, **50**, 78, 104, 171
Muir, David, 6
Mulford, Carla, 11
multiple murder, 24–25
multiple victims and offenders scenario, 32
murder, 79; classification of, 23; definition of, 23; first-degree, 23, 25–27; manslaughter, 23–24; multiple, 24; official murder patterns, 31–32; second-degree, 23
'murder in the first block" syndrome, 46
Murrow, Edward R., 6
Mutual Film Corporation v. Industrial Commission of Ohio case, 158
Mutz, Diana C., 173
MWWS, 136, 137, 139–40
Myers, Henry, 159

Naked City (TV police show), 160–61, 164
National Board of Review of Motion Pictures, 158
National Crime Victimization Survey (NCVS), 29, 119, 120, 122
National DNA Index System (NDIS), 91
National Integrated Ballistics Information Network (NIBIN), 90, 97
National Nightly News, **50**
National Public Radio (NPR), 138
natural disasters, 48–49
NBC (Nightly News), 77
NCIS (crime drama), 34, 57, 124, 174, 188
NCVS. *See* National Crime Victimization Survey
NDIS. *See* National DNA Index System

Neilsen Media Research, 74–75
Nerone, John, 12
Network Contagion Research Institute, 187
network news, 76–77
New Hollywood, 161
New Jersey/New York 24-hour Cable News, **51**
news, 9, 17–18; about 20th Century Limited train voyage, 16–17; block, 40, 54; media as source of information, 17; news divisions, 49; "news you can use" concept, 74; penny press, 11–12, 18; police and court "news," 13; and popular culture, 10–11; portrayal of black people on, 103–5; protections and rights, 10; secret about news organizations, 139; slowing down in fast-paced world, 83–84; stories featuring white victims with Black perpetrators, 134; tease, 42–43; user friendliness, 85; watching, 52; yellow journalism, 15–16
news reporters, 73, 139; competition among, 79
New World Order, 187–88
NIBIN. *See* National Integrated Ballistics Information Network
Nir, Lilach, 173
Nixon, Richard, 165
Normalizing Injustice report, 62
NPR. *See* National Public Radio
NYPD Blue (crime drama), 57

Obama, Barack, 81
O'Donnell, Norah, 6
Oliver, Mary Beth, 64, 65
One America News, 104, 171
Orange is the New Black (TV series), 123, 146–48
Outcault, Richard, 15–16
"over-night photog," 73
overrepresentation of white people, 134

oversexualization of girls in media, 143–44, 153

Paine, Thomas, 5
Parrott, Caroline Titcomb, 106, 124
Parrott, Scott, 106, 124
patriarchy, 117
patrol officers: on duty, 60–61; shift of, 57–59
PBS. *See* Public Broadcasting System
PCA. *See* Production Code Administration
Peaky Blinders (TV show), 179
Pence, Mike, 186
Penny Press, 11–12, 18
People of Color, 30, 62, 65, 102, 105, 134, 135
Percival, Robert B., 43
perpetrator(s) of murder: demographics, 25; official statistics, 29–30, 32; in TV crime dramas, 27–28. *See also* female perpetrators
Peterson, Laci, 134
Pew Research Center, 182
Podlas, Kimberlianne, 93, 94
Poe, Edgar Allen, 14, 17
Poehler, Amy, 7
Poitier, Sidney, 162
police: body cameras, 67–69; brutality picture in Hollywood, 163–64; depiction in crime dramas, 61–63; depiction in nonfiction crime shows, 63; as hypermasculine super-cops, 62, 69; legitimacy, 68, 69; procedural, 160–61, 164, 165
Popeye Doyle (film), 163
press, freedom of, 5–6, 11, 12
Prodigal Son (crime drama), 34
Production Code Administration (PCA), 159–60
The Production Code, 159, 160, 163–65
PSAs. *See* Public Service Announcements
Psych (television show), 123
Public Broadcasting System (PBS), 79

Public Service Announcements (PSAs), 76
Pulitzer, Joseph, 15, 17

Queen of the South, Cristela (TV show), 148

race/racial/racist/racism, 102; bias, 62, 152; institutional, 157; intersectionality of, 135; portrayal in media, 186; racial/ethnic make-up of the group, 185; Sommers findings on, **138**; system, 133
radio market, 74
Ramsey, JonBenét (murder case), 130–31, 143
rape, 116; in crime dramas, 125; kits, 94–96, 97; myths, 121–22
Reasoner, Harry, 6
Reiner, Robert, 62
Revere, Paul, 83
Rice, Tamir, 157
Rizzoli & Isles (crime drama), 96
Robinson, Amanda L., 105
Romer, Daniel, 33
The Roots of Justice (Friedman and Percival), 43
Rossellini, Roberto, 161
Rubio, Solange, 150
Ryan, Erin, 149

Sachs, Nicole M., 82, 183
Safe and Clean Neighborhoods Program, 3
Saks, Michael J., 93
SANE. *See* Sexual Assault Nurse Examiner
Sasson, Theodore, 133
Saturday Night Live (TV show), 177
Saunders, Richard, 10
#SayHerName movement, 136–37
Scharrer, Erica, 61
school shootings, 79–80
Schweitzer, N. J., 93
Scott, Walter, 157
second-degree murder, 23
Sennett, Mack, 157, 158
sensation-seeking. *See* sensationalism
sensationalism, 15, 16, 18, 180
Serani, Deborah, 52, 54
serial killers, 24
serial murder, 24
sex crime or murder, 40
sexual assault, 116; in crime dramas, 125; females as victims of, 119; kits. *See* rape—kits
Sexual Assault Nurse Examiner (SANE), 96
sexualization of young girls in media, 143
sexual orientation bias, 152
Shelton, Hon. Donald E., 93
Shrum, L. J., 32
Sica, Vittorio De, 161
Siegal, Don, 163
Signature Analysis Station, 90
Silence Breakers, 44
Simpson's trial, 39, 40, 46
Singer, Rick, 44
single victim, 24, 29; and multiple offenders scenario, 31–32; and single offender scenario, 31
Sixteenth Street Baptist Church Bombing, 81
Slater, Michael D., 173
slave patrols, 102
Snapchat, 181, **182**
Snappedi (crime show), 63
socialism, 15
socialist feminism, 117
social media, 67, 181; false reports, 183–84; news analysis, **182**; platforms, 132
solid broadcast, 43
Sommers, 93, 131, 134, 136–38, 140; findings on race in media, **138**; media breakdown of categories, 137–38
Sood, Gaurav, 124
Sophocles, 4

Southland (crime drama), 96
Speck, Richard, 24
spree murder, 24–25
standard on crime coverage, 82
Stand By For Crime (police drama), 61
Steiger, Rod, 162
Stewart, Ian, 138
Stillman, Sarah, 131, 136
The Suite Life of Zack and Cody (TV show), 147
Super Bowl case, 76
superpredators, 102
Surette, Ray, 2, 11, 14, 133, 181
Swiderski, John, 47

TASS, 5, 9
Taylor, Breonna, 44–45, 105, 136
Taylor, Don, 160
television (TV): connection between fear and, 4; crime portrayal on, 183; first-degree murder, 25–27; impact on Latina adolescents, 148–50; markets, 74–76; portrayal of Latinos in, 146, 151; portrayal of women in 118; tease, 42; TV networks, political bias of, 170–71; violence on TV, 185
television crime dramas, 22–23, 25–27, 34, 57, 88, 96; affecting people's perceptions of crime, 175; audience of, 178–79; Black perpetrators, 105–7; Black victims, 105–7; comparing TV crime data to official statistics, 29; and crime policy, 172–73; Criminal Minds, 22; and cultivation theory, 32–34; data collection table, **26**; Dragnet, 23; females in, 123–25; fictional, 22, 33; gangster genre in, 160; mirroring official statistics of Black perpetrators and victims, 108–10; perpetrators in, 27–28, 32; police depiction in, 61–63; politics and, 173–74; rape and sexual assault in, 125; rape kits on, 96; role in police officer's work, 69; victims in, 28–29, 32; viewers' favorite dramas,

174–75; *The Wire* (television show), 34–35. *See also* "true" crime shows
terrible highway accident, 48–49
Tiger King (crime show), 63
top layer of wedding cake model, 44–45, 46
top story, sexy, 40, 41–42
Traffic (film), 179
Training Day (film), 163–64
Trial of the Century. *See* Simpson's trial
The Trials of Gabriel Fernandez (crime show), 63
Trielli, Daniel, 124
trigger warning, 54
"true" crime shows: citizen videos on social media, 67–68; *COPS*, 64–65; crime dramas, police depiction in, 61–63; *LIVE PD*, 65–66; nonfiction crime shows, police depiction in, 63; officers on duty, 60–61; police body cameras, 67–69; shift of patrol officer, 57–60. *See also* television crime dramas
Trump, Donald, 186
Twitter, 181, **182**
Tyler, Tom R., 92, 94

UCR. *See* Uniform Crime Report
Unbelievable (crime drama), 96
Unborn Victims of Violence Act of 2004, 134
Uniform Crime Report (UCR), 29, 107, 119, 122
United Parcel Service of America (UPS), 95
"upper-class" papers/journals, 12, 15
UPS. *See* United Parcel Service of America
U.S. Constitution: First Amendment, 5, 9–10; Fourteenth Amendment, 10

Vergara, Sophia, 147
victim blaming of women, 126; just world hypothesis, 120–21;

rape myths, 121–22; victim precipitation, 122
victimization, 116, 118, 120, 122
victims: demographics, 25; gender stereotypes and females as, 116–17; in TV crime dramas, 28–29; multiple, 24; of crime, 120; official statistics, 30–31, 32; precipitation, 122
vigilante groups, 14–16
Violence Against Women Act Reauthorization Act of 2021 (VAWA 2021) 96
violent media, 133, 185
voyeurism, 179–81

Walker, Kenneth, 45
Walker, Samuel, 47, 48
Wallace, Edgar, 14
Walters, Barbara, 6
War on Drugs, 102
Washington, Denzel, 163–64
Washington, George, 10
Weaponizing Women (crime drama), 96
Webb, Jack, 161

Weeds (TV show), 147, 148
Weinstein, Harvey, 44
Welch, Kelly, 102
The West Wing (drama series), 170, 186
White people (men or women), 106, 144, 153
White perpetrator, 106, 111
White victims, 107
Will & Grace (TV show), 147
Williams, Charlotte L., 103–4
Wire in the Blood (crime show), 179
The Wire (crime drama), 34–35, 57, 101
Wizards of Waverly Place (film), 150
woke advertising, 150–51
Wolfgang, Marvin, 122
women. *See* females
Worthy, Kym, 95

yellow journalism, 15–16
Yellow Kid (Cartoon character), 15–16

Zawilski, Valerie, 63
Zayas, David, 146
Zeitchik, Steven M., 179

About the Authors

Beth E. Adubato a 2022–23 Fulbright Scholar, is an associate professor of criminal justice at Saint Peter's University in Jersey City, New Jersey. She has a BA in English, an MA in CJ, an MPAP from the Bloustein School of Planning and Policy, and earned her PhD in 2011—all from Rutgers University. She is a member of Phi Beta Kappa Honor Society. Her Fulbright research is on hooliganism and domestic violence in Belgium and neighboring countries, with a focus on the rise of right-wing extremism and its influence on hooliganism. In addition to academic publications, she is the author of *Grammar for Grownups* and *Life's a Mother,* a novel about single moms.

Before academia, Adubato was a news anchor/reporter in Michigan; a morning news anchor in Erie, PA; and the first woman to anchor sports in Birmingham, Alabama. She then worked for Court TV and News12NJ. She has appeared as a reporter on *Law & Order: Criminal Intent*, *Cupid*, and *The Following*.

Beth is founder and executive director of The LINDA Organization, Inc., a 501(c)(3) nonprofit organization (wearelinda.org). The LINDA Org. collects toiletries, cosmetics, clothing, and children's items for women who have been adversely affected by the criminal justice system. LINDA is presently expanding to form collegiate chapters across the country, employing student volunteers who earn hands-on experience while helping their communities.

Nicole M. Sachs, PhD is a criminal justice researcher and adjunct professor. Her research examines victims and offenders at the intersection of criminal justice and social psychology. Her current projects explore the relation between victim identity and mental health, and between viewing violent crime on television and one's victim identity. She is also conducting several research studies on people under community supervision and is dedicated to examining the impact of and informing policies affecting those returning to their communities post-incarceration. She holds a PhD in Criminal Justice from Rutgers University, an MA in Criminal Justice from Rutgers University, and BAs in crime, law, and justice and psychology from he Pennsylvania State University. She serves as a board member of the LINDA Organization, whose mission is to help women (and their children) reentering their communities, escaping from an abusive situation, and/or struggling with homelessness and mental health and/or substance use disorders.

Donald F. Fizzinoglia has been an independent video and filmmaker since 1978. He continues to pursue his stated goal of balancing "teacher, artist, and professional." A Yale University graduate (BA sociology) with an MA in communication arts and an MS in counseling, he has written, produced, directed, and edited a wide variety of productions including film and television drama, documentaries, talk shows, music videos, commercial, promotional, and educational programs. Early highlights include *Risk*, an AIDS-awareness film targeting teenagers; *LIRR: A Reflection*, an award-winning documentary film chronicling the 150-year history of the railroad line; *All About Telstar*, an independent film set in Texas on the eve of JFK's assassination, and *Turn It Around*, a film-to-tape drug prevention music video featuring Hall-of-Famer Dave Winfield.

In a departure from film history documentaries, Don produced, directed, and wrote *CMT's Most Shocking: College Sports Headlines*, a one-hour documentary examining the issues facing college sports, for Viacom's MTV-CMT network, premiering nationally in 2005.

Don's current documentary project will be examining the women's prison system in the state of New Jersey. He recently published an article on gatekeepers during a time of crisis in the academic journal, *Atlantic Journal of Communication*. Don serves as professor and chair of the Communications Art Department of New York Institute of Technology.

John M. Swiderski, MA is a police officer and adjunct professor of criminal justice. He holds an MA in criminal justice from Rutgers University and BAs in history and labor studies from Rutgers University. Before his career in law enforcement, he served as a corrections officer and as a high school gang resistance and education training educator. His current research interest includes sports and domestic violence. He plays hockey in a police and fire league, which often runs fundraisers to support local families.

www.ingramcontent.com/pod-product-compliance
Lightning Source LLC
Chambersburg PA
CBHW061712300426
44115CB00014B/2655